Language, Society and Power

'This is a book written by real academics, drawing articulately on their own research interests, and using an excellent range of twenty-first century examples to give the book a lively, contemporary feel. The extensive textual analysis is far superior to some of the banal tasks often to be found in introductory textbooks.'
Martin Conboy, *The Surrey Institute of Art & Design*

'This is an excellent, accessible new edition. The large number of examples, worked through in the text, make the book very student-friendly.'
Jonathan White, *Department of English, Dalarna University, Sweden*

This is a completely updated and expanded second edition of *Language, Society and Power*. Lively and accessible, it looks at the ways in which language functions, how it influences thought and how it varies according to age, ethnicity, class and gender. How can a language reflect the status of children and older people? Do men and women talk differently? How can our use of language mark our ethnic identity? The book also looks at language use in politics and the media and examines how language affects and constructs our identities, exploring notions of correctness and attitudes towards language use.

This second edition has been fully updated to include recent developments in theory and research and offers the following features:

- new, relevant and engaging examples drawn from everyday life: conversation transcripts, novels including Ian McEwan's *Atonement*, television and the internet
- new activities designed to give students a real understanding of the area
- an international perspective with examples from the world's press, including the *Washington Post*, the *Daily Mail* and the *New Zealand Listener*
- updated and expanded further reading sections and glossary

Language, Society and Power remains an essential introductory text for students of English language and linguistics, and will also be of use to students of media, communication, cultural studies, sociology and psychology.

Linda Thomas is Head of English and Modern Languages at Roehampton University of Surrey. **Shân Wareing** is Director of the Educational Development Centre at Royal Holloway University of London. **Ishtla Singh** is a Lecturer in English Language at King's College London. **Jean Stilwell Peccei** is a Visiting Lecturer in the English Language and Linguistics Programme at Roehampton University of Surrey. **Joanna Thornborrow** is a Senior Lecturer at the Centre for Language and Communication Research, Cardiff University and **Jason Jones** is Head of English at Strode's Sixth Form College.

Language, Society and Power

An introduction

Second edition

Linda Thomas, Shân Wareing,
Ishtla Singh, Jean Stilwell Peccei,
Joanna Thornborrow and
Jason Jones

This edition revised and edited by
Ishtla Singh and Jean Stilwell Peccei

Routledge
Taylor & Francis Group

LONDON AND NEW YORK

First published 1999
by Routledge
Reprinted twice in 2000, 2001, twice in 2002, 2003

This second edition published 2004
by Routledge
2 Park Square, Milton Park, Abingdon Oxon, OX14 4RN

Simultaneously published in the USA and Canada
by Routledge
270 Madison Ave, New York, NY 10016

Reprinted 2005 (twice)

Routledge is an imprint of the Taylor and Francis Group

Typeset in Times and Futura by
Florence Production Ltd, Stoodleigh, Devon
Printed and bound in Great Britain by
TJ International, Padstow, Cornwall

British Library Cataloguing in Publication Data
A catalogue record for this book is available from the British Library

Library of Congress Cataloging in Publication Data
Language, society, and power / an introduction / [edited by]
  Linda Thomas . . . [et al.]. – 2nd ed.
    p. cm.
Includes bibliographical references and index.
    1. Language and languages.   2. Sociolinguistics.
  I. Thomas, Linda.
  P107.L36 2004   2003012410
  306.44–dc21

ISBN 0–415–30393–1 (hbk)
ISBN 0–415–30394–X (pbk)

For Debbie and Jen

Contents

1 What is language and what does it do?   1

Shân Wareing

2 Language, thought and representation   17

Ishtla Singh

6 Language and ethnicity

93

Ishtla Singh

7 Language and age

113

Jean Stilwell Peccei

8 Language and class   133

Jason Jones

9 Language and identity   157

Joanna Thornborrow

10 The standard English debate 173

Linda Thomas

11 Attitudes to language 193

Linda Thomas

Figures

Newspapers

During the course of our discussions, reference is made to and data are taken from English language newspapers and magazines. A list of these publications is given below.

Daily Mail	UK national daily newspaper
Daily Mirror	UK national daily newspaper
Daily Star	UK national daily newspaper
The Daily Telegraph	UK national daily newspaper
Evening Standard	London daily newspaper
Glasgow Herald	Scottish daily newspaper
The Guardian	UK national daily newspaper
The Guardian Weekend	Supplement to Saturday's edition of *The Guardian*
The Independent	UK national daily newspaper
London Metro	London daily newspaper
National Enquirer	US weekly tabloid news magazine
News of the World	UK national Sunday newspaper
The New Zealand Listener	New Zealand weekly magazine
Northwest Evening Mail	UK daily newspaper
The Observer	UK national Sunday newspaper
Observer Review	Supplement to *The Observer*
The Psychologist	Monthly magazine for members of the British Psychological Society
The Sunday Telegraph	UK national Sunday newspaper
The Sunday Times	UK national Sunday newspaper
THES (*The Times Higher Education Supplement*)	UK national weekly newspaper
Time Out	London weekly magazine

The Times	UK national daily newspaper
The Times Weekend	Supplement to Saturday's edition of *The Times*
USA Today	US national daily newspaper
Washington Post	Washington, DC daily newspaper

Contributors

Jason Jones, formerly a Lecturer in the English Language and Linguistics programme at Roehampton University of Surrey, is now Head of English at Strode's Sixth Form College.

Ishtla Singh, formerly a Lecturer in the English Language and Linguistics programme at Roehampton University of Surrey, is Lecturer in English Language at King's College London (Department of English Language and Literature). Her research interests lie generally in historical and sociolinguistics but a primary area of research is that of language contact, with a particular focus on variation and change in creole-speaking communities. She is the author of *Pidgins and Creoles: An Introduction* (Arnold, 2000).

Jean Stilwell Peccei is a Visiting Lecturer in the English Language and Linguistics programme at Roehampton University of Surrey. She is the author of *Child Language*, 2nd Edition (Routledge Language Workbooks series, 1999) and *Pragmatics* (Routledge Language Workbooks series, 1999).

Linda Thomas is Head of School of English and Modern Languages and Principal Lecturer in English Language and Linguistics at Roehampton University of Surrey. She is the author of *Beginning Syntax* (Blackwells, 1993).

Joanna Thornborrow, formerly a Lecturer in the English Language and Linguistics programme at Roehampton University of Surrey, is now Senior Lecturer at the Centre for Language and Communication Research, Cardiff University. Her main research interests are in discourse and conversation analysis, and stylistics, with a particular focus on media and institutional talk. She is the author of *Power Talk: Language and Interaction in Institutional Discourse* (Longman, 2002) and co-author (with Shân Wareing) of *Patterns* *in Language: An Introduction to Language and Literary Style* (Routledge, 1998).

Shân Wareing, formerly a Lecturer in the English Language and Linguistics programme at Roehampton University of Surrey, is now Director of Educational Development Centre at Royal Holloway University of London. She is the co-author (with Joanna Thornborrow) of *Patterns in Language: An Introduction to Languages and Literary Style* (Routledge, 1998).

Preface to the second edition

The first edition of *Language, Society and Power* was published in 1999, when the majority of the contributing authors were lecturers at Roehampton University of Surrey (then Roehampton Institute London). The book had evolved out of an identically titled course on which we had all taught, and which is still running as a required course for students on the English Language and Linguistics programme, and as a popular option for students in other departments. Since that first edition, several of us have moved to other universities and colleges, but we have all maintained an interest in studying language as a social entity. Thus, even though producing this second edition has required a great deal more co-ordination than the last time, we were all willing to be involved in revising and updating a project which has not only been enjoyable for us but which has also had a favourable reception from its intended audience.

The second edition has remained faithful to the first in many ways. We have maintained a focus on English (primarily British and American varieties). The first edition's glossary of terms potentially new to the reader (printed in bold in each chapter) has been retained but also updated. We have continued to make use of personal reference (something not typically found in academic texts), addressing the reader as *you*, and referring to ourselves as *I* or *we* as appropriate. We have also continued to assume that our readers are generally not, or not yet, specialists in the areas of language study and linguistics, and therefore need an introduction to the kinds of topics which feed into a broader examination of language and society. As such, the book does not offer comprehensive coverage of every possible issue within this vast subject area but instead, provides a stepping-stone to exploring and thinking about at least some of them. Thus, each of the chapters deals with a topic that has been the subject of academic sociolinguistic investigation, and is supplemented with references to useful reading and other sources of material. There are substantial Activities throughout the text to help the reader engage more actively with the ideas being presented.

We have maintained the distinctive authorial 'voices' of the first edition, since they make for a more varied and interesting approach to analysis and discussion. One of the things that the majority of the chapters do have in common, though, is that they seek to interpret the ways in which language and language issues can be deconstructed to reveal underlying ideologies, or beliefs. While all of the chapters have a solid academic grounding, it is important to bear in mind that any interpretation of what people do and say is necessarily going to contain a certain measure of bias. Thus, while we can justifiably analyse a newspaper headline about immigration, for example, and state that its 'slant' reveals an affiliation to politically left- or right-wing principles, it must be remembered that any such approach is in itself ideologically determined: it reveals the analyst's belief that language is not a neutral tool of communication but instead a channel for how we see and construct the world around us. This tenet will become clearer as you read through the text.

Each chapter of this book deals with a different area of language, although there are connections between many of the chapter topics. We have designed the book so that it can be read from cover to cover as a continuous text, but also so that individual chapters can stand alone and be read in their own right. We have divided chapters into subsections, partly to indicate the structure clearly with subtitles and partly to help you find the sections you need to read if you don't need to read the whole chapter.

Chapter 1 interrogates the notion of 'language', and raises some of the underlying questions and ideas that will be relevant as you move into the other chapters. Chapters 2–4 all concentrate on the ideological properties of language, and on how it can be used to influence the ways in which people think and behave. Chapter 2 is concerned with the connections between language, thought and representation, and considers the extent to which language can be said to shape and perpetuate our worldviews. Chapter 3 moves on from the conclusions of Chapter 2 to consider whether, and how, language can be used in politics, and in other fields, to persuade people of particular points of view. Chapter 4 considers how language is used, and to what effects, in media such as newspapers and television with particular reference to news reporting and advertising. Chapters 5–7 deal with language use in connection with particular subgroups within a population. The terms or 'labels' that can be or are applied to members of those groups, and the effect of those labels, are considered. The chapters also look at the kinds of language choices members of those groups sometimes make. Chapter 5 focuses on language and gender, Chapter 6 deals with language and ethnicity and Chapter 7 with language and age. Chapter 8 considers how a further set of subgroup divisions, namely those which go into the construction of social class, affect language use. The last three chapters, 9–11, are concerned with attitudes towards language, and the relationship between language and identity. Chapter 9 deals with language and social identity, and Chapter 10 with the debates that surround the use of standard English. Chapter 11 provides a conclusion to the whole book with an overview of attitudes towards language.

Finally, we hope that you will enjoy reading and using this second edition, and that it will add another dimension to how you think about language and language use. We have certainly enjoyed putting it together, and we hope that at least some measure of our passion and interest in this everyday but extraordinary faculty will prove infectious!

Preface to the first edition

This book is based on a course of the same name that runs in the English Language and Linguistics Programme at Roehampton Institute London, and on which all the authors have taught. It began life as Language, Power, Politics and Sexuality, a short (five-week) introduction to language issues for students studying literature. Over the years the course has grown as interest in language study has grown, and it is now an introductory course for students studying language and linguistics, while continuing in popularity with students of literature. Many of the students taking the course are combining their studies with subjects such as sociology, media studies, women's studies, education and history, where they find that the issues raised are also relevant.

In preparing this book, we have assumed no prior knowledge of linguistics. We hope that students taking courses on the social and political dimensions of language use will find this a useful foundation text. Students of disciplines that include the study of language use, discourse and ideology, power relations, education, the rights of minority groups and equal opportunities should also find this a helpful text. Learners of English may find this a useful route to a better understanding of language use. Since we see language use as being central to many, or most, human activities, we hope that students studying apparently unrelated disciplines may also find it helpful to have a book which covers the range of issues we deal with here. And we have tried to make the text appropriate and interesting for the general reader.

The ideas covered in this book have been explored and developed with groups of students since the early 1980s. They are presented here as eleven topics, currently covered in a modular course on a week-by-week basis. Although they may look it, the topics are not discrete, but have overlapping themes and common threads which we have tried to bring out. Nor are they exclusive. As you read, you may well think of other areas of language use which are worthy of investigation or consideration, such as the relationship between language and health, or language and the law. Issues such as these are not omitted because we think that they are unimportant but because in a book of this length there is not space to cover everything. We hope what we have covered will assist your thinking about the relationship between language and the different dimensions of the societies in which we live.

The authors have taught as a team the course from which this book was generated. We felt that as a group we shared common values both about the topics we taught and our approach to teaching, and that this provided us with a solid foundation for writing this book also as a team. We distributed the topics amongst the six of us, according to our areas of special interest, and met regularly to review the drafts of our chapters and to discuss revisions. Our aim was to produce a coherent text that still reflected the ideas and writing styles of individual team members. To some extent, the different 'voices' of the authors should still be apparent.

Amongst other decisions we had to make as a team of authors, we had to decide on how we would use pronouns such as *I*, *we* and *you*. We could, for example, have decided to write impersonally, and avoid using personal pronouns as much as possible, which is quite common in academic writing. We had to decide whether we should refer to ourselves in the chapters as *I* (the individual writing the chapter) or *we* (the team of writers). We also had to decide whether we should use *you* to address our readers. The conventional, impersonal academic style is often criticised by people with an interest in the social and political functions of language because, as is discussed in Chapter 3, it can be used to make ideas seem less accessible than they need be, and to increase the apparent status of the writers by making them seem 'cleverer' than the readers. In the end, we felt the most honest and sensible thing to do would be to use *we* to refer to the team of authors, to acknowledge the input we have all had in each others' thinking and writing, but to use *I* if we write about our personal experiences. We have addressed you the readers as *you*.

Throughout the book we concentrate on the English language, although we occasionally use another language to illustrate a particular point. The main varieties of English looked at are British and American English.

There is a glossary of terms with brief explanations at the back of the book. Words which appear in the glossary are printed in bold the first time they occur in a chapter. You will also find at the end of each chapter recommended further reading which you can follow up if you want to learn more about a topic. If you want to check whether a topic is covered in this book, and where, the index at the back gives page numbers.

We have included Activities throughout the text. Some ask you to reflect on your own use of, or feelings about, language. Some ask you to talk to other people, to elicit their language use or thoughts on certain issues. Some require you to collect data from other sources around you, such as the newspapers or television. Some you will be able to do alone, and some need group discussion. One of the main reasons we have included Activities is that we believe that the ideas we are discussing in this book really come alive when you begin to look for them in the language which goes on around you. We have seen students' attitudes change from mild interest, or even a lack of interest, to absolute fascination when they have started to investigate language use for themselves.

If the ideas we have presented here are ones you have come across before, we hope we have presented them in such a way as to provoke further thought, or make connections you hadn't previously made. If you haven't thought about some of the ideas we raise here before, we hope that you also find them exciting and spend the rest of your life listening to what people say, reading newspapers and watching television commercials differently.

Acknowledgements

We would like to thank the following people for their contributions: Deborah Cameron and Jennifer Coates who designed the original course, who have given us advice on writing over the years, and to whom this book is dedicated. We hope that both the current course and this text accurately represent their original aims and ideals. We are also indebted to the students who have taken Roehampton's 'Language, Society and Power' course, in its various manifestations, for their interest and excitement, for the opportunity to test our ideas, for the feedback they have given us and the data they have found for us. We would in particular like to thank two of these students, Su Gilroy and Louise McCarron, who read and commented on the draft manuscript of the first edition. We also thank Routledge's anonymous readers, who gave us useful and encouraging advice on both editions; Jennifer Coates for editing advice on the first edition; Doris Stilwell and Sabina Chorley, who helped us find some of the newspaper data; Harry Patel our 'paper man'; Louisa Semlyen and Christy Kirkpatrick, our unfailingly helpful and supportive editors at Routledge, for all their work on our behalf; our copy editor, John Banks, for his invaluable help in preparing the final manuscript; Patrick Thomas and Martin Chorley for not minding too much the work that Shân and Linda did at the weekends for the first edition; Andrew Pitman and Riccardo Peccei for their love and support while Ishtla and Jean edited the second edition. The team would like to thank Jean Stilwell Peccei for preparing the glossary.

The authors and publisher would like to thank the following for permission to reproduce copyright material:

Extract from the *Daily Mail*, 8 January 2003. Reproduced by permission of the Daily Mail.

Extract from 'It's Here: Deadly Terror Poison Found in Britain', the *Daily Mirror*, 8 January 2003. Reproduced by permission of the Mirror.

ACKNOWLEDGEMENTS

Extract from *Miss Smilla's Feeling for Snow* by Peter Høeg published by The Harvill Press. Used by permission of The Random House Group Limited.

While the authors and publisher have made every effort to contact copyright holders of the material used in this volume, they would be happy to hear from anyone they were unable to contact.

Chapter 1

What is language and what does it do?

Shân Wareing

1.1 Introduction

This chapter provides a context for the topics discussed in the rest of the book, by explaining our approach to the study of language and positioning this approach in relation to other ways of thinking about language. Firstly, the chapter considers why language is a phenomenon worthy of study; we use an example of a letter to a newspaper to consider the ways in which language, society and power might be related. Secondly, the chapter considers the nature of language, and how its forms (i.e. its manifestations as spoken or written words, or as signs in sign language) and functions (i.e. what people use language for) may be described and categorised. Thirdly, the chapter explores some of the **variations** found in language systems, and the social meanings which are attributed to different languages, **dialects** and **accents**. Fourthly, the concept of power is introduced, with a discussion of some of the ways in which language creates and maintains power. The chapter concludes with a discussion of the term 'political correctness'.

1.2 Why study language?

People find the subject of language interesting and worth studying for many different reasons. Language can, for example, be used as a way of finding out more about:

- how our brains work, investigating how children learn language, or how damage to our brains results in certain kind of language disorders (psycholinguistics)
- how to learn and to teach different languages (applied linguistics)
- the relationship between meaning, language and perception (philosophy)
- the role of language in different cultures (anthropology)
- the styles of language used in literature (stylistics)
- the different varieties of language people use, and why there are linguistic differences between different groups (sociolinguistics)
- how to make computers more sophisticated (artificial intelligence).

Many of these areas overlap, and the topics discussed in this book employ ideas and methods from more than one area listed above.

Frequently, people who are not linguists are interested in language too. To test the truth of this statement, you have only to look at the letters pages of newspapers and count the number of letters printed per week which are on language-related issues. In the following text, a newspaper columnist complains about the official 'jargon' associated with school teaching in Britain, which she claims she dislikes so strongly that it caused her not to return to teaching:

> I have been taking a refresher teaching course, which reminded me why I gave up teaching in the first place. It wasn't the pupils, or the pay, or the mountains of marking and preparation, or the huge classes. It was the rubbish new language that one must learn and use in order to read and write the reams of plans, forms, observations and assessments which clog the road to teaching – sorry 'providing learning opportunities' – and marking – sorry – 'evaluating learning outcomes'. One look at this page of gibberish gives me the cold shudders. I cannot understand it for toffee.
>
> Michele Hanson
>
> (*The Guardian*, 11 February 2002, p. 9)

A letter making a similar complaint about the use of jargon in education appeared in *The Daily Telegraph* (7 September 1997), responding to a previously published article. (Ofsted is the organisation responsible for monitoring standards in schools in the UK: Office of Standards in Education.)

> *Ofstedspeak*
>
> Lucinda Bredin's concern about the language of Ofsted reports (Review, August 24) is justified. The mysterious world of Ofstedspeak can be difficult to penetrate.
>
> The word 'satisfactory' which smacks of mediocrity, is discouraged by Ofsted. The word 'sound' is encouraged instead.
>
> The bright and shining ones at Ofsted have also given the thumbs down [to] the word 'ability'.[1] Inspectors are asked not to refer to pupils' different levels of ability. They must instead write about levels of attainment, meaning what pupils can do in relation to what might be expected of them.
>
> That happily relieves everyone of having to say of any child that he or she lacks ability. Poor attainment may be the result of poor teaching, or inappropriate curriculum or, come to that, Government policy.
>
> As the second wave of inspections takes place, reports will be written in a different language from before. In particular, where a first

wave report has said that pupils are performing well in relation to their ability, that will be out of order in a second wave report.

There is real danger that Ofsted language will become so arcane as to be unintelligible to ordinary citizens.

Peter Dawson,
Ofsted registered inspector, Derby

This letter actually picks up on many of the issues to do with language which we will be dealing with in this book. First of all, it addresses the concept of whether what we call things does matter, and whether it is a worthy topic of debate. The fact this letter was written at all suggests that what we call things does matter, and is a topic worth debating. A second language issue raised by this letter is the use of jargon; jargon can be impenetrable to anyone outside a small group of 'those in the know', as both Peter Dawson and Michele Hanson state.

The term 'Ofstedspeak' raises a third language issue. The word has been coined by analogy with **Newspeak**, the form of English invented by George Orwell in his novel *Nineteen Eighty-Four* (1949), and creates a reference to Orwell's dystopian nightmare in which people's thoughts are controlled and limited by the language available to them. In *Nineteen Eighty-Four*, Orwell reflects on the relationship between language and our perception of reality, also a theme of this letter. When children are assessed, can their ability be measured, or only their attainment? That is, can their inherent capacity be measured, or only what they achieved on a particular day under particular circumstances? Does it matter which word is used? Peter Dawson obviously thinks that ability can be tested, and the use of the word 'attainment' is a **euphemism** to cover up an unacceptable fact with a 'prettier' word. On the other hand, I prefer the word 'attainment' because I agree with Ofsted that only attainment can be measured, and that ability cannot. If the letter writer and I were to continue this debate, we would be arguing not just about words but about our view of education and our beliefs about the nature of human beings. Words can signal strongly our attitudes to fundamental things; debates that may appear to be about words can actually be about values and world-view. Which word is chosen may also affect people's perception of the world, and of themselves. Pupils who do badly at school because of poor teaching, or an inappropriate curriculum, or government policy, may want to return to learning later in life. Whether or not they do so may well be influenced by whether they thought their previous lack of success in education was due to low ability (and therefore they may feel that they are never likely to improve) or just to low attainment (in which case, under different circumstances, they may feel they would do much better).

Fourthly, the term 'Ofstedspeak' illustrates that human beings use language creatively and make up new words which can nevertheless be understood by others who are familiar with the culture in which the new word was developed.

Fifthly and finally, the letter also illustrates the important matter of who gets to decide how language is used. 'The bright and shining ones at Ofsted' have made a decision about how reports will be written (i.e. using the word 'sound' rather than 'satisfactory' and the word 'attainment' rather than 'ability'). Peter Dawson disagrees with this usage and has written to a national paper to complain about it. However, as a registered inspector for Ofsted, he is likely to have to use these terms, despite his objections, if he wishes to stay in his job. The children whose performances are going to be categorised either under the term 'attainment' or under the term 'ability' however, have no say at all in the discussion about which term is used.

These aspects of language, and in particular the third and fifth mentioned here (the extent to which language reflects and creates our perception of the world, and who makes decisions about what is appropriate language use) are major concerns of this book.

ACTIVITY 1.1

Below are two suggestions for straightforward 'fieldwork' tasks you could carry out if you are interested in finding out more about attitudes to language held in the society around you.

1   Check the letters page of two or more newspapers for a period of time such as two weeks or a month. How many letters about language use appear? Are there common themes in the comments the letter writers make? Do you agree with the arguments they put forward?
2   Keep a mental or a written note of the references people make to language use. Particularly record any comments people make that are regretful or angry about changing language use. Do you agree with the sentiments expressed? If so, why? If not, why not?

1.3 What is language?

Having discussed what you can expect from this book, let's take a closer look at some of the main themes and ideas we'll be dealing with. The first of these is what language actually is. There are several different ways of thinking about language; which way you think about it depends on which aspect of language you are interested in.

1.3.1 Language: a system

One of the obvious ways of thinking about language is as a systematic way of combining smaller units into larger units for the purpose of communication. For example, we combine the sounds of our language (**phonemes**) to form words (**lexical items**) according to the 'rules' of the language(s) we speak. Those lexical items can be combined to make grammatical structures, again according to the **syntactic** 'rules' of our language(s). Language is essentially a rule-governed system of this kind, but there are other ways of thinking about how language works and what we do with it, and it is those which we are concentrating on in this book.

For example, we usually assume that we use language to say what we mean. However, the processes by which we create 'meaning' are actually very complicated indeed, so we're going to begin with some 'models' of meaning. These will help us get started but will soon prove to be too simple to be really accurate, at which point we will have to make the models more complicated.

One model for explaining meaning is to assume that every group of sounds or letters which make up a word has a one-to-one relationship with a meaning. And for every meaning you can think of, there is a corresponding group of sounds (a spoken word) and letters (a written word). When describing this way of thinking about language, traffic lights are often used as a comparison. For the meaning 'stop' we have a red traffic light. For the meaning 'go' we use a green traffic light. An amber light on its own tells you to stop, and that the next light to show will be the red one on its own. In Britain, red and amber lights showing together mean that you should stop, but that the next signal to follow will be green for 'go'. The fact that the lights can show only in certain sequences and combinations is a bit like the syntax which governs word order in sentences, and permits the sequence:

today I went swimming

but not the following sequence (an asterisk * before a phrase denotes that the expression is not one which speakers of that language will accept as well-formed):

*went today swimming I

There are several limitations linked to thinking about language as a system like traffic lights. Firstly, there would only be one signal (group of letters or sounds) for every meaning. If this were the case, Peter Dawson would not be able to disagree with Ofsted about the use of satisfactory versus sound (where clearly there is some overlap in meaning). Secondly, there would be a limited number of meanings and signals available. While it would be possible to use a green and amber combination, what would it mean? You would know if you had been informed already, but what would you do if you were driving along and suddenly came to a traffic light showing amber and green? You might well assume that the lights had malfunctioned, rather than that a new message was being communicated.

1.3.2 Language: the potential to create new meanings

One of the reasons why language is actually a far more complicated entity than traffic lights is that we can use it to create new meanings. Here are some expressions which illustrate language being used creatively to express new meanings:

unleaving
McDonaldisation
being perved at
uptitling
Sweatshirting

These are all expressions which I can remember hearing or seeing for the first time, but which I had no trouble understanding in their contexts.[2]

Perhaps you use some of these expressions yourself, or perhaps they strike you as archaic or peculiar. It's difficult to think of examples of language being used creatively, because successful new uses get adopted very quickly and become just a normal part of everyday language. However, what you can probably still see is that words can be used in new ways to mean new things, and can be instantly understood by people who have never come across that word before. This ability is one of the things that sets human language apart from the kind of communication that goes on, for example, between birds, which can only convey a limited range of messages.

ACTIVITY 1.2

List any expressions you recently heard or started to use for the first time. Can you remember how you felt about using them for the first time? If you are interested in pursuing this area further, ask people of a variety of ages whether they are aware of new expressions coming into use. You could compile a list of expressions based on their answers and, if you have the time available, use the list as the basis of a larger survey to find out how many people are already using these expressions, and whether there's a pattern to who uses them and who doesn't.

1.3.3 Language: multiple functions

Another important dimension of language is the very different purposes we use language for all the time. In the course of a day you will probably use language referentially, affectively, aesthetically and phatically. Below are some examples to illustrate these different ways of using language.

You use language referentially when you say 'put those papers on the table'. Your instruction is referential because it gives information about what you want placed (the papers) and where you want them placed (on the table). This aspect of language, its ability to communicate information, is very important. Examples of contexts where this aspect of language is very obvious are: pilots discussing flight paths with air traffic control; recipes; assembly instructions with self-assembly furniture; school textbooks; directions on how to get to a friend's house. In all these cases, accurate, non-ambiguous information will be a priority.

However, the transmission of information is certainly not the only reason we use language, and there are many linguistic choices we make every day which are not a consequence of information transmission at all. For example, you could use any of the four utterances below and convey the same factual information. But, by selecting one as appropriate and not another, you would be exploiting the affective aspect of language and showing yourself to be sensitive to the power or social relationship between you and the person you are addressing.

> Put the newspaper down on the table.
> Can you put the newspaper on the table.
> I wonder if you'd mind putting the newspaper on the table, please.
> Put the ****ing paper down on the ****ing table right now!

On the other hand, you might say:

> What's black and white and read all over? A newspaper!

In this case you wouldn't be trying to give anyone information. You would be exploiting the ability of language to give us pleasure by its formal properties, its sounds and written appearance: its aesthetic properties.

If later in the day someone came in and said 'Oh, good choice in newspapers!' and you said 'Thanks', you would both be exploiting the phatic properties of language. This is the everyday usage of language as 'social lubrication'. No important information is being exchanged, but you are both indicating that you are willing to talk to one another, are pleased to see one another, and so on.

In this book, we're largely concerned with the first two functions of language: its referential function and its affective impact. These two functions are the ones most clearly associated with power. The referential function is the one associated with what objects and ideas are called and how events are described (i.e. how we represent the world around us and the effects of those **representations** on the way we think, as the letter above about the language of Ofsted reports highlighted). The affective function of language is concerned with who is 'allowed' to say what to whom, which is deeply tied up with power and social status. For example, 'It's time you washed your hair' would be an acceptable comment from a parent to a young child, but would not usually be acceptable from an employee to their boss.

1.3.4 Language diversity

Let's focus on another aspect of language now: the aspect of who speaks what language, and what variety of that language they speak. If you travel to France, you probably expect to be spoken to in French. Language boundaries and national boundaries frequently coincide, but of course the picture is more complicated than that. In many places which are not England or France, English or French is spoken (in India, Canada and many African countries for example). Moreover, in different countries, different versions of English or French are spoken. Indian English is different in some of its grammatical structures from British English, as well as in its pronunciation.

Languages do not vary only between countries; they also vary within countries. Schools in large cities are often attended by children who between them speak many different languages. Not only are many different languages spoken within primarily English-speaking countries such as Britain and the

United States: there is also a great deal of variation within English itself. Chapter 10 looks at variation in English in more detail.

People often have very strong attitudes towards different languages and different varieties of language. Consider this letter from *The Guardian* (20 September 1997), written after the people of Scotland and Wales had voted on whether to have separate elected governing bodies from the main UK government:

> Having survived the nail-biting Wales referendum results on TV, I hope and pray that as soon as their assembly is set up, it will be made illegal to speak the unintelligent [*sic*][3] gibberish called Welsh outside Wales.
> Malcolm Everett, Brighton, East Sussex

It is not clear from the letter how seriously the writer intended his point to be taken. Gibberish, however, is a strong word to use about other people's language and suggests how deeply prejudices can go against language, against other cultures and ultimately, against other people. Clearly, no language is gibberish to those who speak it, and equally, no language, including English, makes sense to a non-speaker.

To conclude this part of the chapter: language is a system, or rather a set of systems (a system of sounds, a system of grammar, a system of meaning); variations in usage are often systematic as well. Within these systems, there is scope for creativity and invention. How individuals use the systems available to them varies according to who the speakers are, how they perceive themselves and what identity they want to project. Language use varies also according to the situation, whether it's public or private, formal or informal, who is being addressed and who might be able to overhear. Integral to these choices we make about language use is the dimension of power, and that will be discussed next.

1.4 Power

Power is a complex and abstract concept, and an infinitely important influence on our lives. Power is defined in *The New Fontana Dictionary of Modern Thought* (1999) as: 'The ability of its holders to exact compliance or obedience of other individuals to their will' (p. 678). The *Dictionary* then quotes the eighteenth-century French philosopher Jean-Jacques Rousseau: 'The strongest man is never strong enough always to be master unless he transforms his power into right and obedience into duty' (p. 678). Language has a key role in transforming power into right and obedience into duty. Some scholars would go further and say that language is the arena where the concepts of right (both in the sense of entitlement and in the sense of what is morally acceptable) and duty are created, and thus language actually creates power, as well as being a site where power is performed.

One of the writers whose theories have had most influence on thinking about language and power is Louis Althusser, the twentieth-century French philosopher. Althusser argued that 'in order to persist over time ... an economic system such as capitalism must continually "reproduce" its relations of production, i.e. the exploitative class relationship arising out of ownership or non-ownership of the means of production' (*The New Fontana Dictionary of Modern Thought*, pp. 24–5). Althusser called the mechanisms by which economic systems reproduce their relations of production 'Ideological State Apparatuses' (ISAs). ISAs include the political parties, trade unions, religious and educational institutions, the family and culture, including the mass media. 'All these act to integrate individuals into the existing economic system by subjecting them to the hegemony of a dominant ideology, a set of ideas and values which ultimately supports the dominance of the capitalist class' (*The New Fontana Dictionary of Modern Thought*, p. 25). In other words, the values and beliefs we hold which seem to be 'normal' and 'commonsense' are in fact constructs of the organisations and institutions around us, created and shared through language. It is more effective and efficient for a system to control our behaviour by controlling our perception of reality than it is to control us with force (such as the police, prisons and the military).

The concept of power has already surfaced in this chapter: the power of Ofsted inspectors to decide what words to use; the power of one person which makes it possible for them to give another person a command such as 'Wash your hair' without jeopardising the relationship; the status of some languages compared to others, such as the relative standing of English and Welsh. For the rest of this chapter, I will present some examples of language and power at work together, to illustrate some of the ways these two phenomena are inter-linked.

To begin with, consider these statistics published by the State of the World Forum (September 2000).[4]

- Number of pages on the World Wide Web: 320,000,000
- Percentage of all websites in English: 80
- Percentage of world population that understands English: 10

These statistics indicate the extent to which the Web is dominated by the English language, and to which the majority of the world's population are excluded linguistically from most of the material on the Web, even if they

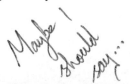
Maybe I should say...

11

had the physical means of accessing it. The Web is frequently talked about as a democratising medium, one which enables everyone to have their say, or publish their ideas. These statistics show that this description of the Web is really true only for English speakers. What language/s you speak is one way in which you immediately have access to, or are excluded from, some kinds of power. Bearing in mind these statistics, how appropriate is the term 'World Wide Web'?

We also find power at work in our everyday use of language. **Discourse** structures create power relations in terms of how we negotiate our relative status through interaction with others. Two examples of this follow. The first is an email I received at work:

> Pfs2 crashed at 11:04PM Sat reporting fan failure and excessive temper-ature in the SSA (where user data is held). It failed in its re-boot because two disks had gone. It is now back and the fan assembly appears to be working normally. However two disks have gone which means that one of the user volumes is running un-mirrored. The disks will be replaced by Sun and that will entail further down-time, possibly today but prob-ably tomorrow morning although I have no timescale currently. Y drives were re-available at 10:25AM today. As pfs2 was considered available by sun to the extent that it was pingable after the crash, that system was effectively unavailable due, e.g., to network timeouts on NFS mounts.
>
> A.

Although this email was not intended for me, as it was sent to me by mistake, I tried to read it. It immediately triggered feelings of frustration and inade-quacy as I struggled to understand it, reminding me of the many times I have needed to ask the advice of a computer expert but not understood their response. Sometimes I have suspected that the expert knew that I didn't understand their reply but enjoyed feeling they had knowledge that I didn't have, that they had the power to make me feel ignorant, and that, as a result of the power imbalance, I would not be brave enough to demand an explanation in language I could understand. This particular email was not sent to me to intimidate me; that was an unintended side-effect. However, the phenomenon of a layperson not understanding an expert is one illustration of the dynamics of power and language. The layperson becomes increasingly aware of their lack of know-ledge; perhaps feels confused, embarrassed or frightened, possibly too scared to ask for an explanation; or, perhaps having asked and received an explana-tion as confusing as the original statement, they have given up. Many of us have encountered this situation in dealing with experts in the fields of computing, medicine or law. In the World Wide Web example, we saw that which language you speak can be a pathway to power. In this example, what variety of language you speak, and how you make use of that variety, are sources of power.

Power can also be played out in other ways in ordinary conversation, and we all have experience of this; indeed it is probably true to say that power is a dimension of every single conversation we have, in one way or another. This extract from Ian McEwan's novel *Atonement* illustrates two characters, Cecilia and Mrs Jarvis, battling for power in a conversation. Briony has visited her sister, Cecilia, and has not so far been invited in, so both are in the hall of Cecilia's lodgings

> At that moment, the door snapped open and the landlady stood right in front of Briony, so close to her that she could smell peppermint on the woman's breath. She pointed at the front door.
>
> 'This isn't a railway station. Either you're in, young lady, or you're out.'
>
> Cecilia was getting to her feet without any particular hurry, and was retying the silk cord of her dressing gown. She said languidly, 'This is my sister, Briony, Mrs Jarvis. Try and remember your manners when you speak to her'.
>
> 'In my own home, I'll speak as I please,' Mrs Jarvis said. She turned back to Briony. 'Stay if you're staying, otherwise leave now and close the door behind you.'
>
> Briony looked at her sister, guessing she was unlikely to let her go now. Mrs Jarvis had turned out to be an unwitting ally.
>
> Cecilia spoke as though they were alone. 'Don't mind the landlady. I'm leaving at the end of the week. Close the door and come up.'
>
> Watched by Mrs Jarvis, Briony began to follow her sister up the stairs.
>
> 'And as for you, Lady Muck,' the landlady called up.
>
> But Cecilia turned sharply and cut her off. 'Enough, Mrs Jarvis. Now that's quite enough.'
>
> Briony recognised the tone. Pure Nightingale, for use on difficult patients or tearful students. It took years to perfect. Cecilia had surely been promoted to ward sister.[5]

Cecilia asserts her authority through her body language (getting up slowly), her speech acts (giving direct commands, such as 'try and remember your manners', and 'Enough Mrs Jarvis', and through speaking as if the landlady were not present), presumably through her accent, which indicates her higher social class (hence the comment 'Lady Muck'), and through her use of a tone associated with her authority at work ('Pure Nightingale'). The landlady retaliates by her body language (turning away from Cecilia to address Briony), by giving commands to Briony ('either you're in ... or you're out'), and by insulting Cecilia ('Lady Muck'). This book looks at insults in Chapter 5 on gender and Chapter 6 on ethnicity, on talking as if others weren't there in Chapter 7 on age, and attitudes to accent in Chapter 11.

Finally, let us return to the matter raised by the letter about Ofsted and the use of language in the education system: who decides which terms are acceptable and which are not. In the 1980s, campaigns to change language use (where language was sexist, racist or discriminatory to people with disabilities) attracted considerable media attention and the term 'political correctness' (or PC) was and still is used to describe such campaigns. Language reform has been around for a long time: it was very influential in the eighteenth century, for example, so the implication that no one argued about the use of language prior to the emergence of 'political correctness' is false, and is one example of the way the term is manipulated. According to Cameron (1995), the term 'political correctness' was probably first used in a straightforward way, in the sense of political actions which the speaker approved of. However, it took on an ironic sense and was used among people active on the political left as a self-mocking joke to describe the extreme and unrelenting standards of behaviour of some of their fellow activists. In this sense it was directed at those who were overly pious or 'holier-than-thou'. While 'politically correct' was used in this ironic sense, to be politically 'incorrect' was to mean 'something like "I am committed to leftist causes, but not humourless or doctrinaire about it"' (Cameron 1995: 122). The term 'political correctness' was then appropriated by the political right as a slur against all left-wing activity. This, as Cameron points out, leaves those on the political left in a difficult position. How, for instance, do they answer the question 'Are you politically correct?' when they're not sure if the answer 'Yes' means 'Yes I'm left-wing' or 'Yes, I'm bigoted/extreme/doctrinaire/joyless'. This appropriation of meaning is what Cameron calls a 'triumph of linguistic intervention' and its success is apparent in that the negative connotations of 'political correctness' are so well established that it is now virtually impossible to use the term in any positive sense. So anything you label as 'PC' takes on the negativity of the label, obscuring the real issues about whether the thing itself is worthwhile or not. The term 'political correctness' is thus a good illustration of the way terms can 'slide around', having slightly different meanings for different people, and being a 'site of struggle' (in this case, a struggle over who controls the meaning and thus whether 'political correctness' is a good thing or a bad thing, a joke, a serious threat or a worthwhile cause). It is ironic that, having been a 'site of struggle' over meaning itself, the term 'political correctness' can be used as a weapon against proposals for language reform, on the basis that such proposals are interference with language and its meaning. Such attacks have resulted in sets of joke coinages such as 'vertically challenged' (short), 'chronologically challenged' (old) and 'follically challenged' (bald), which effectively undermine serious attempts at language reform and deflect attention away from the underlying issues. (For more on political correctness see Chapter 3 below; Cameron 1995; Dunant 1994.)

1.5 Summary

This chapter has outlined why the topics of language, society and power might be worth studying, and why in this book we are assuming that the three topics are related. Several ways of thinking about, or 'modelling', language have been offered and some of the kinds of variations in language you might encounter have been commented on. The chapter concluded by looking at some of the ways language, power and society are related. The study of language is worthwhile, we believe, because it is such an important part of all our lives. We also believe that by studying it we can learn a great deal about how society is structured, how society functions, and what are the most widespread, but sometimes invisible, assumptions about different groups of people.

Some people find that this knowledge is valuable because it contributes to their understanding of themselves and their relationships with others. Knowledge about language, society and power may enable people to make choices in their language use which make them feel better about themselves. People can also find knowledge about the areas discussed in this book valuable because it can be used to challenge what they perceive as unfairness in society. Whatever your reasons for reading this book, we hope you find it interesting and useful.

Notes

1   The use of square brackets in this sentence indicates that the original text has been altered in some way, and that what is contained within the square brackets is the addition of the present author. In this case, the text was shortened slightly, by removing some words from either side of the word 'to'.

2   *Unleaving* is a word invented by the poet Gerard Manley Hopkins (1844–89) from the poem 'Spring and Fall'. From the context, it refers to the fall of leaves from trees. The *McDonaldisation* of diets refers to the global increase in high-fat fast-food consumption. I found *being perved at* in a fashion column, which was describing the consequences of wearing to work summer clothes which showed a lot of flesh. *Uptitling* was coined to describe the practice of changing

jobs titles to make them sound more prestigious. *Sweatshirting* is a word I encountered as a heading in a mail order catalogue for the pages with sweat-shirts and jogging bottoms on them.

3   The use of the Latin term *sic* here indicates that what may appear to be a mistake made in this publication is in fact a correct transcription of the original. In this case, the letter writer may have confused the words 'unintelligible' (language which cannot be understood) with 'unintelligent' (not clever). He may have made a mistake in writing his letter, the newspaper may have made a mistake in their reproduction of his letter, or he may have deliberately chosen 'unintelligent' to cast a slur on the Welsh people.

4   http://www.simulconference.com/clients/sowf/dispatches/dispatch2.html.

5   Ian McEwan, *Atonement* (London: Jonathan Cape, 2001), p. 334. 'Nightingale' is a reference to Florence Nightingale (1820–1910), the founder of trained nursing as a profession for women.

Suggestions for further reading

Andersson, Lars-Gunnar and Trudgill, Peter, *Bad Language*, Harmondsworth: Penguin, 1992. This is a small, accessible book written for the general reader which aims to start you thinking about language issues.

Dunant, Sarah (ed.), *The War of the Words*, London: Virago, 1994. A collection of essays directed at the general reader, including 'The culture war and the politics of higher education in America', 'Sex and the single student: the story of date rape' and 'Liberté, Égalité and Fraternité: PC and the French'.

Montgomery, Martin, *An Introduction to Language and Society* (2nd edition), London: Routledge, 1996. An introductory text which covers a wide range of social and linguistic issues.

Fairclough, Norman, *Language and Power* (2nd edition), London: Longman, 2001. Linguistic analysis of political and advertising texts. See in particular Chapter 3, 'Discourse and power'.

Klein, Naomi, *No Logo*, London: Flamingo, 2000. A political text for the layperson, critically analysing the ideological mechanisms of consumerism and branding.

Chapter 2

Language, thought and representation

Ishtla Singh

2.1 Introduction

On 2 July 2001, three underground trains on the London Victoria line were halted in a tunnel, where they remained for over an hour. Passengers had to be evacuated, and over six hundred treated for heat exhaustion – a consequence, it seemed, of too little ventilation and too many people. An investigation was subsequently launched into what was termed 'overcrowding' on underground trains. On 23 January 2003, however, London Underground officially stated that there was 'no such thing as an *overcrowded* Tube train', since the term meant 'excess over a defined limit', and no restriction on passenger numbers had ever been set (*London Metro*, 24 January 2003: 11). Trains could therefore only ever be *crowded* and there was subsequently no cause for alarm.

Such examples of linguistic sleight-of-hand are not uncommon. Indeed, many of us are very aware of similar types of 'trickery' in advertising, news reporting and even (or especially?) political speeches. The fact that it is so common implies a perceived link between how we talk about things and how we construe them: London Underground, for example, chose to represent conditions on the train in a way that not only mitigates their responsibility to passengers but also potentially alleviates fears about commuter safety. A similar example arose in the 1990s when the tobacco industry in Britain was accused of not explicitly warning consumers of the dangers of *low-tar* cigarettes, which were instead marketed as a 'healthier' alternative to the standard, high-tar varieties. A spokesperson for the anti-tobacco league stated in a radio interview that such 'irresponsible advertising' was akin to telling people that they'd be safer jumping out of a second, rather than fifth, storey window.

It's not just people in the public eye who exploit the links between language use and perception. All language users can, and do, make similar choices about the 'angles of telling' (from Simpson 1993) they adopt. Indeed, it has even been argued that such alternative 'angles on reality' exist not only within the resources of individual languages but also between languages themselves. The following sections explore both of these ideas, and we begin by looking at a well-known theory of language as a representational system devised by Ferdinand de Saussure. Section 2.3 then looks at the premises of the Sapir–Whorf Hypothesis, which posits a relationship between experience, perception and language, and section 2.4 discusses examples of 'angles of telling' within one language.

2.2 Saussure and language as a representational system

The Swiss linguist Ferdinand de Saussure (1857–1913) is perhaps best known as the deviser of structuralism, which not only formed the basis for much modern linguistic enquiry but was also adapted into many other fields, notably literary criticism. His theories about language are too numerous to detail here and the following is therefore a summary of the ideas most pertinent to our discussion.[1]

Saussure theorised that speakers of different languages engage in an arbitrary division of reality; that is, that 'different languages cut up reality in different ways' (Andersen 1988: 27). Thus, every language can be said to be a particular system of representation that mirrors, and indeed so reinforces, the 'world' of its speakers. The mental links that speakers make between concepts or perceptions and the labels used to 'name' them, is made at the level of *langue*, which is 'our [innate] knowledge of the systematic correspondences between sound and meaning which make up our language (including the knowledge of what utterances are possible ... and what utterances are not)' (Andersen 1988: 24). To make this idea of innate knowledge a bit more

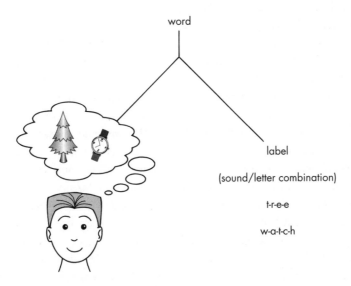

Figure 2.1 Words represent labels and concepts

transparent, think of words such as *tree*, or *tomorrow*, or *summer* or *elephant*. As soon as you hear or read these, you 'know' what concepts they refer to. You also know, again without explicit explanation, that they are acceptable English words – their sound or letter combinations (in speech and writing respectively) are all possible. Furthermore, you are able to make such judgements with words you have never heard before, or don't know the meaning of, such as *gleek* or *xng*. You would probably rate the former as a possible English word, but not the latter, which does not conform to English sound combinations.[2] And finally, you would also know, without instruction, that

I hope to see an elephant standing under that tree tomorrow

is an acceptable English construction, while

*hope standing an to elephant see under that I tomorrow

is not.

In essence, *langue* comprises an 'abstract system of units and rules' (McMahon 1994: 25) that members of a speech community subconsciously share. This innateness of *langue* means that it is very difficult, if not impossible, ever to come to a true and accurate description of how it is actually constructed in each language (though Saussure felt that this should be the ultimate concern of linguistics). The only glimpses into the workings of *langue* that we are afforded are through analysis of *parole*, the actual use of language in both speech and writing. Whereas the 'hardwiring' of langue is shared by a speech community, *parole* encompasses the *individual* use of language. It is on this level that we demonstrate the choices that result in the 'angles of telling' referred to in section 2.1. To return to our earlier example, even though the sound or meaning correspondences between *overcrowded* and *crowded* are both 'known' at the level of *langue* to English users, different groups (here, the safety watchdog and London Underground) have made deliberate choices in which representation they favour at the level of, in this instance, written *parole*.

One of the things you may not have been consciously aware of while you've been reading so far (but of which you will be now!) is that, as an English user, you understand *overcrowded* and *crowded* not only because of their established sound and meaning correspondences in your *langue* but also because of their relationship to each other. In other words, you 'know' that an element of the meaning of *crowded*, for example, is that it is not *overcrowded*, and vice versa. Saussure's theory of the **linguistic sign** elucidates both of these principles. Firstly, the notion of the linguistic sign formalises what we have so far been calling 'sound and meaning correspondence'.

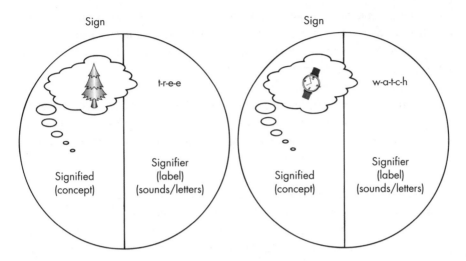

Figure 2.2 Signs are made of signifiers and signifieds

Saussure terms the sound sequence which makes up a label a **signifier**, and the meaning or concept associated with it the **signified**. The correspondence between the two constitutes the linguistic sign. Saussure was careful to stress (as we shall here), that the actual sign is not one or the other of its component parts but instead the association that binds them together (see Figure 2.1). Saussure stated that, once the correspondence between the signifier and the signified has been established in a langue, it tends to appear 'natural' and indivisible to speakers: 'Just as it is impossible to take a pair of scissors and cut one side of paper without at the same time cutting the other, so it is impossible in a language to separate sound from thought, or thought from sound' (*Cours de Linguistique Générale*; quoted in Harris 1988: 29).

However, Saussure did maintain that the link between the signifier and the signified is arbitrary. In other words, there is no pressing reason why the concept of a tree, for example, *has* to be symbolised by the exact sequence of sounds or letters in *t-r-e-e*. This is underlined by the fact that different languages label the same concept with different signifiers: *arbre* in French, for example, or *Baum* in German. In addition, because the link is ultimately arbitrary, there is also no reason why either might not change over time, and a new 'natural' link established. Indeed, this is a common development in any language's history. The English *werewolf*, for example, preserves Anglo-Saxon *wer*, which once meant 'man'. We can safely assume that the speakers who coined and used this **compound** also perceived a link as natural and indivisible between the sound and meaning of *wer* as that which we still retain for *wolf*.

The second major point in Saussure's theory of the sign relates to the idea that we mentioned earlier, namely that signs partially derive meaning from their relationship with other associated signs. For example, we understand what a *werewolf* is by virtue of the fact that it is not a *wolf*, and vice versa. However, if we were to extract *wer* from the compound and do a quick survey, we would be hard pressed to find English users who could confidently tell us its meaning. The simple fact that it is no longer part of modern English *langue* means that those of us unfamiliar with *wer* have no mental reference point for it, no grid of associations that could help us shape it – it could mean absolutely anything.

Interestingly, while the fossilised *wer* in *werewolf* persists, along with its associated terrors, English users have gone on to coin a relatively new compound, *wolfman*. At first glance, this could be interpreted as simply a more transparent rendition of the older sign. However, we could argue that the two are somewhat different: *werewolf* refers to a sinister transformation of a person into a wolf-like monster, whereas *wolfman* appears to denote someone who takes on, or has, superficially wolfish characteristics but remains essentially, a (somewhat unfortunate) person. Thus, to paraphrase a famous movie title, we're more likely to anticipate being scared when we see *An American Werewolf in London*, and to look forward to a few laughs with *An American Wolfman in London*.

If this is indeed our interpretation of the two signs then, as in our example *crowded* and *overcrowded*, part of our understanding of *wolfman* is predicated on the fact that it does not refer to the traditional *werewolf*. Thus, as stated earlier, at the level of *langue*, signs do not exist in isolation, but in systems of associative relationships. Furthermore, as our example indicates, these associative relationships can shift to make room for new signs. We could therefore argue that an older system of *wolf~werewolf~man* has altered somewhat to accommodate *wolfman* so that, now, *werewolf* embodies an increasingly ominous element as compared with the friendlier newcomer. A more down-to-earth example is discussed in Chapter 5, with reference to the introduction of *Ms* to the associative relationship that holds among female-referring titles.

The idea that language users partly derive their understanding of signs from the latter's associative relationships ties into Saussure's theory that we can truly get at the essence of a sign only by contextualising it in its current system of use. For example, even though Anglo-Saxon texts have been able to tell us that the signifier *wer* was tied to signified 'man', we can't confidently say that we fully understand how it was used in everyday Anglo-Saxon life. What were the associative relationships of *wer*? Could it be used as a general term for 'male', or, more specifically, for a particular type of man? Did *wer* have favourable connotations in speech (that is, did it refer to a male who possessed qualities valued in that society)? To better understand the subtle layering of meaning a sign accrues through its use; consider a modern English sign such as *paki*, a term of racist abuse in the UK denoting someone who appears to have ethnic affiliations with the Indian subcontinent. If we had to separate it into its component parts, we could say that the signifier *paki* is tied to the signified or concept 'person ethnically linked to the Indian subcontinent'. However, to leave it at that would be to ignore the fact that socially negative perspectives have become encoded into the signified component. They may be difficult to deconstruct and objectify, but the fact that this sign is used in racist *parole* testifies that they are nevertheless present and potent. In the UK, *paki* exists in a system of associative relationships with signs which negatively label other ethnic groups. UK English users know, at the level of *langue*, the relative potency of these signs: my students for example tell me that *paki* is 'worse' than *frog* (which denotes the French), which in turn is worse than *taffy* (which refers to the Welsh), but that nothing is as bad as *nigger*. Someone outside the speech community in which these signs and their associative systems are current will not necessarily have the same 'understanding' of them when they initially surface in *parole*. As a personal example, some of the racist signs in my native *langue* were very different from those I encountered when I settled in England. For example, my **creole** *langue* contained signs such as *red* and *dougla*,[3] which had no currency in Britain. I wasn't familiar with signs such as *paki*, or *frog* or *taffy*, and they each seemed (and still do) equally appalling to me. The importance of considering signs within their current systems of use is further emphasised when we compare them across languages. For example, the English sign *mutton* might superficially appear to be equivalent to the French *mouton*, from which it was originally adapted. Both signifiers are linked to the signified 'cooked meat of the sheep' and, in English, we maintain a distinction between *mutton* and the associated *sheep*, which denotes the live animal. However, in French, the signifier *mouton* also refers to the live animal as well and so exists in a different set of associative relationships. Thus, considering linguistic signs in the context of their systems is crucial to understanding how individual speech communities 'cut up reality'. Their *parole* makes explicit, to a certain extent, assumptions and correlations that have become implicit at the level of *langue*.

It is noteworthy that individual languages are made up not just of linguistic signs: as we have seen, we also have knowledge, at the level of *langue*, of the structural principles which allow us to create utterances that are meaningful in our native languages. We can refer to our 'native knowledge' of these structural rules as our **grammar**, and the systems of each also vary from language to language. As we shall see later, the grammatical systems of one language might specify that only certain types of nouns can be marked for plurals, or that all nouns have to be gendered as masculine or feminine. Thus, the arbitrary division of reality that Saussure theorised is embodied in different languages through the interaction of the grammar and linguistic signs of each. Furthermore, it is arguable that the representations of 'reality' offered by the resources of each language are not just reflections of particular ways of looking at the world; they also reinforce those perceptions for their users. The following section further explores this link between representation and perception as formalised in the Sapir–Whorf Hypothesis.

ACTIVITY 2.1

You will need other people for this activity. Take two familiar objects and agree that you will reverse their names (for example, you will call dogs *tulips*, and you will refer to tulips as *dogs*). Now ask each other questions, including the reassigned names, which the other person must answer. For example,

QUESTION: Have you ever been bitten by a tulip?
ANSWER: Yes, but not badly. I didn't need a tetanus injection.

When you have exhausted the questions you can think to ask, discuss whether you found the activity difficult, and whether you can imagine a world where all the names were swapped overnight.

2.3 The Sapir–Whorf Hypothesis

The notion of an arbitrary but significant link between perceptions of 'reality' and linguistic representation is neither new nor particular only to Saussure. Since at least the time of the Ancient Greeks, scholars have argued for a causative link between culture and language (that is, a community's cultural experience and resultant worldview 'shapes', in Saussurean terms, their *langue*). In the eighteenth and nineteenth centuries, this idea was promoted through the notion of *Weltanschauung* ('worldview') in the work of philosophers such as von Humboldt, Kant, Herder and Hegel. In the twentieth century, exploration of *Weltanschauung* was mainly taken up by anthropologists, ethnologists and sociologists, and carried into American scholarly traditions by Franz Boas and, later, Edward Sapir. The work of the latter in particular, and that of his student Benjamin Lee Whorf, gave impetus to the theory that 'culturally based "ways of speaking"' exist: a concept that would form the basis of what is known today as the Sapir–Whorf Hypothesis.

The hypothesis comprises two parts, **linguistic relativity** and **linguistic determinism**. Linguistic relativity theorises that the languages of different cultures comprise distinct systems of representation which are not necessarily equivalent. Linguistic determinism proposes that a language not only encodes certain 'angles on reality' but also affects the thought processes of its speakers. More specifically, Whorf's position seems to have been that language is linked to 'unconscious habitual thought' and that there is 'at least some causal influence from language categories to non-verbal cognition' (Gumperz and Levinson 1996: 22). Users of a language are generally unaware both of the relative nature of their linguistic system and of its impact on how they think. Thus, as Whorf stated:

> the forms of a person's thoughts are controlled by inexorable laws of pattern of which he is unconscious. These patterns are the unperceived intricate systematizations of his own language ... every language is a vast pattern-system, different from others, in which are culturally ordained the forms and categories by which the personality not only communicates, but also analyzes nature, notices or neglects types of relationship and phenomena, channels his reasoning, and builds the house of his consciousness.
>
> (quoted in Gumperz and Levinson 1996: 21)

In one of Whorf's most famous explorations of relativity and determinism,[4] he posited a relationship between linguistic representation, cognition and behaviour, exemplified by observations he had made when working as a fire inspector. He had found, for instance, that in certain storage facilities, people were much more careful around what were labelled *gasoline drums* than with *empty gasoline drums*. People's interpretation of the linguistic sign *empty* influenced their perception of these drums as being safer than their *full* counterparts, and obscured the fact that they still contained explosive vapour. In a more recent example, the US Council for Energy Awareness, which handles publicity for America's nuclear industry, conducted a research poll on the public's evaluation of certain *Nukespeak* terminology. They found that a significant number of interviewees responded positively to nuclear plants which were termed *walk-away safe*. On the basis of their understanding of these two signs (and presumably, because they had not been informed otherwise), members of the public interpreted this label as meaning that 'people living nearby could walk, rather than run, from the area in the event of an accident' (Ann Bisconti, quoted in *Bulletin of the Atomic Scientists*, April 1990: 5). However, within the 'technical community' (ibid.) of Nukespeak users, the phrase is used instead to denote a plant which can automatically shut itself down if necessary.

Studies that test relativity and determinism continued throughout the twentieth century and quite a few have yielded interesting results. John Lucy (1992), for example, compared the effects of noun pluralisation in American English and Yucatec Maya (spoken in south-eastern Mexico). Both languages categorise and pluralise their nouns differently. In Yucatec Maya, speakers distinguish between three main noun types: (1) those which refer to animate, discrete entities (e.g., *dogs*); (2) those which refer to non-animate, discrete objects (*cups*); (3) those which refer to 'tangible substances with malleable form' (*mud*) (quoted in Skotko 1997: 9). Nouns in category (1) will carry plural marking, and those in (2) and (3) will not. American English speakers typically distinguish between 'count' and 'mass' nouns: the former refer to entities, animate and non-animate, which are discrete, and the latter to entities that inherently contain the sense of 'more than one' (as in, for example, *people*). Speakers of this language will typically pluralise count nouns, but not mass ones.

In Lucy's experiment, twelve speakers of each language were given four tasks based on a picture series. They were first asked to look at and verbally describe a drawing (picture A) which depicted a hut next to four trees and a well. Picture A also contained a boy, a bottle lying in front of the hut, a hen and a man feeding corn to three pigs. In Task II, informants were asked to describe Picture A but without looking at it, thus depending on their short-term memory. Task III required them to pick, from a series of five pictures which differed slightly from picture A, the one most similar to the original. In picture B the boy was missing, in C the bottle was removed, in D a broom was added, in E there was extra corn by the hen, and in F extra corn near the pigs. In the final task, respondents were presented with all six pictures, and asked to identify the original picture A. In all four tasks, a significant element of the English speakers' description and recollection of the pictures was that of **number** for almost every animal and non-animate discrete object (such as the hut, or broom). However, they hardly noticed differences of quantity in substances such as the corn. The Yucatec Maya speakers, on the other hand, noted and remembered number less than the English speakers did overall. However, the plurals they did recollect were mostly for nouns denoting animals. Given that the results of each group of speakers accorded with the pluralisation patterns of their native language, Lucy concluded that this particular grammatical structure had a significant effect on how speakers perceived and remembered visual stimuli. The Yucatec Mayan speakers, for whom plural marking is less frequent, 'view[ed] picture scenes differently and notic[ed] less variations opposed to the English speakers' (Skotso 1997: 11).

Scientific American (Minkel 2002: 2) cites another example of an experiment designed to test linguistic determinism. Lera Boroditsky of MIT, in one study, looked at whether the **grammatical gender** assigned to nouns in languages such as French and German influenced the perceptions speakers had of the objects' attributes. She asked bilingual German–English, and Spanish–English respondents to describe, in English, items that were grammatically gendered as masculine or feminine in their other native tongue. A sign such as *key*, for example, is gendered as feminine in Spanish, and masculine in German. The native Spanish speakers used adjectives such as *lovely, tiny, magic* to describe this object, in contrast to the native German speakers' *hard, jagged* and *awkward*. Of course, there is nothing inherently feminine or masculine about such attributes, and any such associations we make will be based on our stereotypes of gendered qualities, but it is none the less interesting that speakers seem to perceive and describe the same object in such different ways. If Boroditsky is right, then the use of grammatical gender may play at least some part in the qualities that speakers subconsciously encode in the relevant linguistic signs.

Though we have spent the last few pages looking at relativity and determinism across different languages, you'll remember that we also hypothesised that various 'angles of telling' are possible within the resources of one language. The following section explores this notion further with reference to discourses in English.

2.4 One language, many worlds

In one episode of the sitcom *Friends* (Episode 175254, Series 9), the character Rachel tells the group that Ross, the father of her baby, still consults his childhood paediatrician. In order to stall their teasing, Ross protests that the doctor 'is a great diagnostician!'. His brother-in-law, Chandler, retorts: 'diagnostician, or boo-boo fixer?' As in our earlier example of *overcrowded* versus *crowded*, the crux of the matter lies in the labelling: how you name it links to how you perceive it. While this version of Ross's 'reality' generated a healthy giggle from the audience, there are many who would argue that some real-life choices of representation are no laughing matter. One of these is Carol Cohn (1987), who wrote of her first-hand experiences of the *technostrategic* language used in the US nuclear industry. In 1984, she began a year of immersion in 'the world of defense intellectuals', in order to understand better 'the nature of nuclear strategic thinking'. One of her significant conclusions was that the language used by this Nukespeak community reflected and reinforced a particular perspective; namely that nuclear weapons are safe. We can refer to this perspective as the group's **ideology**. Simpson (1993: 3) defines ideology as 'the taken-for-granted assumptions, beliefs and value-systems which are shared collectively by social groups'. Thus, the people whom Cohn met appear to have subconsciously participated in a particular, positive 'reality' about nuclear power, as natural and as obvious to them as is the horror-filled alternative to many of the rest of us.

Cohn identified a high use of 'abstraction and **euphemism**' (1987: 1) in technostrategic language. For example, certain nuclear devices are labelled as *clean bombs*, directing perception away from the dreadful results of their high-energy blasts. *Counter value attacks* obscure the destruction of cities, and *collateral damage* neatly hides the resultant human corpses. She notes too that there is an explicit element of sanitisation in some aspects of representation: *clean bombs* are employed in *surgically clean strikes* where an opponent's weapons or command centres can be *taken out*, meaning that they are accurately destroyed without significant damage to anything else. As Cohn (ibid.: 2) states, 'the image is unspeakably ludicrous when the surgical tool is not a delicately controlled scalpel but a nuclear warhead'.

Among the other categories that Cohn identified as being important in Nukespeak were sexual **metaphors**, domestic imagery and religious terminology. Lecturers in the industry talked of *penetration aids*, advisers of 'releasing 70 to 80 percent of our megatonnage in one orgasmic whump', and of the fact that nuclear weapons were 'irresistible, because you get more bang for the buck'. On one trip to a nuclear submarine, Cohn and her group were invited by an accompanying officer on the tour to reach out and *pat the missile*. According to Cohn, patting denotes intimacy and sexual possession; here, transposed to the appropriation of what she terms 'phallic power'. However, as she also points out, patting can also embody an element of domestication. Thus, *patting* the missile also means rendering it familiar and harmless. Representations that support this perception include naming launch-ready missiles in their *silos* as *Christmas tree farms*, the fact that weapons systems *marry up* and that *buses deliver* the nuclear explosives on certain missiles. Finally, Cohn identified a significant use of religious terminology. The first atomic bomb test was named the *Trinity*, and famously, Oppenheimer (the lead scientist on the project) thought of the Hindu avatar Krishna's words on a battlefield in the *Bhagavad Gita*: 'I am become death, destroyer of worlds'. Certain members of this Nukespeak world also refer to themselves as the *nuclear priesthood*, making, as Cohn points out, an 'extraordinary implicit statement about who, or rather what, has become God' (ibid.: 5).

Overall, Cohn believes that the 'angle of telling' embodied in such modes of representation makes it easier to ignore the human cost of nuclear war. It is weapons, not people, that are seen as *vulnerable*, which have to *survive*, and which can get *killed*, sometimes through *fratricide* (the destruction of one warhead by another from the 'same side'). Nukespeak is relative to the perspective of the creators and controllers of nuclear weapons: the worldview it encodes is not that of the victim. Thus, Cohn felt that, as she gained fluency in this 'new language', the less concerned she became about nuclear war. She believes that as she learnt it, her ideology changed simultaneously: 'I no longer stood outside the impenetrable wall of technostrategic language and once inside, I could no longer see it. I had not only learned to speak a language; I had started to think in it. Its questions became my questions, its concepts shaped my responses to new ideas' (Cohn 1987: 3). However, as Cohn demonstrates by voicing her concerns about Nukespeak, her perceptions were not completely determined by its representations. Indeed, she even states in her article that she was at times able to step 'outside the wall' and 'remember' that she was actually scared of, not excited by, nuclear power. She calls for greater awareness within the industry of what Nukespeak 'allows us to think as well as to say' (ibid.: 1) so that others too have the choice of stepping 'outside the wall'.

It's ok to be in love.

ACTIVITY 2.2

Jon Hooten (2002) suggests that many English-speaking communities have increasingly included 'war terminology' into everyday usage, normalising it and de-sensitising speakers to the actual horrors of such conflict. Thus, headlines such as *Farmers battle Summer Drought, Mayor defends Budget* and utterances such as *Your new car is da bomb* or *Did you see that comedian bomb last night?* demonstrate how 'the extra-ordinary metaphor of war has infiltrated the everyday' (ibid.: 2). Can you think of similar instances of normalisation from *warspeak* or from any other specialist domain? Do you think that such 'infiltration of the everyday' can in fact influence our perceptions of the 'extra-ordinary' as ordinary?

In section 2.3, we saw that the differences in representation encoded in individual languages are a result not just of their distinct systems of signs but also of particular features in their discrete grammars. The same principle holds for the structural choices available within one language: the ways in which users construct utterances are also significant in the representations they make. For example, the *London Metro* (24 January 2003) article mentioned at the beginning of this chapter also printed a comment made on BBC Radio 4 by London Underground's safety director, Mike Strzelecki, about the evacuation of passengers from the three halted trains. He had said, as part of his statement to the press, 'mistakes were made'. This is an interesting choice: note that he *didn't* say 'we made mistakes', or even 'London Underground made mistakes'. The latter two alternatives give a clear sense of who might have been responsible for those errors, but in Mr Strzelecki's comment such information is imperceptible and, as such, the reader or listener is not 'directed' to look for it. The differences in perception that the real and fictional examples engender is due to the use of two **voices**: Mr Strzelecki's comment makes use of **passive voice** and my alternatives of **active voice**.

The following illustration makes use of a simplified model detailed in Simpson (1993: 4). This is the **transitivity model**, used in the analysis of utterances to show 'how speakers encode in language their mental picture of reality and how they account for their experience of the world' (Simpson, ibid.: 89). Utterances potentially comprise three components: (1) *process*, which is typically expressed by a verb; (2) *participants* in the process: the participant who is the 'doer' of the process represented by the verb is known as the *actor*; the *goal* is the entity or person affected by the process; (3) *circumstances* associated with the process: in utterances such as *she cried loudly* or *he jumped from the cliff*, the underlined components provide extra information about the process, and can in fact be omitted.

In active voice, utterances typically follow the structure *actor + process + goal*. Thus, our earlier fictional examples would be structured as:

We/London Undergound   made   mistakes
actor   *process*   *goal*

Here, the foregrounding of the actor makes their involvement perceptually important. In passive voice, on the other hand, it is the goal which becomes foregrounded, and the actor is moved to the end of the utterance:

mistakes   were made   (by us/London Underground)
goal   *process*   *actor*

I've bracketed the actor in the above example to signal that it can be either retained or omitted, making agency less or not at all visible. The marginalisation or exclusion of the actor in such constructions can contribute to a perception that it is relatively unimportant. Consequently, a reader or listener may be more likely to concentrate on the foregrounded information and spend less, if any, time thinking about the actor.

Thus, the combination of structural and sign choices is integral to the creation of certain representations. A good illustration of this can be seen in newspaper headlines, which typically condense an 'angle of telling' on a particular story. For example, in January 2003, police raided a flat in Manchester,

England, which contained ingredients for making the poison ricin.[5] A police-man, Stephen Oake, was fatally stabbed. The incident was widely covered in the British press, and headlines such as the following appeared on 15 January. (See Chapter 4 for examples and analysis of another Ricin incident.)

Daily Mirror

Ricin Raid Copper	Knifed	to Death
participant (goal)	process	circumstance

The Times

Policeman	Murdered	in Ricin Raid
participant (goal)	process	circumstance

Northwest Evening Mail

Butchered

Process

In the current post-9/11 political climate,[6] many British newspapers reflect (and in so doing, perpetuate) a particular ideology which draws a distinction between an *us*, a category which includes 'Western' outlooks and ways of life, and an oppositional, threatening *them*. These headlines have been written within this ideological framework but tell their stories in somewhat different ways.

The *Daily Mirror* and the *Times* headlines both make use of passive voice, foregrounding the victim of the stabbing. In addition, neither makes explicit mention of the alleged actor of the 'knifing' or 'murdering', but it is noteworthy that later reports in various British newspapers went on to make explicit links between this incident and threat from *terrorists*: currently, a highly negative sign. The *Northwest Evening Mail*, on the other hand, omits explicit mention of both actor and goal and focuses instead on the all-important process which has resulted in death. One-word headlines such as this are extremely interesting, because they highlight the fact that the signs used are chosen with some meas-ure of deliberation. Why not simply *Killed*, for example, or *Murdered* or *Knifed*? Indeed, if we were to consider the three signallers of process as being in an associative relationship (see section 2.2), as in *murdered~knifed~butchered*, we might agree that while they all share certain elements of mean-ing, such as a sense of deliberate violence and untimely death, *butchered* is much more horrifically emotive than the other two, carrying as it does very strong connotations of cruelty and inhumanity when used in reference to a human being. The *Evening Mail*'s choice of representation, therefore, is likely to skew the reader's perception towards a certain angle of telling in the narra-tion of this episode, as indeed are the choices of the other two newspapers.

The *Daily Mirror* and *The Times* differ also in their labelling of the victim: the former chooses the more colloquial *copper*, and the latter the more formal *policeman*. Both use the phrase *ricin raid*, but in somewhat different ways. The *Daily Mirror* foregrounds it with *copper* in a **nominalisation**, which effectively summarises and establishes an immediate context for the stabbing of Constable Oakes. In *The Times*, however, this *ricin raid* context is given less perceptual prominence than the 'murder' of the policeman. Although neither headline explicitly mentions who might have been responsible for the stabbing, it is arguable that the notion of the threatening *them* is implicit in *ricin raid*, since the media have consistently been carrying numerous warnings on the potential manufacture and use of such poisons as chemical weapons by *terrorists*. Indeed, the *Daily Mirror*'s 'familiarisation' of Constable Oake as a *copper*, an ordinary man just like *us*, going about his (law-abiding) job and inadvertently becoming a victim, contrasts effectively with the 'anarchy' of the *them* involved in poison manufacture and killing.

It is arguable that such headlines reflect the political orientations of their respective newspapers.[7] *The Times*, a more formal broadsheet, is typically considered to be aligned to the political right whereas the *Daily Mirror* (more of a tabloid paper) is assumed to be more politically left. A quick trawl through some of the editions of the *Northwest Evening Mail* has indicated that it too has alliances with the political right, as well as quite conservative views on issues such as immigration. However, in the current climate, an opposition between a threatening terrorist *them* and a threatened *us* seems to be the de facto ideology underlying newspaper reporting of the majority of such stories, and as such, it is extremely difficult to find relevant headlines which clearly reflect different political affiliations. None the less, it is important to remember that newspapers do not write themselves but are necessarily put together by people who, by virtue of being people, necessarily have perspectives on how the world unfolds. Such viewpoints consciously and unconsciously become linguistically encoded and readers are arguably influenced into either going along with or rejecting them. Thus, as Simpson (1993: 6) states, we can assume that language is not a transparent, objective medium for communication but, instead, a 'projection of positions and perspectives . . . a way of communicating attitudes and assumptions'. And in Nukespeak, or headlines, or comments made by spokespeople for safety or indeed, in whatever type of discourse we choose to examine, 'the elusive question of the "truth" of what [is said] is not an issue; rather, it is the "angle of telling" adopted' that necessitates our scrutiny.

ACTIVITY 2.3

Look at the headlines and the first lines of reports of the same story from three or four different newspapers on a particular day. Using the discussion of the newspaper headlines in section 2.4 as a guideline, compare how information is being presented in each. What are the perspectives being presented, and how are they being linguistically encoded?

2.4 Summary

In this chapter we have explored the notion that each language can be considered a unique and arbitrary system of representation which 'cuts up reality' in different ways. The resources of each language allow for different discourses, which can reflect and reinforce the ideologies of the groups they are used by. Thus, 'language is not used in a context-less vacuum' but 'in a host of discourse contexts . . . which are impregnated with the ideology of social systems and institutions (Simpson 1993: 6). It follows, therefore, that socially powerful groups can use language to perpetuate their ideologies. Because we do not always interrogate language use, assuming it instead to be a 'natural, obvious' medium of representation, we can become normalised to the ideological perspectives that discourses encode, seeing them instead as 'common sense'. Indeed, this is what Carol Cohn experienced when she stated that integration into the Nukespeaking community made it increasingly difficult to think outside of the worldview embodied in the discourse. Thus, since language can be used to naturalise us into accepting certain ideas about 'the way things are and the way things should be' (Simpson 1993: 6), we must learn to challenge its representations and, as Sapir once stated, fight its implications. These ideas will be explored in more detail in the following chapters.

Notes

1   For an excellent discussion of Saussure's ideas see Carroll (1956).
2   *Gleek* appears to have once meant 'a joke, a jeer, a scoff', according to the Revd Alexander Dyce's *Glossary to the Works of Shakespeare* (1902). *Xng* occurs in one of the Bantu languages, where it means 'to run'.
3   *Red* can be used derogatorily to refer to someone with African and European ethnicities, and *dougla* to refer to someone with both African and Indian ethnicities.
4   Whorf (1939).
5   Ricin is distilled from a poisonous protein in the bean of the castor oil plant. It is a highly toxic poison: one milligram can kill an adult.

6   '9/11' is the term used in the United States to refer to the attack on the World Trade Center on 11 September 2001.
7   See Tony Trew's (1979) work on newspaper headlines, quoted in Simpson (1993).

Suggestions for further reading

Montgomery, Martin (1996) *An Introduction to Language and Society* (2nd edition), London: Routledge. Chapter 10 of this introductory text discusses the issue of language and representation and is clearly illustrated with data from news reporting.

Fairclough, Norman (1989) *Language and Power* (2nd edition), London: Longman. An introductory text to the area of language use and power. Chapter 4 provides a clear discussion of how ideology becomes entrenched in discourse and accepted as 'common sense'.

Simpson, Paul (1993) *Language, Ideology and Point of View*, London and New York: Routledge. A useful and engaging discussion and analysis of how language works in texts to reflect ideologies and perspectives.

Chapter 3

Language and politics

Jason Jones and Jean Stilwell Peccei

3.1 Introduction

In this chapter we look at how language can be used to achieve political ends. We start with a discussion of what politics is, and how it is possible to see many of our ordinary choices and decisions as having political consequences. We then consider political language in light of the the relationship between language and thought which was explored in Chapter 2. We will discuss the ways in which language can be used to create and reinforce certain value systems, focusing on the role of discourse in shaping the beliefs which affect people's behaviour, motivations, desires and fears, and in establishing certain ideologies as 'common sense'. Finally, we examine some of the rhetorical devices used by politicians to make an impact on the public.

3.2 What is meant by 'politics'?

George Orwell claimed that 'in our age there is no keeping out of politics. All issues are political issues' (1946: 154). Politics is concerned with power: the power to make decisions, to control resources, to control other people's behaviour and often to control their values. Even the most everyday decisions can be seen in a political light. In the supermarket, some brands of coffee are marketed on the basis of fair wages having been paid to the workers in the countries where the coffee was produced. Every time you buy coffee, you choose between these brands and brands which are often both cheaper and advertised more prominently, but which don't make this statement about fair wages. When you choose, you make a small contribution to the continued existence of either a company that claims to pay workers fairly or one that doesn't make this claim. You make political decisions when you decide whether or not to buy recycled paper goods, organically grown vegetables or genetically modified food. When food is imported from countries with political regimes or particular policies opposed by people in your country, you will be lobbied not to buy goods from those countries, as was the case with the boycott on South African produce during the apartheid era. There is no avoiding political decisions, even in the most domestic, everyday areas. In this chapter, we will largely use the language of 'career' politicians who govern countries to illustrate our ideas about political language. However, as we have argued, politics stretches far wider than this narrow definition, and political language is in use all the time, all around us.

ACTIVITY 3.1

Consider the uses of the word 'politics' in the expressions below. If you had to explain what these expressions meant, perhaps to a speaker from another culture, how would you rephrase them? Avoid using the word 'politics' in your rephrasing.

1   They made careers for themselves in politics
2   Sexual politics
3   Don't get involved in office politics
4   The personal is political
5   Philosophy, Politics and Economics
6   Environmental politics

From your answers to this activity, it will probably be clear that politics can refer to a wide range of activities. Your answers might have included: (1) the process of deciding national policy; (2) gender equality; (3) the jockeying for position which goes on in small, tightly knit groups, often achieved by the process of leaking and withholding information; (4) the way people negotiate roles in their private lives (also related to gender); (5) the history of political systems; (6) a whole range of activities to do with transport, housing and consumption. Indeed, there is indeed no keeping out of politics!

3.3 Politics and ideology

Politics is inevitably connected to power. The acquisition of power, and the enforcement of your own political beliefs, can be achieved in a number of ways; one of the obvious methods is through physical coercion. Many events regarded as significant in history involve the imposition, by force, of the rule of one group of people on to another group. This is what, in essence, most wars are about. Under dictatorial regimes, and military rule, those in power often control people by using force. In democracies, physical force is still used legally, for example to restrain people accused of criminal activity.

Other kinds of coercion are implemented in a democracy through the legal system. For example, there are laws about where you can park your car, about not destroying other people's mail, about where and when you can drink alcohol. If you break these laws, you can be fined, or even arrested and imprisoned. These are all examples of political ends achieved by coercion.

However, it is often much more effective to persuade people to act voluntarily in the way you want, that is, to 'exercise power through the manufacture of consent . . . or at least acquiescence towards it' (Fairclough 1989: 4), instead of continually having to arrest them for wrongdoing. To secure power, it makes sense to persuade everyone else that what you want is also what they want. By encouraging citizens to embrace his or her goals of their own accord, any cost-conscious ruler is able to save money on armed forces and police officers. To achieve this, an ideology needs to be established: one which makes the beliefs which you want people to hold appear to be 'common sense', thus making it difficult for them to question that dominant ideology.

The concept of ideology was first introduced by followers of Karl Marx, notably Louis Althusser. Althusser wondered how the vast majority of people had been persuaded to act against their own best interests, since they worked long hours at laborious tasks and lived in poverty, while a very small number of people made enormous amounts of money from their labour, and enjoyed lives of luxury. In order to explain why the impoverished majority didn't just refuse to work in this system and overthrow the rich minority, Althusser reasoned that the poor had been persuaded that this state of affairs was 'natural', and nothing could be done to change it.

Today, 'ideology' tends to be used in a wider context, to refer to any set of beliefs which, to the people who hold them, appear to be logical and 'natural'. 'Ideology' is not necessarily a pejorative term, because it can be argued that virtually everything we know and think is in fact an ideology. People can question the ideologies of their culture, but it is often difficult. Not only can it be a challenging intellectual task, but it can also result in social stigma. People who question the dominant ideology often appear not to make sense; what they say won't sound logical to anyone who holds that ideology. In extreme cases, people who ask such questions may even appear to be insane. So, while it is possible to question the dominant ideology, there is often a price to be paid for doing so.

As was proposed in the previous chapter, it is possible to regard our understanding of reality as entirely mediated by the language and the system of signs available to us. That system of signs, according to this argument, is in fact not an unbiased reflection of the world but a product of the ideologies of our culture. In the next section, we will see two examples (one fictional, the other real) of the powerful role of language in establishing and maintaining ideologies.

3.3.1 Language as thought control: Newspeak and political correctness

Chapter 2 discussed the theory of linguistic determinism, which suggests that language can be said to provide a framework for our thoughts, and that it is very difficult to think outside of that framework. If we look at this argument within the context of politics and ideology, we can see that it might be possible to use language to manufacture an ideology which could steer the way people think. Politicians throughout the ages have owed much of their success to their skilful use of rhetoric, whereby they attempt to persuade their audience of the validity of their views by their subtle use of elegant and persuasive language. We will explore the use of persuasive language in sections 3.4 and 3.5. However, there is a more extreme side to this line of argument: that language can be used not only to *steer* people's thoughts and beliefs but also to *control* their thoughts and beliefs. It is this extreme view that we will now consider.

If we accept that the kind of language we use to **represent** something can alter the way in which it is perceived, then you might wonder whether, by controlling the discourse, one can control how another person thinks. This is the premise explored by George Orwell's novel *Nineteen Eighty-Four* (first published in 1949). A totalitarian society of the future has Ingsoc (English Socialism) as the dominant political system. The system is enforced by the mandatory requirement for all citizens to use a language called **Newspeak**, a radically revised version of the English language from which many meanings available to us today have been removed. In an appendix to *Nineteen Eighty-Four* entitled 'The principle of Newspeak', Orwell explains that 'the purpose of Newspeak was not only to provide a medium of expression for the world-view and mental habits proper to the devotees of Ingsoc, but to make all other modes of thought impossible' ([1949] 1984: 231). The principles of Newspeak are therefore grounded in the Sapir–Whorf Hypothesis: that language determines our perception of the world (see Chapter 2). Orwell wrote:

> It was intended that when Newspeak had been adopted once and for all and Oldspeak forgotten, a heretical thought – that is, a thought diverging from the principles of Ingsoc – should be literally unthinkable, at least so far as thought is dependent on words. Its vocabulary was so constructed as to give exact and often very subtle expression to every meaning that a Party member could properly wish to express, while excluding all other meanings and also the possibility of arriving at them by indirect methods. This was done partly by the invention of new words, but chiefly by eliminating undesirable words and stripping such words as remained of unorthodox meanings, and so far as possible of all secondary meanings

whatever. To give a single example. The word *free* still existed in Newspeak, but it could only be used in such statements as 'This dog is free from lice' or 'This field is free from weeds'. It could not be used in its old sense of 'politically free' or 'intellectually free', since political and intellectual freedom no longer existed even as concepts, and were therefore of necessity nameless . . . A person growing up with Newspeak as his sole language would no more know that equal had once had the secondary meaning of 'politically equal', or that free had once meant 'intellectually free', for instance, than a person who had never heard of chess would be aware of the secondary meanings attached to queen and rook.

([1949] 1984: 231)

Of course, this is only a fictional situation. You might well question not only the viability of enforcing the exclusive use of a language such as Newspeak but also its ability to prevent people from thinking of certain concepts simply by removing the words that encode those concepts. In fact, Orwell himself stated that he did not believe thought to be entirely 'dependent on words'.

Nevertheless, the principles of linguistic determinism on which the fictional Newspeak is founded could be argued to underlie aspects of moves towards 'political correctness' in language. Newspeak, admittedly, was the product of a malign dictatorship in Orwell's novel, while 'political correctness' could be viewed as a benign attempt to improve the world. However, the two interventions into language use, one fictional, one real, may share certain assumptions, which we will now explore.

The origins of the term and indeed the concept of 'political correctness' (PC) are interesting and complicated. (See also Chapter 1.) Several linguists have proposed that, although the term originated with left-wing politicians, it has now been largely 'hijacked' by those on the right. (See, for example Cameron 1994, 1995; and Lakoff 2000.) The term has been used as an insult, as a joke and in sincerity by people who believe in its importance. When used by the latter group, it is underpinned by the assumption that the terms used to represent minority groups matter. Examples of 'PC' terms which have had an impact on language use include *visually impaired*, *blended family* (households incorporating children from several relationships) and ethnic origin terms such as *African-American*. Non-PC terms are considered by some not only to be offensive but to create or reinforce a perception of minority groups as unequal to the majority, which in turn may have a detrimental effect on the way a society is organised.

It could be argued that the use of 'PC' language is particularly significant in relation to disability, since many changes could be made to the way most organisations operate which could in turn have a positive effect on the lives of people with disabilities. For example, some people make a distinction between impairment and disability, using *impairment* to refer to a condition (such as loss of vision or a limb), and *disability* to refer to activities which are difficult or impossible to undertake (for example, reading small print or climbing stairs). This is intended to draw attention to the fact that someone's inability to read a book or reach the top floor of a shop is as much a consequence of the lack of adequate facilities as of their actual impairment.

Although 'political correctness' is not an attempt to control people's thoughts in the way that Orwell's Ingsoc did through Newspeak, it nevertheless represents an attempt to alter people's perceptions of certain **signifieds** (concepts) by replacing old **signifiers** (labels) with new ones. It should also be noted that there are those who do not support the argument that the language used to refer to a person has any significant impact on the way we actually think about them, but support 'politically correct' language on the grounds that it is important not to be offensive or disrespectful. Interestingly, the discourse of some opponents of 'political correctness' appears to share many assumptions concerning the relationship between language and thought with those who support it, at least on the surface. In this respect, Robin Lakoff proposes that the opponents' repeatedly cited descriptions of the PC phenomenon in the media 'suggest something much more threatening than is actually the case. "The new McCarthyism", "thought police", "Orwellian", "Fascist" and "totalitarianism," among the favored terms, conjure up a *Nineteen Eighty-Four* world of inexpressibility, constriction, and savage repression' (Lakoff 2000: 98).

So far in this chapter, we have considered the use of language to influence people's view of the world, using the examples of Geórge Orwell's invented language Newspeak and of 'political correctness'. You may think that any deliberate intervention into language use which attempts to influence the way people think is wrong. However, it may be worth considering whether intervention for a good reason (such as to improve the lives of disadvantaged people) can be justified, while the intervention for a bad reason (such as to limit people's lives) cannot. Of course, what constitutes a 'good' or a 'bad' reason is a question for political debate, which takes us back to politics again.

In the following sections we will return to the less extreme line of argument which suggests that language can be used to influence (rather than control) people's political and ideological views by exploring in detail the ways in which politicians can use language to their own advantage.

3.4 The implications of implications

One of the goals of politicians must be to persuade their audience of the validity of their basic claims. In this section we look at two of the ways this can be achieved in political discourse – **presuppositon** and **implicature**. These tools can lead the hearer to make assumptions about the existence of information that is not made explicit in what is actually said, but that might be deduced from what was said. In addition, implying rather than baldly asserting an idea leaves speakers with a 'get out clause', since they didn't actually state X but merely implied it. The use of implicature and presupposition is an integral part of all human communication. However, it is particularly useful in advertising and political discourse because it can make it more difficult for the audience to identify and (if they wish to) reject views communicated in this way, and can persuade people to take something for granted which is actually open to debate.

3.4.1 Presupposition

Presuppositions are background assumptions embedded within a sentence or phrase. These assumptions are taken for granted to be true regardless of whether the whole sentence is true. Take this sentence from the 2001 British Conservative Party Manifesto: 'We want to set people free so that they have greater power over their own lives.' Such a statement presupposes that people are not currently free. Even if we negate the sentence, 'We *don't* want to set people free so that they have greater power over their own lives', the presuppositions still hold that currently people are not free and have less power over their own lives. Presuppositions can be 'slipped' into a sentence in several ways via:

- *adjectives, particularly comparative ones.* 'A future Conservative Government will introduce a *fairer* funding formula for schools' (Conservative Shadow Education Secretary, Damian Green, 16 March 2003). This presupposes that the current funding system is not fair.
- *possessives.* 'You will never hear me apologising for highlighting *Labour's* failures time and time again' (Iain Duncan Smith, Leader of the British Conservative Party, 16 March 2003). This presupposes that the Labour Party has failed.
- *subordinate clauses.* 'We have arrived at an important moment in *confronting the threat posed to our nation and to peace by Saddam Hussein and his weapons of terror*' (George W. Bush in the White House press conference of 6 March 2003). This presupposes that Saddam

Hussein is a threat to the United States and to peace. Note also the use of the possessive *his* which presupposes that Saddam Hussein has weapons of terror.

- *questions instead of statements.* 'Is it not now time for him to ensure that his Government get control of the situation in Belfast?' (David Trimble, leader of the Ulster Unionist Party addressing Prime Minister Tony Blair in Parliament on 3 July 2002). This presupposes that the government does not have control of the situation.

Presuppositions are widely used not only in political debates and speeches but also by journalists to 'position' politicians in an interview or press conference. Here is an example from the BBC *Newsnight* television programme of 6 February 2003. Jeremy Paxman to Prime Minister Tony Blair: 'Yes, an unreasonable veto, as you put it. But if that happened, would you be prepared to go to war despite the fact that apparently the majority of people in this country would not be with you?'.

Not only does Blair have to answer whether he is prepared to go to war, he potentially has to deal with the presupposition that the majority of people in his country are not behind him. If he answers only the question on his preparedness to go to war, he tacitly admits that the majority of people in his country are not behind him. 'How' questions can be particularly useful for positioning the interviewee, as we can see from a 1990 interview with Margaret Thatcher, the British Prime Minister at the time. Gerry Foley, of ITV news starts off with: 'Prime Minister, how isolated do you think you now are on [European] economic and monetary union?'. In this case, the fact that she is isolated is presented as a 'given'.

ACTIVITY 3.2

Listen to or read transcripts of interviews with politicians and find instances where the presuppositions in the interviewers' questions can help put the politician on the spot. Pay close attention to the politicians' answers. Do they sometimes explicitly try to deny the presuppositions as well as answering the main question? Or do they ignore them? There are now many resources on the internet where you can access transcripts of political debates, speeches and interviews. Here are a few suggestions:

US sites

    www.pbs.org

    www.cnn.com

www.americanrhetoric.com
www.loc.gov (Library of Congress)

UK sites

www.parliament.uk
www.bbc.co.uk
www.itnarchive.com/
www.margaretthatcher.org

3.4.2 Implicature

Like presuppositions, implicatures lead the listener to infer something that was not explicitly asserted by the speaker. However, unlike presuppositions, implicatures operate over more than one phrase or sentence and are much more dependent on shared knowledge between the speaker and hearer and on the surrounding context of the discourse. Here, Oliver Letwin, a Conservative MP, addresses a question to David Blunkett, the Labour Home Secretary, concerning the government's plans to institute a system of national identity cards:

> This issue is too important an area of our national life, too central to the protection of society against fraud, and too fundamental to the preservation of our liberties, for us to accept such obscurity and spin. Will the Home Secretary assure the House that in the coming days and weeks he will make it clear what he is actually asking us to debate?

Although in some respects implicature is more indirect than presupposition, what Letwin was implying was clearly not lost on the Home Secretary:

> There appears to be a presumption by the Opposition that if they mention the word 'spin', the whole world will believe that someone has been spinning. Although I specifically instructed all those around me not to spin, appeared on no programmes – unlike the right hon. Gentleman – and kept away from saying anything about this over the last few days, I am accused of spin. I will tell the House what I am spinning. I am spinning the right of the British people to decide over the next six months whether they want a sensible way of confirming their own identity.
>
> (Hansard, 3 July 2002)

In that exchange, Blunkett acknowledged the power of implicature, but also made the point that it is often easy to see through it. Here is another example of implicature which caused quite an uproar in some sections of the British press, although this time it was from a journalist not a politician. Is it obvious to you what Jeremy Paxman was implying in this exchange with Prime Minister Tony Blair?

PAXMAN: The question is what freedom he has under the current inspection regime but we've discussed that already, I want to explore a little further about your personal feelings about this war. Does the fact that George Bush and you are both Christians make it easier for you to view these conflicts in terms of good and evil?

BLAIR: I don't think so, no, I think that whether you're a Christian or you're not a Christian you can try perceive what is good and what is, is evil.

PAXMAN: You don't pray together for example?

BLAIR: No, we don't pray together Jeremy, no.

PAXMAN: Why do you smile?

BLAIR: Because – why do you ask me the question?

PAXMAN: Because I'm trying to find out how you feel about it.

(BBC *Newsnight* broadcast of 6 February 2003)

3.5 Persuasive language – the power of rhetoric

Rhetoric is the skill of elegant and persuasive speaking, perfected by the ancient Greeks. The *Oxford English Dictionary* defines it more precisely as 'the art of using language so as to persuade or influence others; the body of rules to be observed by a speaker or writer in order that he may express himself with eloquence'. Although politicians today do not follow the original Greek rules in their strictest form, they often adopt identifiable habits of speech and observe a broader 'body of rules' which govern the linguistic structures and devices which they use to increase the impact of their ideas. In the following sections we will look in more detail at some of these devices.

3.5.1 Metaphor

Basically, metaphor is a way of comparing two different concepts. A distinction is often made between metaphor and simile in that a metaphor asserts that something is something else, e.g. 'The mind is but a barren soil', while a simile only asserts that something is similar to something else, e.g. 'The mind is like barren soil'. However, in both cases the mechanism is similar. As listeners or readers we know that the mind is not literally barren soil. Rather, the speaker or writer is inviting us to understand the mind in terms of barren soil. One of the challenges politicians face is that they often have to talk about abstract concepts in ways that make them seem more concrete, partly so that they can be more easily grasped, and partly to avoid boring their audience. The economy, which is regularly referred to in political speeches, is a case in point. It is not a concrete entity; it is an abstract model for thinking about a very large quantity of diverse financial data, including rates of inflation and patterns of employment and spending. A very frequently appearing metaphor for the economy in political discourse is *economy as machine*. For example, Margaret Thatcher on inflation in the 1970s in a speech to Confederation of British Industry, 19 April 1983, said: 'That vast wealth-producing engine of the West began to splutter, to hesitate and occasionally to backfire.' Graham Stringer of the Manchester Airport Board on the planned construction of a second runway said: 'The airport is already acknowledged as the *economic motor* of the region' (*The Times*, 16 January 1997). You can find many more examples by typing the phrase the *engine of the economy* into a search engine such as www.google.com, which at the time of this writing produced over a thousand occurrences of this metaphor.

Personification is a special type of metaphor that entails giving human characteristics to inanimate objects or abstract ideas. In political discourse, it is frequently used when referring to countries. Sometimes this is done largely for poetic effect, as in US President Lyndon Johnson's address on the assassination of Martin Luther King: 'Once again the heart of America is heavy.' At other times, the goal is more clearly ideological. For example, various British television news broadcasts during the 1990s referred to Germany's strong and influential position in the European Union with the metaphor 'Germany is the bully in the playground'. One advantage to a politician of a phrase such as *bully in the playground* is that it represents a complicated series of events in international relations much more simply and ties them into something which many people will have personally experienced, in this case negatively. The potential of this kind of metaphor for helping to construct or reinforce a particular perception of events or of whole societies can be seen by thinking of other metaphors for Germany's predominance in Europe that could have been used instead, e.g. *the conductor of the orchestra* or *the captain of the ship*.

In this respect, it is worth remembering that many of the metaphors we use in daily discourse, not just political discourse are so commonplace, so frequent and so pervasive that we scarcely realise that they are metaphors. For example, Lakoff and Johnson (1980) have proposed that Western culture metaphorically conceptualises argument as a war, citing the following typical expressions that we use when describing arguments:

Your claims are *indefensible.*
He *attacked* my position.
His criticisms were right *on target.*
He *shot down* all my arguments.
I've never *won* an argument with him.

Tony Smith of the University of Sydney writes of the language used in the Australian Parliament:

Not all language is literal, and metaphors describing Parliament are over-whelmingly masculine. In the Assembly, Members still speak beneath the weapons of war that symbolically emblazon the wall, but combat and the military are declining as sources of analogy and being replaced by contact sports, especially football. The image of football is constantly present, with its reflection of manly rites of passage. After an interstate Rugby League match against Queensland, a match billed as 'mate against mate, state against state', the Speaker called for order, saying, 'If the Member does not stop conversing, I will do to him what New South Wales did to Queensland last night.' Here, he produced a rubber hammer in New South Wales' colours and whacked it on his desk.
(*Lingua Franca*, broadcast, ABC National Radio, 29 May 1999)

Of course, we could think outside the framework of *argument as war* (or its close relative *argument as contact sport*), but it can be quite difficult. As a demonstration, Lakoff and Johnson invite us to imagine a culture where argument is seen as a dance, the participants as performers and the goal as producing an aesthetically pleasing performance. How easy would you find it to describe an argument in that culture?

ACTIVITY 3.3

Think about the effects of conceptualising the economy not as an engine but as a flower, a fire or an octopus. Then rewrite Margaret Thatcher's statement on inflation in the 1970s (see p. 46) in line with each of these new metaphors.

3.5.2 Euphemism

A euphemism is a figure of speech which uses mild, inoffensive or vague words as a means of making something seem more positive than it might otherwise appear. Euphemisms are commonly used when talking about taboo subjects, such as death or sex. We might talk about *passing away* instead of *dying*, or *making love* rather than *sexual intercourse*. It is a device which can help to make what might actually be seen as questionable ideas or issues more palatable and 'normal' and is a potentially useful tool for politicians when engaging in what Orwell called the 'defense of the indefensible'.

As we saw in Chapter 2, the use of euphemism is particularly extensive when discussing military matters. Two of the examples, 'surgically clean strikes' and 'clean bombs', achieve their effect in part from the positive connotations of *clean* and the associations that exist in everyday discourse between *clean* and *healthy*. In the 1990s Slobodan Milošević, President of the former Yugoslavia, embarked on a programme of what he termed 'ethnic cleansing'. In reality, this referred to the forcible removal of the non-Serbian civilian population in an attempt to redesign Yugoslavia along purely ethnic lines. He did this by bombarding towns with heavy artillery, besieging villages and massacring civilians. The term *ethnic cleansing* could be seen as an attempt not only to 'hide' these details from public discourse but also to present them in a positive light.

We might consider the term *ethnic cleansing* to be a prime example of euphemism, although the degree to which it fooled anyone for very long is highly debatable. A NATO-led aerial bombardment campaign was initiated to force the Yugoslav government to accept international requirements to cease ethnic cleansing, permit the return of already expelled refugees and accept an international peace-keeping mission within Kosovo. When Yugoslavia disintegrated into several states, Serbia, Milošević's stronghold, was expelled from the United Nations, and in 1999 Milošević was indicted at the International Court of Justice in The Hague for 'genocide, crimes against humanity, grave breaches of the Geneva Convention and violations of the laws or customs of war' (Case No. IT-01-51-I, The International Criminal Tribunal for the former Yugoslavia). Today *ethnic cleansing* is not a euphemism at all. It is a highly pejorative and emotive term, which has become virtually synonymous with the very acts that the euphemism was trying to disguise. In recent political discourse it has been applied (although not necessarily accurately) to the government policies of, among others, Israel, Chechnya, India, Macedonia, the Philippines and Sudan. It has been applied retrospectively to Nazi Germany's treatment of the Jews and Hungary's treatment of the Slovak minority in the late nineteenth century. It has even been applied by conservationists to the poisoning of pike (an invasive non-native fish) by the California Fish and Game Department.

Rather more subtle and arguably more benign uses of euphemism are frequently to be seen in the discourse of diplomatic negotiations. Thus, when a spokesman describes a diplomatic meeting as 'a free and frank exchange of views', people familiar with 'diplo-speak' interpret this as 'a flaming row'. If nothing else, however, this sort of euphemism prevents the parties involved in negotiations from painting themselves into a verbal corner. Indeed, much of the work in a successful negotiation is finding 'a formula of words' that both sides can live with. However, as Applebaum (2000) has pointed out in her analysis of the language of the Northern Ireland peace process, this work can be quite tortuous. The original term used in the 1998 Good Friday Peace Agreement, for the Irish Republican Army (IRA) eventually giving up its weapons was *decommissioning*. It had been deliberately chosen for its 'neutrality' but, she proposes, it proved difficult for Sinn Fein (the political wing of the IRA) to sell this to the IRA rank and file because it soon came to be interpreted by them as a euphemism for *disarming*, which in turn was interpreted as a euphemism for *surrender*. By 2001, the IRA proposed the term *putting weapons beyond use* instead. However, the opponents of the IRA interpreted that as a euphemism for *keeping weapons*. The negotiations continue at the time of this writing.

ACTIVITY 3.4

US post-Cold-War foreign policy has been described both in the press and by successive administrations in a variety of terms: 'global leadership', 'world policeman', 'new world order', 'strategy of enlargement' and 'assertive multi-lateralism'. To what extent would you consider any of these expressions to be euphemisms, and if so what for?

3.5.3 The 'rule of three'

One of the best-known structural devices in political rhetoric is the use of the 'three-part statement'. For some reason, we seem to find things that are grouped in threes particularly aesthetically pleasing. Goodman (in Cockcroft and Cockcroft 1992) has looked at the predominance of 'triads, threes and eternal triangles' in cultures from all around the world. She points out the frequent occurrence of the number three in fairy or folk tales (e.g. *Three Little Pigs*;

Goldilocks and the Three Bears; *Three Blind Mice*) and of groups of three in films (e.g. *The Good, the Bad and the Ugly*; *Sex, Lies and Videotape*; *Truly, Madly, Deeply*). The importance of the three-part statement as a rhetorical device is widely found in political documents and oratory. Three of the most famous three-part statements from the eighteenth and nineteenth centuries are to be found in:

- the cry of the French Revolution: 'Liberté, Égalité, Fraternité' (liberty, equality, brotherhood)
- the American *Declaration of Independence*, 'We hold these truths to be self evident: that all men are created equal; that they are endowed by their Creator with certain unalienable rights; that among these are life, liberty, and the pursuit of happiness.'
- Abraham Lincoln's *Gettysburg Address*: 'that government of the people, by the people and for the people shall not perish from this earth'.

Here are two examples from the 1997 British parliamentary elections. The first uses a three-part group of words, the second a three-part group of sentences.

This is the result of four years of Liberal Democrat and Labour *waste, whinge and weakness.*

(British Conservative Party election pamphlet, 1997)

We cannot secure peace by standing aside from war. We cannot end danger by putting safety before our friends. We cannot conquer fear by fearing to act ourselves.

(Iain Duncan Smith, Leader of the Conservative Party in Britain, addressing the party's annual conference, 10 October 2001)

ACTIVITY 3.4

Listen to or read the transcript of a politician delivering a speech in Congress or Parliament or on an occasion such as a party conference, convention or political broadcast. How many times does s/he make use of three-part statements? Would the ideas expressed have been more or less effective if they had been delivered in any way other than as a triad? (See Activity 3.2 for a list of online transcript sources.)

The three-part statement is such a powerful structure that politicians have used it even when they have only one point to make. At the 1996 Labour Party conference, Tony Blair claimed that the three main commitments of the Labour Party were 'education, education, education', while at the Conservative Party conference in the same year, that party's main concerns were presented as 'unity, unity, unity'.

3.5.4 Parallelism

When politicians want to draw attention to a particular part of their message and make it stand out from the rest of the speech, they often use parallelism, a device which expresses several ideas in a series of similar structures. This can serve to emphasise that the ideas are equal in importance and can add a sense of symmetry and rhythm, which makes the speech more memorable.

> *We shall* fight on the seas and oceans, *we shall* fight with growing confidence and growing strength in the air, *we shall* defend our Island, whatever the cost may be, *we shall* fight on the beaches, *we shall* fight on the landing grounds, *we shall* fight in the fields and in the streets, *we shall* fight in the hills; *we shall* never surrender.
>
> (Winston Churchill, Speech to the House of Commons, 4 June 1940)

> And so *let freedom ring* from the prodigious hilltops of New Hampshire. *Let freedom ring* from the mighty mountains of New York. *Let freedom ring* from the heightening Alleghenies of Pennsylvania. *Let freedom ring* from the snow-capped Rockies of Colorado.
>
> (Martin Luther King, Jr., 28 August 1963)

In both Winston Churchill's and Martin Luther King's speeches, we see not only the repetition of specific phrases, *We shall* and *Let freedom ring*, but also parallel structures. Note the repeated use of prepositional phrases by Churchill: *on the beaches, on the landing grounds, in the field*, etc. Martin Luther King's speech shows an even more extensive parallelism. The four sentences end with identically patterned prepositional phrases:

from +	the +	adjective +	noun (hills/ mountains)	+ of +	noun (American state)
		prodigious	hilltops		New Hampshire
		mighty	mountains		New York
		heightening	Alleghenies		Pennsylvania
		snow-capped	Rockies		Colorado

Antithesis also involves parallelism but uses it to establish a relationship of contrast. As Harris (2003) points out, antithesis, by juxtaposing opposite or nearly opposite truths, can convey a sense of complexity in a person or an idea and can clarify or highlight differences which might be otherwise over-looked. We can see an extended example of antithesis in former US President Richard Nixon's 1969 Inaugural Address, which was made during a period of increasingly widespread domestic opposition to America's involvement in the Vietnam War:

> We find ourselves rich in goods but ragged in spirit, reaching with magnificent precision for the moon but falling into raucous discord on earth. We are caught in war wanting peace.

3.5.5 Pronouns

Even the pronouns that political speakers use to refer to themselves or their audience can be a significant part of the message. They can be used either to foreground or to obscure responsibility and agency. Consider, for example, former US President George Bush's use of pronouns in the extract below; why do you think he changes from *we* to *I*?

> As we announced last night, we will not attack unarmed soldiers in retreat. We have no choice but to consider retreating combat units as a threat and respond accordingly [. . .] From the beginning of the air oper-ation, nearly six weeks ago, I said that our efforts are on course and on schedule. This morning, I am pleased to say that coalition efforts are ahead of schedule. The liberation of Kuwait is close.
>
> (*The Guardian*, 27 February 1991)

One explanation for the shift would be that he uses *we* when the focus of his speech is relatively controversial, as it is unclear whom *we* refers to, and *I* when he is on safer ground and wanting to claim responsibility for positive achievements.

In the following speech, his son, President George W. Bush, is talking about possible military action against those he believed to be responsible for the September terrorist attacks on the United States. Even with the strength of feeling and emotion in the aftermath of the attacks, military action is always controversial. The consistent use of *we* helps to represent his response to the attacks as 'everyone's' response:

> Whether we bring our enemies to justice or bring justice to our enemies, justice will be done . . . We ask every nation to join us . . . Great harm has been done to us. We have suffered great loss. And in our grief and anger, we have found our mission and our moment.
>
> (Address to Congress, 20 September 2001)

The next example, Prime Minister Tony Blair, addressing the Labour Party Annual Conference in October 2001, shows a shift in pronouns between *I* and *you*, with a similar effect. The switch from *I* to *you* brings together his audience and, more importantly, encourages them to identify with the emotions that he felt at the time.

> Just two weeks ago, in New York, after the church service I met some of the families of the British victims . . . And as you crossed the room, you felt the longing and sadness, hands clutching photos of sons and daughters, imploring you to believe them when they said there was still an outside chance of their loved ones being found alive, when you knew in truth that all hope was gone.

3.6 Summary

In this chapter we have argued that politics is a widespread phenomenon, not restricted to people who make their career as politicians. We proposed that ideology is important in constructing a worldview and that people in a society tend to collaborate in the production of certain value systems and ways of talking about things, which can make other ways of thinking or talking seem rather strange or anti-social. This idea was then taken one stage further, as we considered the possibility of language controlling or influencing thought using illustrations from Orwell's *Nineteen Eighty-Four* and the 'political correctness' debate. In the section on the language of persuasion we examined the uses of presupposition and implicature which can be used to convey ideas without explicitly stating them and can make notions which are in fact debatable seem like 'givens'. Finally we looked at a variety of frequently occurring rhetorical devices in political discourse, metaphor, euphemism, the three-part statement, parallelism and pronoun use and at ways they can be used to achieve ideological and communicative potency. The themes in this chapter tie in closely with those discussed in the previous chapter. The next chapter continues these themes, looking at language use in the media, and how language choices can influence our perception of events, their causes and their effects.

Suggestions for further reading

Bolinger, Dwight (1980) *Language – The Loaded Weapon*, London: Longman. A classic in the field. Chapters 10–12 are particularly relevant to the discussion of language and politics.

Fairclough, Norman (2001) *Language and Power* (2nd edition), London: Longman. This text looks very closely at the use of language to manufacture consent and influence what people accept as 'common sense'.

Lakoff, Robin (2000) *The Language War*, Berkeley: University of California Press. Taking the view that the struggle for power and status is largely being played out as a war over language, Lakoff analyses the significance of a range of American media events from the 1990s: 'political correctness', the Anita Hill and Clarence Thomas hearings, Hillary Rodham Clinton as First Lady, O. J. Simpson's murder trial, the ebonics controversy, and the Clinton sex scandal.

Chapter 4

Language and the media

Joanna Thornborrow

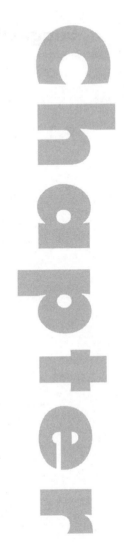

4.1 Introduction

The media (usually understood to refer to the press, radio and television broad-casting) have become one of the most pervasive phenomena in our culture. We can also add the World Wide Web to the list of communications media, but we will be dealing here mainly with newspapers and broadcasting media (television and radio). The aim of this chapter is to examine how our know-ledge about the world is mediated through press and broadcasting institutions, and to suggest ways in which the analysis of language can provide insights into how that mediation can affect the **representation** of people, places and events.

The mass media have become one of the principal means through which we gain access to a large part of our information about the world, as well as to much of our entertainment. Because of this, they are a powerful site for the production and circulation of social meanings, i.e. to a great extent the media decide the significance of things that happen in the world for any given culture, society or social group. The language used by the media to represent partic-ular social and political groups, and to describe newsworthy events, tends to provide the dominant ways available for the rest of us to talk about those groups and events. We will be looking here at some examples of these.

Lastly, as access to television and radio discourse is widening, more programmes, such as the ever-popular talk shows and phone-ins, are being dedicated to the 'voices' of the ordinary public, rather than limited to jour-nalists, politicians and media experts. Also, with the development of the internet, a vast amount of information is now available from many different sources. But does this necessarily mean that a broader spectrum of people and opinions are being represented as a result, or do media institutions to a large extent still maintain control of who can talk and what gets said? We will also be addressing this question here.

4.2 The function of the media

We use the media for many different purposes; for information, for entertain-ment and for education, through a range of programmes for schools as well as university broadcasts. We listen to the news on radio and television for information about local, national and international events; many people spend hours every week being entertained by a variety of programmes from regular soap operas to weekly quizzes and chat shows. Sometimes, the boundaries become blurred between information and entertainment, and a new term has been coined to refer to programmes which serve both functions: 'infotainment'. Wildlife programmes, docu-dramas and the growing number of talk shows could all be described as having a dual role: to entertain as well as to inform. There is also an ongoing debate about what television is for, often centred on the quality of programmes such as the popular 'reality TV' series *Big Brother*. This kind of television gives us another kind of viewing experience, seen positively by some people as an interesting social and psychological media experiment, negatively by others as being voyeuristic and banal.

The mass media provide the means of access to much information and represent a potentially powerful force in our society. This is partly due to the fact that the media can select what counts as news, who gets into the papers and on to television and radio and, most importantly for linguists, the way that stories about people and events get told and the frameworks in which people get to appear and talk. However, we must be careful when talking about the media as powerful. Any newspaper story goes through several stages before it appears on the page, and many different people can be involved at each stage. The same is true of broadcast news stories. Rather than seeing the media as being a group of individuals who control and in some way manipulate what we read or watch, we need to think of each medium as a complex institution. This institution is characterised by a set of processes, practices and conventions that the people within it have developed within a particular social and cultural context. These practices have an effect both on what we perceive as news and on the forms in which we expect to hear or read about it.

The media are always there, and have come to be taken for granted as an integral part of most people's lives. Scannell (1988), in an account of the social role of broadcasting, argues that even the language we use to talk about television programming reflects this ordinariness, this taken-for-granted place in our lives. The expression 'there's nothing on TV' has come to mean 'there's nothing I want to watch', rather than describing an actual state of affairs where there is really nothing being broadcast if you switch on your set. The fact that, with the increase of twenty-four-hour broadcasting and multiple channels, there is practically always something on television is now quite unremarkable for most of us.

We should not be too quick to see the media as all-powerful, and the public as mere puppets of media control. The relationship is not a straightforward one. The reading, listening and viewing public can also choose not to buy, listen or watch; they can switch off, change allegiances and in some cases challenge versions of events. For example, as a result of the events surrounding the Princess of Wales's death in August 1997, a new set of laws may be passed in Britain restricting the rights of 'paparazzi' journalists to take intrusive photographs, and this is due in some part at least to the public reaction to her death. On the other hand, the same public were always ready to buy the papers and watch the programmes that featured reports of her both when she was alive and after her death, and in that sense, the media were providing, and continue to provide, what sells their product.

4.3 Media, language and power

As we noted in the last section, one of the most important and interesting aspects of the potential power of the media from a linguistic point of view is the way that people and events get reported. Since the early 1970s, linguists have been interested in the relationship between how a story gets told, and what that might indicate about the point of view that it gets told from (Lee 1992; Simpson 1993; Montgomery 1996). This level of language use is called linguistic representation (see Chapter 2), and we will now look at some linguistic structures that can determine how events are represented, and thus lead to different versions, or views, of the same event.

On Tuesday 7 January 2003, the news broke that the previous Sunday police had raided a flat in north London, where they found a small quantity of a poison called ricin, and that seven people had been arrested, one of whom was later released. (Ricin had previously been used in the 1978 assassination of a Bulgarian dissident, Georgi Markov, on the London Underground. The poison had been smeared on the tip of an umbrella.) The group was quickly suspected as having links with al-Qa'ida, and as being part of the terrorist network responsible for 9/11 and the Bali nightclub bombing in 2002. The next day, the front pages of many newspapers carried the story of the police raid, but as we can see from the following articles, they presented the story in rather different ways. (See Chapter 2 for an analysis of another similar incident.)

The *Daily Mail* is a daily tabloid newspaper with right-wing sympathies, which generally disagrees with the current New Labour government headed by Prime Minister Tony Blair. The *Daily Mirror*, also a red-top tabloid, tends to have more left-wing opinions but can also be critical of New Labour.

If we analyse the language used in these articles, we find contrasts in how the story was told in each newspaper, and what the implications of this event might be. Looking at the linguistic choices made in the two texts means asking: what kinds of words or phrases are being used to refer to people or places or events, what kinds of actions are involved, and who is responsible for them? These choices are part of the process of **representation** in discourse. By examining the way events are represented, we can begin to see more clearly how different points of view, or **ideologies**, are constructed linguistically.

The following are the headlines carried on Wednesday 8 January:

Daily Mail	*Daily Mirror*
POISON GANG ON THE LOOSE	IT'S HERE
Huge hunt for terrorists armed with deadly ricin	Deadly terror poison found in Britain

The large-print front-page headline from the *Mail* refers to a 'poison gang', who may still be at large and in possession of ricin, foregrounding the people involved and that some of them have still not been arrested. The accompanying smaller headline expands 'poison gang' as 'terrorists armed with deadly ricin', and the 'huge hunt' refers to police action to find those who are still 'on the loose'.

The large-print headline from the *Mirror*, 'It's here', foregrounds the substance itself. The phrase is *deictic*, which means that the reader has to work out what the pronouns 'it' and 'here' refer to in this context. This is simple enough given the accompanying smaller headline 'deadly terror poison found in Britain', but the use of the deictic phrase is more dramatic than if, for example, we replace the pronouns with a corresponding fully lexicalised phrase. Which of the following is more sensational?

Ricin in Britain
Deadly poison found in Britain
It's here

The choice in how to summarise this particular story in the headline text is handled in different ways by each paper, with the *Mail* focusing on the people involved (the gang and the police) and the *Mirror* on the poison ricin and where it is (in Britain). The *Mirror* headline focuses on what the police have found, while the *Mail* headline focuses on what the police are doing.

How is the story developed? In the paragraphs that follow the headlines, further differences between the two papers can be seen in the way the story is constructed, and which elements are given prominence. Some of the elements are the same, for example, both texts share the adjective 'deadly' to refer to the ricin, but the way the elements are put together makes the emphasis of the story slightly different in each case.

Britain was on red alert for a
bio-terror attack last night as
a hunt was launched for a gang
of suspected Al Qaeda activists
armed WITH A DEADLY POISON.

Police who raided an Al Qaeda
poison factory in London fear
most of THE DEADLY RICIN is
missing and in the hands of
terrorists.

The *Mail* continues to foreground the hunt for the 'gang of terrorists', and tells the story in terms of the action being taken, with the first clause describing the state of the country, and the second the search for the gang of activists:

Britain was on red alert for a bio-terror attack
a hunt was launched

The *Mirror* tells the story with a focus on the whereabouts of the missing substance, beginning with the main clause describing police 'fear' which develops the sense of suspense and public danger found in the headline:

Police fear most of the deadly ricin is missing and in the hands
of terrorists

Here is the continuation of the story as it appeared in the next five paragraphs in each paper:

Anti terrorist police arrested seven North Africans after the discovery of traces of ricin, which can send a person into a coma and kill within hours.

One of those held is believed to have worked as a science teacher. Security sources said at least three members of the alleged terror cell were still at large and may be in possession of the chemical.

The amount seized is too small to launch any 'mass casualty' attacks but the real fear is an assassination attack on a major public figure, such as the prime minister, by spraying the toxin in his face or injecting it.

Britain was on alert last night for an attack, possibly by aerosol spray or by smearing the substance on door handles at busy public buildings or shopping centres.

Confined spaces such as a commuter train carriage, a Tube station or a lunchtime restaurant were thought to be possible targets of the original plot.

Six men and one woman were arrested on Sunday in swoops on the ricin 'plant' – a flat in Wood Green, North London – and other addresses in the north and east of the capital.

It could also be ingested through the skin after being smeared on door knobs or handrails. 'People who come into contact with it will die,' said a government source.

Westminster sources revealed that levels of security surrounding Tony Blair have been 'significantly upgraded' over the past few days.

The males – in their late teens, 20s and 30s – are all said to be Algerians linked to Osama bin Laden's network. The woman has been freed.

Up to 30 more confederates are feared to be operating in Britain, most of them living in London.

The following paragraphs appear a little further down in each article.

Scotland Yard swooped at 10am on Sunday in a flat above a pharmacy in Wood Green, North London, after receiving a tip-off over the New Year.

Up to 20 officers wearing white protective suits found equipment covered in chemical traces and began removing items in protective black bags.

Armed special Branch officers in white chemical warfare suits smashed their way into the rented Wood Green property in the early hours.

A small quantity of ricin – used in the 1978 umbrella murder in London of Bulgarian dissident Georgi Markov – was found amid a kitchen laboratory for making more of it.

Who is involved? In the *Mail* there are a number of phrases used to describe the police involved in the hunt:

Anti-terrorist police
security sources
Scotland Yard
up to 20 officers

and to describe government officials and spokespersons:

Tony Blair
Westminster sources
a government source

The *Mirror*, on the other hand, refers only to 'police' and 'armed special branch officers'. The sources of information are not directly attributed, as the two phrases below use passive sentence construction, where the agent of the verb is deleted. In other words, who 'says' and who 'fears' is omitted from the account:

the men . . . ARE ALL SAID to be
up to 30 more [. . .] ARE FEARED TO be

The *Mail* gives official sources:

Westminster sources revealed
a government source said

There is also a difference in the level of certainty expressed by the two papers with regard to who the arrested people are. The *Mail* uses a number of mitigating strategies which function to distance them from strong claims about the identity of the 'gang':

SUSPECTED Al Qaeda activists
seven North Africans
one [. . .] IS BELIEVED to have worked as a science teacher
members of the ALLEGED terror cell

The *Mirror* however uses the unmitigated phrase 'terrorists', and only one mitigated identity description:

the men . . . are all SAID TO BE Algerians linked to Osama bin Laden

The difference here then, is that the *Mail* seems to be more cautious than the *Mirror* about the identity of the gang. Another difference is the *Mirror's* reference to the attack on Georgi Markov. The attack had a classic undercover 'secret agent' spy-thriller character, and adds to the drama being created in the *Mirror's* story.

The *Mirror* uses three different noun phrases to describe the kitchen in the north London flat where the ricin was found:

an al Qaeda poison factory
the ricin 'plant'
a kitchen laboratory

while the *Mail* describes it as:

a flat above a pharmacy in Wood Green

What is the effect of these different choices in representation? We could argue that in line with the headline text, the *Mail* is placing less emphasis on the substance, and more on what is being done. The *Mirror* on the other hand continues to increase the semantic load by using phrases which categorise the kitchen as a 'factory', 'plant' and 'laboratory'. A similar semantic loading can be found in the description of the clothing worn by the police officers who raided the flat:

Up to 20 officers wearing WHITE PROTECTIVE SUITS found equipment
Armed special Branch officers in WHITE CHEMICAL WARFARE SUITS smashed their way in

The *Mail*'s use of 'white protective suits' is made more dramatic and sensational by the *Mirror*, which describes the clothing as 'white chemical warfare suits'.

The story in the *Mail* represents the main threat from the 'poison gang' as being to public figures (like the Prime Minister Tony Blair). The *Mirror*, in contrast, sees the main threat as being to ordinary members of the British public, and lists six places where the poison could be used: door handles, shopping centres, public spaces, commuter trains, Tube stations and lunchtime restaurants. The *Mail* only mentions 'door handles' and 'handrails', without specifying any places.

In these two short articles, we have shown how the same event can generate two rather different stories. Apart from the differences in style, where the semantic loading and reduced level of mitigation tend to emphasise the dramatic nature of this event in the *Mirror*, there is also a difference in the two papers' interpretation of what this event means. For the *Mail*, it is the danger to the establishment (senior public figures), which underlies the urgent hunt for the rest of the gang; for the *Mirror*, it is the danger to the British public at large which is foregrounded if the rest of the substance is not found.

Do these two stories reveal two different ideological stances taken by the two papers? The *Mail*'s and the *Mirror*'s reporting of this event cannot be described as an expression of 'right-wing' and 'left-wing' political opinion. However, the differences that our analysis has begun to reveal do seem to reflect a difference in perspective on this story: a concern with the Establishment and the maintenance of order (increasing security measures, hunting the gang) in the *Mail*, and a concern for the British people (locating the poison, the danger of ricin in public places) in the *Mirror*.

ACTIVITY 4.1 ─────────────────

This analysis has dealt with only some of the differences between the two texts. To take the analysis further, you could list all the verb phrases that occur in the two stories and compare them. Would this support the findings that (1) the *Mirror* story uses more dramatic language than the *Mail*, and (2) that the *Mail* is concerned with the Establishment while the *Mirror* is concerned with the people?

4.4 Sources of news

The attribution of a source is important to the level of 'factuality' that can be claimed for a story. In the following extract from a story about Princess Diana and British rugby player Will Carling, the 'facts' of the case are far from clear. Although sources are given, the original source of the information on which the newspaper bases its report is masked by the way this paragraph is written. A complex series of reporting phrases appears to indicate the source, but effectively succeeds in making it quite difficult to retrieve. These phrases are italicised in the text below:

> The newspaper *claimed* Mr Carling arranged to take former England foot-baller Gary Lineker to lunch with the princess at Kensington Palace earlier this year. A friend of Mr Carling's *is reported as saying*: 'He [Mr Carling] *told* me later Gary had bottled out *saying*, "that woman's trouble".'
>
> (*The Guardian*, 7 August 1995)

There are four sources of information mentioned in this passage: Lineker, Carling, Carling's friend and a newspaper (*News of the World*). Their reports range from the direct 'said' and 'told' to the more mitigated 'is reported as saying' and 'claimed', suggesting that the paper is anxious not to claim outright that this third- or fourth-hand information is absolute fact.

In this section we have shown how the linguistic choices made in a text can construct different accounts, or linguistic representations, of events in the world. In doing so, we may have mentioned some terms for linguistic structures which are not familiar to you, but if you want to find out more about these structures, and how to use them in an analysis of a media text, you may find it useful to refer to Fairclough (1989, particularly Chapter 5) and Thornborrow and Wareing (1998).

Look at two newspapers on the same day and compare two versions of the same story. What differences can you detect in the way language is used? Do these differences influence or affect your interpretation of the event?

4.4.1 Commonsense discourses

The tendency to represent people, situations and events in regular and predictably similar ways results in the linguistic choices that are used in these representations becoming established in our culture as the most usual, prevailing ways of talking or writing about types of people and events. Once something has been represented in a particular way, it becomes more difficult to talk 'around', or outside that representation, to find an alternative way of describing a social group *X*, or a political event *Y*. As discussed in Chapter 3, we call these prevailing choices in representation **commonsense** or **dominant discourses** (see also Chapter 2, and Fairclough 1989).

An illustration of how one event can become the frame for representing subsequent events is the tendency to refer to any story of American presidential cover-up scandal as some kind of 'gate'. Since Nixon and the Watergate scandal, there has been Reagan and 'Irangate', Clinton and 'Whitewatergate', followed by 'Zippergate', and 'Fornigate'. While the history and circumstances of each individual situation may be distinct, the use of the term 'gate' categorises them according to the notion of an American president deliberately setting out to deceive the American public. The category has also been taken up by the British press and has been used in the context of the British royal family. 'Camillagate' was the story of the long-standing relationship between Prince Charles and Camilla Parker-Bowles, which hit the headlines some years after his marriage to Diana Spencer, when her problems with him and other members of the royal family had entered the public domain.

4.4.2 The power to change?

If the media are powerful as a site for producing and maintaining dominant discourses, as we have claimed in the previous section, they can also be a possible site for change. One of the most publicly discussed changes in recent years has been the move to use non-sexist language, and to encourage **symmetry** in the representation of men and women. Sometimes the press can be seen to be trying to adopt grammatical forms which are neutral, such as the **third person pronoun** 'they' or 'them' as a non-specified-gender **pronoun**.

The following extract is from a story about Texan farmers suing the talk show host Oprah Winfrey for damaging their business when she invited people on to her show to talk about the risks involved in eating American beef:

> And this year the average American will chew their way through 63lb of Texan beef, compared to only 51lb of chicken and 46.7lb of pork. It's an ill-advised man who stands between an *American* and *his* burgers.
> (*The Guardian*, 10 February 1998)

This extract shows the use of the **unmarked** possessive form their (rather than his or her) in the phrase 'chew their way through' to refer back to the earlier noun phrase 'the average American'. So far, so non-sexist. But in the following sentence, this is not sustained, and we have the **marked** male forms 'it's an ill-advised man' (rather than 'it's an ill-advised person') representing the actor in this sentence as male, and 'an American and his burgers', which also represents the average American as male. (For more on the use of **asymmetrical** language in the representation of gender see Chapter 5.)

In this section we have introduced the concept of **dominant discourses** within the context of the media, and have suggested that these discourses are produced by recurring similarities in the way information is represented. We have looked at some examples of linguistic choice in reporting newsworthy events, and how different newspapers can represent the same event in different ways. In the next section we turn to the question of 'voice' in the media, looking at whose voices are represented, and who gets to say what.

4.5 Media voices: accent and register

ACTIVITY 4.3

When you listen to the news on your local radio station, what **accent** does the newsreader have? Is this the same as those on the national, or more prestigious, radio station? Listen to the television news at different times of the day; do you notice any difference in the accents of the newsreaders at these times?

In the early days of news broadcasting in Britain, the accent used almost exclusively by presenters was one called advanced **Received Pronunciation** (advanced **RP**). This was the accent of the educated and the wealthy, which gave no indication of what part of the country the speaker came from. This accent gave rise to the expression **BBC English**, so strong was the link between this accent and the British Broadcasting Corporation. This has now given way to what is known as 'mainstream RP', an accent which sounds less formal than advanced RP and is the one that most people in Britain generally hear when they listen to newsreaders on national television.

This established use of mainstream RP is linked to the continuing perceived status of RP as an accent of authority. In radio and television discourse, the occurrence of marked regional variation in accent in the national news tends to be organised according to a hierarchy within programmes: the main newsreaders in the television studio read in standard English, with a mainstream RP accent, while the accents of specialist reporters outside the studio 'at the scene' are much less constrained and may sometimes be regionally marked (for example, one well-known BBC TV journalist and political commentator, John Cole, had a marked Northern Irish accent). Voice-overs in documentaries are also likely to be mainstream RP, while the accents of sports commentators, weather presenters, political commentators and other media 'voices' tend to be more regionally varied.

At one time this difference was especially noticeable on British television when a particular sports journalist would modify slightly his accent depending on which programme he was reporting for. On the national six o'clock evening news he would give the sports news bulletin in a mainstream RP accent, and half an hour later, on the local London South East news, he would shift into a more marked London accent.

Allan Bell (1984) uses the term **audience design** for speakers changing their style of speech according to the person or people they are addressing. Bell also suggests that, since radio and television presenters are addressing a distant, unknown audience of viewers and listeners, then they may design their speech according to certain linguistic 'values' or **norms**. In this case, newsreaders may be selecting one **variety** over another according to the conventionally prestigious norms of RP rather than according to the actual audience they are addressing. This is a particular type of audience design that Bell calls 'referee design'.

4.5.1 Variation in register

Register has been defined as **linguistic variation** according to the context of use (Halliday 1972). This means that we expect to find language used in different ways according to the situation it occurs in, and according to different types of media. For example, the register of weather forecasting in Britain depends on three features: its topic or **field** (the weather around the country), its **tenor** (the way it is delivered by the presenter) and its communicative **mode** (speech, writing and some visual modes in the form of maps and icons). We expect a weather bulletin to contain technical vocabulary relating to temperature, high and low pressure, cyclones, etc., but we also expect the presenter, unlike newscasters, to address the audience directly, by saying things like 'look at this rain moving in from the west here'. On television weather reports, there is also usually some visual representation of the weather being described, for example a small sun to represent sunshine, arrows for the direction of the wind, and snowflakes for wintry conditions. The register of weather forecasting depends also on the cultural context of the broadcast. The British format has just been described, but the format can vary from country to country.

The same expectations of linguistic register (language variation according to context) apply to other media **genres**, where there are conventions of appropriate language use for specific types of programme. When these conventions are well established, often the form of how something is reported can outweigh the content, or the information itself.

A famous media hoax used a well-established media format (the documentary) to broadcast information that was false. A report of a 'spaghetti harvest', broadcast on BBC One's documentary programme Panorama on 1 April 1957 (1 April being a traditional date for practical jokes) showed strands of pasta growing on trees, while a male RP voice-over provided a serious commentary on traditional spaghetti farming in Italy. Radio, television and newspapers in Britain still successfully play hoaxes on the public on 1 April. Similarly, though unintentionally, misleading was the radio broadcast in the United States on 30 October 1938 of Orson Welles's reading of H. G. Wells's short story *The War of the Worlds*. It apparently caused panic among listeners who believed that New Jersey was being invaded by Martians.

These occurrences demonstrate the potential power of the broadcast word to be received by the public as authoritative, factual and believable. On the other hand, research into how audiences react to and interpret news programmes (Morley 1980, 1992; Richardson and Corner 1986; Moores 1993) has suggested that the viewing public is not always so ready to believe events as they are presented through the news media, and has other resources for interpreting what it sees and hears on the news.

However, it does remain the case that the media are constantly shaping our expectations about the way different kinds of information are transmitted, and these conventional formats can play an important part in the way we interpret the messages they contain. Language plays a central role in structuring these conventions through the association of particular registers with specific types of programme, such as the language of documentaries, where voice-over commentaries can often produce an effect of authority and objectivity in their account of events on the screen (see Fairclough 1995).

The effect of an institutional, authoritative, objective voice can be compared to the effect produced by voices which are beginning to be heard on television in new media genres such as BBC Television's *Video Nation* slots. These are very short video film sequences, lasting only a few minutes, made by 'ordinary' (i.e. non-institutional) people, about themselves, or any topic they feel strongly about. The growth of public participation programmes and phone-in radio shows also provides a space for lay people to contribute to the variety of voices represented in the media, as we shall see next, although the final 'gatekeeping' to decide who gets access, and who does not, remains with the broadcasting institutions.

4.6 Public participation in the media

Programmes which involve audience participation, such as *Oprah Winfrey* and *Donahue* in the United States, *Kilroy* and *Esther* in Britain, have been growing in popularity and number, and achieve very high viewing ratings. There is some disagreement about whether these programmes provide the opportunity for more democratic debate in the media, or whether they in fact depoliticise important issues by presenting them in this format. Some theorists (e.g. Livingstone and Lunt 1994) have argued that these programmes open up access to an important public domain for people whose voices and opinions are not usually heard on television, and that talk shows provide a powerful space for the voices of ordinary, lay members of the public to be privileged over the voices of institutional representatives and experts whose opinions and views usually predominate elsewhere in other media genres. Others (e.g. Fairclough 1995) have argued against this view, saying that audience participation programmes are structured in such a way that the discourse of the experts and the institution is still the framing, dominant discourse, while the discourse of lay participants is always mediated and constrained within the institutional format.

An example of this can be found in a study of the interaction between host and callers to a London talk radio show. Ian Hutchby (1996) explores the strategies available to participants in argument sequences, and shows that typically the caller 'goes first', by stating their position in relation to a particular topic, while the host 'goes second', challenging the caller's opinion without necessarily having to produce one of their own. The following transcript illustrates this phenomenon:

```
1   Caller:            When you look at e:r the childcare facilities in
2                      this country, .hh we're very very low (.) i-on
3                      the league table in Europe of (.) you know if
4                      you try to get a child into a nursery it's
5                      very difficult in this country. .hh An' in fa:ct it's
6                      getting wor::se.
7   Host:       What's that got to do with it.
8   Caller:            .phh Well I think whu- what 'at's gotta d-do
9                      with it is . . .
```

(Hutchby 1996: H:21.11.88:I1.I)

This resource of 'going second' in an argument is available to both caller and host, but in this context is principally used by the host, making them interactionally the most powerful participant through their position as challenger to a previously stated claim.

Another strategy which also contributes to the interactional power of the television host over audience participants is illustrated in the following transcript of a sequence in a British talk show, *Kilroy*. Here, the talk of the lay audience member is directed and to some extent controlled by the host's intervention and questioning:

```
1   Host:    Tell me about this (.) household
2   Alice:   erm well both my parents are very loving (.)
3            very accepting of lots of things (.) and (.)
4            therefore that rubs off (.) on my sister and
5            I – erm
6   Host:    – how old are you
7   Alice:   nineteen
8   Host:    how old's your sister
9   Alice:   sixteen
10  Host:    mmm
11  Alice:   and erm (1.0) I've lived with both separately (.)
12           I've lived with Dad for the last couple of years
13           – now
14  Host:    – does Dad have a lover
15  Alice:   Yes he does (.) – Pedro
16  Host:    – You live with Dad and lover
17  Alice:   yes
18  Host:    How old were you when you lived with Dad and
19           lover
```

20	Alice:	erm (1.0) I was seventeen when I moved to
21		Melbourne
22	Host:	cause you problems
23	Alice:	no
24	Host:	did you find it strange
25	Alice:	no
26	Host:	find it difficult
27	Alice:	no it's just like living with any other
28		parent and their lover
29	Host:	it's just like living with any other parent
30		and their lover

(Thornborrow 1997: Adoption/Kilroy/1994)

In this extract, Alice is asked by the host to tell the story of how she came to live with her father and his male partner. However, she is not left to tell her own story without the intervention of the host. She starts by focusing on the quality of the relationship between her and her parents (lines 2–5), but the host interrupts her several times, asking her questions which elicit certain kinds of information (about her age, her father's relationship and how she felt about it), resulting in a story which is jointly produced, rather than a story told by Alice in her own words.

4.7 Language, society and virtual power

To conclude this chapter we look briefly at the development of computer-mediated communication (CMC) over the past two decades. This new form of communication can take a variety of forms, from email exchanges to synchronous (real-time) interaction in chat rooms and MUDs (Multi-User Dimensions), to asynchronous (postponed-time) interaction in newsgroups and bulletin boards. David Crystal (2001) provides a comprehensive overview of the linguistic features of CMC, and the language we use to communicate on the web. This has been given various names including 'netspeak', 'netlish', 'weblish, 'wired-style' and 'cyberspeak', and some of the words and expressions first coined in this context have now become part of the language we use every day. Crystal gives examples of terms such as 'multi-tasking', 'dot.com', and 'he's 404' (2001: 19) which are used 'offline' as well as 'online'. But many of the questions we ask in this book about how language can be powerful apply to social relations in virtual realities just as much as they do to social relations in 'real' life (IRL). What are some of the issues involved?

4.7.1 Social identity

In the early days of CMC it was thought that this new medium would result in more democratic communication, because a person's social identity (their gender, ethnicity, age) can be hidden in the virtual world. In cyberspace, people can also play with identity and present themselves in different personas, so the internet would be a place where social hierarchies become levelled out, and people could encounter each other in a more equal way. However, this has turned out to be not quite so simple. As Nancy Deuel found in her study of virtual sex interactions, stereotypical interpretations of gendered behaviour still prevail:

> Sexual aggression is assumed to be a male trait and one participant notes: 'It seems to me that if a female character shows any bit of intelligence and sexual recognition, people will think she's a male IRL. If she flirts shamelessly and has a smutty description, people will think she's a male IRL.'
>
> (1996: 134)

So while it may be possible to disguise your identity on the Net, the people you interact with will still make assumptions about who you are based on what you say and how you say it.

4.7.2 'Netiquette'

The internet makes it possible for people who are geographically scattered thousands of miles away from each other to interact either in real time or with a very small time delay. This has led to the concept of cyberspace as a 'global village' (Crystal 2001: 5) where people who use the Net are members of a virtual community. As in any other community, rules and codes of behaviour have developed in order to control the way that members of the community behave. Entering a chat room as a 'newbie' means having to learn the conventions and rules of interaction in that space. Many newsgroups have a FAQ (frequently asked questions) file which sets out what these rules are, some even have moderators or 'wizards': people who are prepared to spend time monitoring the use of a group and making sure that rules are kept. Inappropriate behaviour can get you sanctioned, and possibly excluded from, a group. 'Flaming' (aggressive verbal behaviour), 'spamming' (sending unwanted long messages) and 'grandstanding' (posting your opinions widely with no respect for the topic of a newsgroup) are all activities that can lead to sanctions. One example of this is using a 'kill file', a kind of shield which can be used to prevent unwanted, offensive messages from getting through to you. Kollock and Smith (1996) describe this kind of shield as a powerful interactional device, one that can 'make invisible any objectionable person' (120). However, it works only on an individual, not a community, level, and, even if you banish someone from your screen, other users may not, so you will still see future postings if other participants comment on them. What is particularly interesting about the rules that attempt to control social interaction in cyberspace is that it is the people who use the Net who establish those rules. Cyberspace is a community regulated not yet by a 'top-down' authority but by a 'bottom-up' process developed by internet users.

4.7.3 Cyberspace: a socially powerful community?

In her study of a community protest, Laura Gurak (1996) explains how a database called 'MarketPlace: Households' (listing details about millions of American households and produced by a company called Lotus) was prevented from becoming commercially available. The release of this product became the subject of an intense debate about privacy, not just in newspapers but across internet newsgroups and bulletin boards. For two months across the United States, people were posting information about the database, and how to contact Lotus to complain about the violation of their privacy. The speed and efficiency of this medium resulted in a highly effective campaign to stop the database going on sale. Gurak makes the point that what she calls 'rhetorical communities', diverse groups of people who participate in protests and campaigns via the internet, can be socially and politically powerful. In cases such as this, CMC can provide a public forum for action and protest, as so many participants can become involved very quickly in a campaign.

ACTIVITY 4.4

If you regularly use internet sites such as chat rooms, or post to a newsgroup, what are the rules that govern behaviour in these cyberspaces? How do you know what they are, and what happens if you break them?

4.8 Summary

In this chapter we have discussed the power of the media to determine what counts as news, and also how it gets represented. We have outlined the conflicting views of the media, on the one hand as organs of democracy, providing essential public information and on the other as powerful monopolies which relentlessly pursue their own interests. With the increase of public access to broadcasting space, and particularly with the arrival of the World Wide Web, and its potential for unregulated mass communication, these questions remain central to the debates about the function and power of the mass media. Are they providing an emerging forum for public debate, or are they still closely monitored institutions with hierarchies of discourse and systems of 'gatekeeping' which continue to control who gets to say what, and how? An analysis of the language and discourse used in mediated contexts provides a valuable way of finding evidence to support or counter these claims.

Suggestions for further reading

Fairclough, Norman (1995) *Media Discourse*, London: Edward Arnold. This book covers a wide range of language use in the media from a Critical Discourse Analysis (CDA) perspective.

Graddol, David and Boyd-Barrett, Oliver (eds) (1994) *Media Texts: Authors and Readers*, Clevedon: Multilingual Matters. A collection of essays which cover a range of different themes in media discourse, from the style and structure of news stories and the role of visuals to more theoretical discussions of the concept of 'author', and the interpretative role of the audience.

Simpson, Paul (1993) *Language, Ideology and Point of View*, London and New York: Routledge. This is an accessible account of the relationship between linguistic forms and point of view in a wide variety of media.

Thornborrow, Joanna and Wareing, Shân (1998) *Patterns in Language: An Introduction to Language and Literary Style*, London: Routledge. A practical introduction to how to approach texts using linguistic tools of analysis. Chapter 7 deals specifically with examples of media language.

Readings on the World Wide Web

Many studies are beginning to appear of the way we use language in CMC. David Crystal's book provides an overview of the linguistic features of 'Netspeak', while Susan Herring's collection of articles provides some interesting insights into aspects of the social and cultural issues involved in this new form of communication.

Crystal, David (2001) *Language and the Internet*, Cambridge: Cambridge University Press.

Herring, S. (ed.) *Computer Mediated Communication: Linguistic, Social and Cross-cultural Perspectives*, Amsterdam and Philadelphia: John Benjamins.

Chapter 5

Language and gender

Shân Wareing

5.1 Introduction

In the preceding chapters, we have focused on the ways in which **representation** in language can have an impact on perception, and on forms of language use which are typical in two contexts: politics and in the media. This chapter also looks at representation and at typical forms of language use, in this case, in relation to gender. We will consider **asymmetrical** representations of women and men, and why these can be considered sexist. We will then look at whether women and men use language in different ways, and the possible reasons for gender-based differences in conversational styles. The chapter ends by probing the concept of gender.

It may help to start with an explanation of what is meant by the terms 'sex' and 'gender'. 'Sex' refers to biological category, which is usually fixed before birth. 'Gender' refers to social category, which is associated with certain behaviour. Bicycle design neatly illustrates the difference between the two: bike saddles designed for women are usually wider than saddles designed for men, because women have a wider pelvic girdle (a sex difference). Bikes without a crossbar, so riders can wear skirts, are designed in response to a gender difference, since there is no biological reason why, in some cultures, women wear skirts and men don't.

So what is meant by 'sexism'? Sexist language represents women and men unequally, as if members of one sex were somehow less completely human and less complex and had fewer rights than members of the other sex. Sexist language also presents stereotypes of women and men, sometimes to the disadvantage of men, but more often to the disadvantage of women.

It is debatable whether language can actually be sexist against men (as opposed to just rude), or only against women. Clearly language can represent men as less complex, less fully human or entitled to fewer rights than women. However, whether this counts as sexist or not can be argued to depend on the distribution of power in society as a whole. Generally speaking, men still hold more 'high-status' occupations in this society than women do; men still own more property and earn more than women. There are still more male politicians, more male company directors, more male judges, professors, surgeons, head teachers and film directors. Men also tend to have more physical power; domestic violence is perpetrated more often by men against women than the other way around. It is debatable whether using language to diminish men has the same effect as using language to diminish women, since the power relations underlying the language use are different. The following statistics relating to gender inequality are from State of the World (2000):

- On average, in developed countries, women earn 23 per cent less than men. In developing countries, they earn 27 per cent less.
- Women work two-thirds of the world's working hours, produce half of the world's food and yet earn only 10 per cent of the world's income and own less than 1 per cent of the world's property. Almost a quarter of the global population lives in extreme poverty – on less than the equivalent of $1 per day. Seventy per cent of these people are women.
- Gender violence causes more deaths and disability among women aged fifteen to forty-four than cancer, malaria, traffic accidents or war.
- In Great Britain, where one woman in ten is severely beaten by an intimate partner every year, the cost to health and social services is estimated at over £1 billion per annum.
- In Switzerland, Japan and Belgium, for every hundred men enrolled in higher education there are respectively just fifty-three, sixty-three and seventy-eight women.
- Women hold only 1 per cent of executive positions in the world's biggest international corporations. Women hold only 6.2 per cent of all ministerial positions worldwide.

Given the distribution of power suggested by these facts, in this chapter we will mainly be looking at sexist language which diminishes women, but one example of language which represents men in demeaning ways appears in section 5.2.6.

5.2 How is English sexist?

Sexist language can be discussed in two ways: firstly, as the extent to which the English language system is inherently sexist, and secondly, as the extent to which some ways of using language are sexist. To consider the first approach, the extent to which the English language system is sexist, one of the things we look for is **symmetry** versus **asymmetry** in the vocabulary or **lexis**.

5.2.1 Symmetry and asymmetry

A clear example of symmetry can be found in English terms for horses. Horse is a **generic** term which covers animals of both sexes:

(1) generic   *horse*
    female   *mare*
    male   *stallion*
    young   *foal* (either sex)
    young female   *filly*
    young male   *colt*

The terms for human beings follow a similar system, but are not so symmetrical in the way they are used:

(2) generic   *Man*
    female   *woman*
    male   *man*
    young   *child*
    young female   *girl*
    young male   *boy*

Example (2) indicates the ambiguity of the term *Man/man*. Speakers and writers often blur the distinction between the use of the word *Man* generically, to mean women, men, girls and boys, and the use of *man* to mean only men (and not women or children). This is illustrated in example (3) below, where the first mention of *Man* appears to be in its generic sense, but the next sentence makes it clear that in fact *Man* here means men and not women.

(3) For decades, pubs have been Man's best friend. He could take his wife, his girlfriend, but not his children. But now that's all about to change.

> (*News at 10*, ITV,[1] 3 January 1995,
> on changes in the laws regarding children
> in licensed drinking bars)

Another kind of asymmetry in the way the system shown in (2) is applied, is the use of *girl* to describe adult women, where *man* would almost certainly be used if the reference were to an adult male. Consider this headline and the first sentence of an article from the *Daily Mail* (24 September 1997):

(4)   **Police girl wins sex bias case by a split verdict**
A policewoman who allegedly threatened to kill her chief constable and have the legs of a senior officer broken won a controversial sex discrimination case yesterday . . . The 34-year-old officer, who said her high-flying career was ruined by bullying male colleagues, now expects to receive up to £250,000 in compensation.

Since women's status tends to be far more dependent on their attractiveness than men's, the use of *girl*, rather than *woman*, to imply that you are not yet 'old' is usually assumed to be a compliment. Would a male police officer (aged thirty-four) be called a *police boy* in a headline?

The use of titles is also asymmetrical:

(5)   woman   *Miss / Mrs / Ms*
man   *Mr*

An adult male can be assumed to use the title *Mr* before his family name, unless he has another title such as *Dr* or *Judge*. However, an adult woman (who does not use another title) may use one of three titles: *Miss*, *Mrs* or *Ms*. Thus any woman who gives her preferred title on a form is revealing far more information about herself than a man does. *Miss* reveals she is unmarried (or chooses to present herself as such). *Mrs* indicates that she is married. *Ms*, a relatively new title, was introduced to end the inequality in the system but instead you could say that the inequality has increased. Instead of having only one title (which does not reveal marital status, in line with titles for men) there are now three possible titles in circulation, and all three appear alongside *Mr* on many forms. If you choose not to tell the world your marital status by selecting *Ms*, some people will assume you are divorced; others will assume you are a feminist; i.e. the use of *Ms*, if you had the choice of using *Miss* or *Mrs*, can seem to carry information about your political opinions. Furthermore, since the introduction of *Ms*, selecting *Miss* or *Mrs* as your title can seem to indicate that you do not want to appear to be a feminist. Therefore not only do two of the titles women use reveal marital status, all three titles can appear to carry information about the user's political affiliations. This is not a situation men face! The titles *Miss* and *Mrs* are a reminder of a time when the power relations between women and men were much more markedly unequal than they are today for most women living in Europe or the United States. Women were then regarded as the responsibility, or indeed the property, of either their father or their husband. Some forms of marriage service still require women to be 'given away' by their father (or other male relative) to their husband. Women's political and economic rights changed considerably over the twentieth century, with, among other changes, the advent of votes for women, equal opportunities policies and effective birth control. However, our language still allows us to indicate the marital status of a woman in way that does not exist for men.

5.2.2 Unmarked and marked terms

Another useful concept when analysing sexism is that of **unmarked** and **marked** terms. This is still asymmetry, but of a specific kind. For example, *lion*, an unmarked form, can refer to a male or female lion. However, the term used for a male lion is also *lion*, while a female lion is referred to by a marked term, *lioness* (it is 'marked' because it has the additional suffix *-ess*). It is quite common for 'unmarked' terms to refer to males, while to refer to a female, the terms are 'marked' by adding a suffix. This may make terms for females appear to differ from the 'standard'. For example:

(6) *waiter   waitress*
     host   hostess
     actor   actress

The marked terms on the right are used less nowadays, and the unmarked terms on the left are often used for women as well as men, which indicates that language and attitudes are changing. However, it is also true that some terms which can apparently refer to females or males, such as *surgeon*, *doctor*, *professor* and *nurse*, are in fact sometimes used as if they really only applied to one gender. People refer to a lady doctor, a woman professor or woman surgeon, implying that the norm is male, and to a male nurse, implying that the norm is female. It should be noted that nurses are of lower status than the other occupations mentioned. Therefore one way which these examples can be interpreted as sexist is that they imply that 'normal' (or, in the case of the medical profession, 'high status') people are men.

5.2.3 Semantic derogation

The process of words which refer to women acquiring demeaning or sexual **connotations** has been widely observed, and has been termed **semantic derogation**. (*Semantic* is a linguistic term referring to meaning; *deroge* means 'to cause to seem inferior'.) Examples (7) to (10) illustrate this process.

(7)   gentleman or lord   lady

Lady is used in contexts where is it highly improbable that *gentleman* or *lord* would be used. In the UK, *lady* is commonly used to form the expressions such as *dinner lady* (a woman who serves meals to schoolchildren) or *lollipop lady* (a woman who helps schoolchildren to cross roads). Would you expect men filling these roles to be referred to as *dinner gentlemen*, or *dinner lords*? As *lollipop lords* or *lollipop gentlemen*? Probably not! *Lady* is used in contexts where *man* or a gender-free term is used if the job is done by a male. To illustrate the point here's an newspaper extract describing a television programme about how animals communicate:

> How does a randy polar bear find a mate? Not very easily is the answer. After all, most of them mope about solitary, icy territories the size of Britain. And even when a lady polar bear does come mooching along, males have about as much chance of spotting her white coat against a sea of ice and snow as David Seaman has of tracking a 30-yard lob.
> (*The Observer*, 30 June 2002, p. 5)

(8)   master   mistress

'He is my master' usually means 'he is my boss' or 'he has more power than me'. 'She is my mistress' is most likely to be interpreted as meaning 'she is my illicit lover'. This demonstrates two phenomena: firstly that words for women tend to lose status (being someone's illicit lover usually is a much less powerful position than being their boss), and secondly, that words for women often end up referring to women in a sexual capacity. This has clearly happened to *mistress* and not to *master*. Even the term 'woman' is also sometimes used to refer to women as sexual activity, as in the phrase *wine, women and song*.

(9)   sir   madam

Sir and *madam* can both be used to refer to high-status people, but *madam*, unlike *sir*, is also used to refer to a brothel keeper.

(10)   bachelor   spinster or old maid

All three terms refer to an unmarried person, but *spinster* and *old maid* appear to be rarely used nowadays, perhaps because their associations are so negative. *Bachelor*, however, usually has positive connotations. The *bachelor life* and a *bachelor pad* (an apartment for a single man) are generally regarded as glamorous; a bachelor is someone who has succeeded in not getting tied down.

Spinster and *old maid* on the other hand suggest to many people someone old, grey, ugly and unable to 'get a man'. *Bachelor girl* can be used to refer to an unmarried woman, to avoid the stigma of the other terms; however, this expression follows the pattern of unmarked and marked terms discussed above (*bachelor* is the 'norm', *bachelor girl* the marked form), as in the newspaper headline from the *Daily Mail* (2 March 2002, p. 11): 'Are these the most eligible bachelor girls in Britain?'.

The examples cited above are all asymmetrical, and diminish women rather than men, by representing women as the property of men, as being of lower status, and as being primarily sexual beings. If we agree with the arguments laid out in Chapter 2, these usages not only represent women unequally, but they may also contribute to perceptions held by both men and women which contribute to women have less power over their own lives and other resources than men.

ACTIVITY 5.1

Look at a selection of newspapers over a few days and collect as many examples as you can find of asymmetrical references to women and men. Do you think your national newspapers (if they are not British) are less sexist than suggested by the examples above, or perhaps sexist in other ways?

5.2.4 Sexism in discourse

In section 5.2, it was stated that sometimes sexism is located not in specific words but in the **discourse**, that is, by meanings created in a whole utterance or sentence, or a longer text. Below are some examples of apparently non-gender-specific terms being used in a context which in fact shows they are being used to refer exclusively to men. The information which indicates that the use is specific is contained elsewhere in the discourse. Sometimes this additional information is described as **disambiguating** the generic term (that is, it indicates more exactly to what the term refers). Generic (non-gender-specific) terms are shown in *italic*; gender specific terms are in SMALL CAPITALS.

(11) *People* feel entitled to the car, the GIRL, etc. If *they're* let down, *they* blame *themselves*.

(Oliver James, quoted by Emma Cook in
The Independent, 31 August 1997)

(12) Scanners that could determine *our* political beliefs, pinpoint *our* involvements in crime, or even uncover extramarital liaisons are being developed by neurologists . . . Such research raises the prospect that attitudes and feelings *we* try to conceal will one day be uncovered by researchers. *Lying politicians, spin doctors* and CHEATING SPORTSMEN (and HUSBANDS) will suddenly find life uncomfortable.

(Robin McKie in *The Observer*, 10 March 2002)

(13) Several of Hollywood's most powerful *players* have arrangements with what in pre-palimony terms were 'common-law WIVES' – Kurt and Goldie, Tim and Susan, and Hugh and Elizabeth – one has to wonder: why do *stars* bother to get married at all?

(Alison Powell, *The Guardian*, 13 September 1997)

(14) *People* in *their* twenties and thirties will have to work until *they* are 72 unless *they* do more now to save for *their* retirement, a new report says. A *worker* making typical contributions to a company pension scheme will either face a big cut in HIS income at 65 or have to keep working for another seven years, according to research by the Pensions Policy Institute.

(*The Times*, 27 February 2002)

(15) According to disapproving church writers, the Vikings were addicted to drink, gluttony and WOMEN.

(The Jorvik Viking History Centre, York (seen in 1997))

ACTIVITY 5.2

Can you identify the gender-specific references and the generic, or gender-neutral, references in these descriptions of dress codes in London restaurants?

Who dresses for dinner?

The Causerie Restaurant, Claridge's Hotel

The rule of jacket and tie at all times has become more relaxed. The public rooms require smartness without formality; the restaurant remains firmly jacket and tie. Those who come without a tie are invited to choose one from a selection held at the door – 'all very fine ties'. The restaurant used to ask any gentleman who removed his jacket during the meal to put it on again, but this practice appears to be dying out. The recalcitrant 'star' who came in less than formal clothes would be admitted, but respectfully asked to improve next time.

The Ritz
Tries very hard to ensure no denims or trainers. Smart casual is the norm for breakfast, while at lunch, tea and dinner, jacket and tie are mandatory. A spokeswoman draws attention to 20 silk Turnbull and Asser ties, and a selection of jackets, for guests who do not provide their own. Ladies' only requirement is to be smart. 'It's hard with the ladies but we try not to make an issue of it.'

The River Café, Hammersmith
Owned by the wife of architect Sir Richard Rogers, and one of the most fashionable restaurants in London, it has no code at all, but a spokesman did indicate that bare chests would not be allowed, 'although people haven't actually started stripping off', he adds.

(James Bristow, *The Independent*, 20 September 1996)

You will probably have noticed that 'guests' are assumed in all three paragraphs to be male, since jackets and ties are rarely regarded as appropriate formal wear for women, and the Ritz paragraph distinguishes explicitly between guests and ladies. You may also have noticed that the owner of the River Café is not identified by name at all, only by her relationship to her husband!

5.2.5 Other explicit examples of sexism

One aspect of sexism in language which we have not discussed yet is probably the most obvious kind: direct insults or other remarks which make inequality explicit, aimed at women rather than men. On *PM*, BBC Radio 4's early evening news programme, a journalist from *The Independent* newspaper (28 February 2002) explained why media award ceremonies, such as the Oscars, are given so much media coverage: 'We get to see beautiful actresses and interesting actors', making explicit the dynamic which places greater emphasis on women's looks and on men's personalities. In 2002, a well-known chocolate bar appeared with a new label, which appears to work by establishing the credentials of the chocolate bar as masculine, or macho (as it has always been marketed). In dark blue foil, the wrapping has a circular icon of a woman with a superimposed diagonal red line (similar to a 'No Smoking' sign) and the additional text 'IT'S NOT FOR GIRLS!' and 'NOT AVAILABLE IN PINK'. It seems to use the term *girl* and the icon as insults, a marketing strategy which might appear rather risky if it discourages women from purchasing the product.

Insults and obscene words are often to do with sexual behaviour and parts of the body. To investigate whether there is a sexist bias in insults and obscene terms, make a list of as many as you can think of (you can do this on your own or in class). Now group the terms you have collected into separate lists according to what they describe. Compare the lengths of your lists and the kinds of terms they contain; for example, are they funny? Blasphemous? Very obscene or only mildly? How many are to do with sexual behaviour or parts of the body? Decide whether your lists provide you with evidence of sexism in English.

It is common, as a result of this activity, to find that there are far more terms to describe promiscuous women than men, that insults for women are often harsher and less funny, and that the words that many people find most obscene describe women's sexual organs, not men's. This can be illustrated by an extract from a television guide, joking about a television chef who on a previous programme had sworn on air. Among a range of swear words, the writer (or editor) decided just one of them should not apear in full, but should have some of its letters replaced by asterisks:

> See? He's human! I can picture the spin-off recipe book – Jamie's Fuckin'
> Kitchen. 'Here's a recipe I call Shit-Hot Spag Bol – 1lb minced cow
> bollocks, 2 onions, garlic, a tin of fucking tomatoes and a pissload of
> spaghetti. And if you don't like it, you're a c***.'
>
> (Charlie Brooker, *The Guardian*, 2 November 2002)

(See also Chapters 6 and 7 for examples of insult terms centred on ethnicity and age.)

5.2.6 Sexism against men?

In introducing this section, I raised the question of whether language could be sexist against men. The following example seems to illustrate the other side of the coin:

> Last week I asked for alternative suggestions for the phrase toy boy.
> Hundreds have poured in from men and women. Here's my pick of the
> best: HRT (Husband Replacement Therapy), Youthfool, Wrinkle picker, Joy

Boy, GIBBET (Good In Bed But Extremely Temporary), Mantress, Sugar laddie, POW (Prefers Older Women), Mutton Fodder and Booster Rooster. Glad Lad, Juvenile Lead, Studlet, Born-Later-Babe, Bimboy, Bounty Hunter, Nappy Chappy, Ego Booster, Mini Mate, Play Mite, Lap Chap and Tom Kitten. Muscle Tussle, Handsome Sansom, Younger Monger, Romp Tot, Cub Class, Game Boy and Sapling. Homelette, Boncubine, Little Soldier, Beddyboy, Passion Puppy, Honkybonk, Kideology Kid and Himbo.

(*Daily Mail*, 28 May 1997)

Do you think the sexist effect here is the same as in the previous examples discussed? Do you think there is a difference between sexism directed at women and at men, or does sexism always have the same effect?

5.3 Do women and men talk differently?

Perhaps some of the examples discussed above seem to you more likely to be used by women or by men. There is plenty of anecdotal evidence around that there are differences in the way men and women talk. A common stereotype is that women talk more than men; perhaps you have heard people say things like: 'women never stop talking'. Women's talk is often described in terms seldom used about men's talk: *gossip, chatter, nag, rabbit, yak* and *natter* are all terms used to refer predominantly to women's conversations. They all imply that women's talk is plentiful but rather pointless. (See also Chapters 6 and 7 on the value placed on the language or talk of other groups.)

There has been a considerable amount of research in this area; the majority of the research on which the remainder of this chapter has been based has been conducted in English-speaking countries such as the United States, Britain and New Zealand, in a variety of ethnic and social groups. The research findings have been that there are quite dramatic differences in the ways men and women talk, which are sometimes the opposite of what you might expect. For example, the evidence strongly suggests that men on the whole talk far more than women, in contradiction of the stereotype. This is an important finding, because it shows **ideology** at work (as discussed in Chapter 3). It is so much a part of our 'common sense' that women talk more than men that we tend to assume it's true despite plentiful evidence around us to the contrary. The fact that we do tend to believe that women talk too much, when research shows that men on average talk more than women, also indicates how women, and women's activities, have tended to be undervalued.

The differences between women's and men's use of language are remarkably many and varied. For example, there is evidence at the level of **phonology** that women and men vary in their pronunciation. If you are interested you should read Trudgill (1972), Milroy (1987) and Coates (1993: 61–86). There is also evidence of **syntactic** differences, i.e., the kinds of grammatical constructions we use (see Coates 1993: 76–7). In this section we will concentrate on the area of discoursal differences, that is, variation in the kinds of things we talk about, and how we conduct conversations.

5.3.1 How much talk?

As stated above, stereotypes of women's and men's talking styles usually portray women talking far more than men (see Coates 1993: 16–37 for an overview of common stereotypes and prejudices). As also stated above, men (and boys) in fact appear from the research to talk more in mixed-sex groups than women (and girls) do. Studies on this which you might want to check for more information include Fishman (1980), Spender (1980) and Swann (1989). Spender (1990: 41–2) gives an overview of the research. The proportions most frequently quoted are that in a mixed-sex conversation, the average amount of time for which a man talks is approximately twice as long as the average amount for which a woman talks. There is evidence that women who talk for more than one-third of the available time in mixed conversations involving three or more people will be regarded by others as talking too much.

This unevenness in how much women and men are expected to talk is also found in school classrooms, where boys talk more in front of the whole class than girls do, and absorb more of the teacher's time. As a consequence of this research, changes to teaching styles in the UK have been made to distribute the amount of classroom talk, and the teacher's time, more fairly.

5.3.2 Turn construction and interruption

One of the very famous findings from research into language and gender differences is the extent to which men interrupt women. It appears that men interrupt women more than they interrupt other men, far more than women interrupt men, and more than women interrupt other women (see Coates 1993: 107–13; and for a critical review see James and Clarke 1993). The finding that men interrupt women so frequently is often argued to indicate that men act as if they have more right than women to speak in mixed-sex conversations, and that women act as if they had less right to speak than men. The research in this area also discovered that women, particularly in single-sex conversations, are more likely to overlap one another's talk than men are. This overlapping talk differs from interruptions because two or more speakers can continue talking at the same time on the same topic without any apparent sense of their right to speak being violated. These data are often used to argue that women value co-operation and collaboration very highly in their conversations, while men perhaps feel uncomfortable with the degree of intimacy that overlapping talk involves.

5.3.3 Back channel support

Research suggests women are often more active than men in supportive roles in conversation. It appears that women give more back channel support than men do. Back channel support is the verbal and non-verbal feedback listeners give to speakers. Listeners can give feedback by saying things like *mmm, uhuh, yeah,* by nodding, smiling, frowning and by other body language including gestures and body posture. People who have written on this include Zimmerman and West (1975), Fishman (1983), Coates (1989) and Jenkins and Cheshire (1990).

Not only do the studies suggest that women give more back channel support than men, some studies suggest that women's sense of when it is appropriate to give back channel support is more 'finely tuned' than men's, so that speakers really feel they are being listened to. Not being given back channel support is usually reported as making speakers feel unsure of themselves, and can lead to speakers hesitating and repeating themselves and sometimes to their just ceasing to speak. If you are interested in testing this out, experiment with giving different amounts of back channel support and monitor the effect it has on the conversation.

5.3.4 Mitigated and aggravated forms

Women have been shown in some studies to use more **hedges** and **epistemic modal forms** than men. Hedges are linguistic forms which 'dilute' an assertion; for example: *sort of, like, I think* and *kind of.* Epistemic modal forms indicate explicitly the speaker's attitude towards their utterance. For example, *should, would, could, may* and *might* (which are all **modal auxiliary verbs**) can be used to indicate that you don't want to sound completely certain about something. Other words with a similar function are *perhaps, really* and *maybe.*

The studies suggest that women exploit hedges and epistemic modal forms more than men, although why this happens is disputed. Some scholars claim it is because women are less confident than men and feel nervous about asserting anything too strongly (see Lakoff 1975, one of the first people to publish on this area). Other studies claim that women prefer to avoid conflict and so use forms which, by being less direct, allow disagreement to take place without explicit confrontation.

Here is an example of a fifteen-year-old girl using hedges to mitigate the force of her statement, in which she is questioning the interpretation made by another girl of a character in a play they are studying in school:

> Laura: – But (.) but (.) *do you not think* that's *just* a big a. (.) it *could* be *just* a big act (1) he *might* not

(The dots in brackets indicate a pause shorter than 0.5 of a second; the figure 1 in brackets indicates a pause of one second.) Laura is suggesting that her classmate's interpretation is wrong and that the character is just putting on 'a big act'. To make her objection, however, she uses very mitigating language, emphasised here with italics.

5.3.5 Topic development

Another way women's and men's conversations appear to vary is in the topics they choose to discuss. Women, it is said, select more personal topics: their family, their emotions and their friendships. Men, on the other hand, are said to prefer more impersonal topics, often based on factual or technical knowledge, such as football, cars or home improvements. These require fewer intimate revelations, and also emphasise the exchange of information as the reason for the conversation. Women's conversations, it is claimed, focus more on the development and maintenance of the relationship between speakers, fostered by the exchange of intimate details and supportive listening (as discussed above).

ACTIVITY 5.4

Ask their permission to tape a group of people talking. Transcribe approximately three minutes' worth of conversation and see which, if any, of the features discussed above you can identify. Does your recording follow the gender-specific uses outlined above? Transcription is a very time-consuming activity, but worthwhile because it reveals so much.

5.4 Possible explanations

So why might these differences exist? The situation is different from those which give rise to people speaking different languages or different dialects, which are usually associated with geographical or social distance. Women and men, on the other hand, grow up in the same families, go to school together, work together and socialise together.

5.4.1 Dominance

One explanation offered for these variations is 'dominance' theory, which takes the difference in power between women and men as the main cause of discoursal variation. As stated above, it is statistically the case that men tend to have more power than women, physically, financially and in workplace hierarchies. The ways we talk may be a reflection of the material differences between the sexes, and may also reinforce those differences, making them seem 'normal', part of the 'natural order of things'.

Research which supports this explanation includes Fishman (1980), and DeFrancisco (1991). The strength of this explanation is particularly clear in some situations, such as business meetings, where women often report that they have difficulty in gaining the floor (i.e. the right to speak), that they are more often interrupted and that their points are not taken as seriously as men's are.

5.4.2 Difference

Two of the problems with dominance theory are, firstly, that it may appear to cast all women as 'powerless victims', and, secondly, that it casts men as undermining, excluding and demeaning women. 'Difference theory' is a response to these difficulties. It suggests that women and men develop different styles of talking because, in fact, they are segregated at important stages of their lives. Deborah Tannen's work (1990, 1991) is often taken as an illustration of difference theory.

According to 'difference' theory, playing in single-sex groups as children, and having same-sex friendships in adult life, leads men and women to have separate 'subcultures' each of which has its own 'subcultural norms', that is, rules for behaviour and, in particular, for talking. Within their own subcultural groups, women's and men's conversational norms work perfectly well for what they want to accomplish. Women, the theory explains, desire from their relationships collaboration, intimacy, equality, understanding, support and approval. Men, on the other hand, allegedly place a greater premium on status and independence, and are less concerned about overt disagreement and inequality in their relationships. The rub comes when women and men try to communicate with one another: their different styles can lead to misunderstandings.

Some people link these characteristics to biological factors: that men's different hormonal balance means they are more aggressive than women. Others link it to socialisation: that girls are rewarded very early for behaving politely and putting the needs of others before their own, but are told off more than little boys for rough behaviour. Little boys, on the other hand, are praised for being 'active' and 'spirited'. These gendered socialisation patterns are not neutral, as you will probably have noticed: they still prepare women for being less socially powerful than men.

5.4.3 Analysis of gender

The weakness of both the models described above is that there is a tendency to regard 'women' as being all more or less the same: talking in the same ways and having the same expectations from relationships. In fact differences of age, nationality, religion, class, sexual orientation, regional and cultural background mean that two women may have different ideas of what it means to be 'a woman', and different expectations of their friendships and sexual relationships. Equally, men are not an homogeneous group with shared values, but have diverse ways of thinking about their identity.

Another way of looking at the differences between the ways in which women and men use language is to see the differences in the way we use language as part of what creates our perception of gender. Newborn babies cannot easily be identified as 'girls' or 'boys' if they are dressed identically. However, in many cultures, babies are frequently dressed in ways to make their gender clear, for example by the colours of their clothes. The use of colour to indicate gender is particularly marked when it comes to dressing boys. Many people would feel quite disturbed by the thought of dressing a baby boy in pink. We use clothes, and other physical attributes we control such as our jewellery, hairstyles and use of makeup, to indicate our gender. Similarly, perhaps women and men adopt certain styles of talking as part of the process of demonstrating to the world what their gender is. Finally, it is worth considering how many of the differences we observe are linked less to what people actually do when they talk and more to our perception of gender, and how we interpret the differences we notice. For example, in studies of interruption, it is notoriously difficult to agree on exactly what an interruption is and when one has occurred, making it a slightly ambiguous area. And, because of this ambiguity, it is easy for our expectations to affect what we notice, and how we interpret what we notice, while ignoring other evidence which does not fit so neatly into our preconceptions.

5.5 Summary

In this chapter we looked first at sexism in English, created through asymmetry, marked and unmarked terms, and semantic derogation. We also looked at how it's possible to be sexist in discourse using terms which in another context might not be sexist at all. You were asked to consider whether it is possible to be sexist about men in the same way as it is about women. Bearing in mind the arguments made in Chapter 2, that representation reflects, and has an effect on, the way we perceive the world, you might consider whether the evidence of sexism in language is also evidence of sexism in society.

In the second part of the chapter, we looked at differences in the way women and men talk, and how evidence of these differences sometimes contradicts our 'commonsense' ideas. Two possible explanatory theories were put forward: dominance and difference theory. We ended with a word of warning: that it is very hard to be objective in our analysis of gender, since our perceptions in this area can easily be distorted by our expectations.

Note

1   Commercial television in Britain.

Suggestions for further reading

Cameron, Deborah (1998) *The Feminist Critique of Language* (2nd edition), London: Routledge. A wide and fascinating range of essays on the topic of women and language.

Coates, Jennifer (1993) *Women, Men and Language* (2nd edition), London: Longman. The definitive overview of differences in women's and men's speech (phonological, syntactic and discoursal), written in a clear, accessible style.

Coates, Jennifer (ed.) (1997) *Language and Gender: A Reader*, Oxford: Blackwell. For taking your studies further, a state-of-the-art collection of articles.

Mills, Sara (1995) *Feminist Stylistics*, London: Routledge. Sexist language and how to analyse it: examples from literature, songs and advertisements.

Chapter 6

Language and ethnicity

Ishtla Singh

6.1 Introduction

During my time in Britain, I have met a number of people who make very interesting (if inaccurate) assumptions about the type of person I must be. When I first arrived, my ability to 'speak English really well' was often commented on as surprising and laudable, and seemed to contribute in some measure to my acceptability into the community I had entered. One person, deaf to my protestations, praised me for giving up my 'native Jamaican' for English (even though I'm from Trinidad and a creole speaker). On the other hand, this mistaken assumption also led someone else, equally unshake-able in their convictions, to call me a 'coconut' (White on the inside, Black on the outside), and to accuse me of 'forgetting my roots'. I have been called a 'fucking nigger' by a random passer-by, and advised by another not to be a 'traitor to my people' in a foreign country. The notion of 'my people' has also generated quite a bit of comment. Many were incredulous at the fact that there is a significant Asian presence in Trinidad, others insisted that I couldn't possibly be '"pure" Asian' because I had been born in the Caribbean and therefore must have African branches in my family tree. On one memo-rable occasion, someone explained at length that the reason I wasn't a good swimmer but a good runner lay in my alleged 'Ethiopian genes and race memory'.

It's important to note that these types of occurrences did not make up the bulk of my experiences. I also met, and continue to meet, many people who do not appear to make such assumptions. However, what interested me about these instances was what they revealed about people's varying ideas and stereotypes of ethnicity, and of the perceived relationships between ethnic grouping and language use. Let's now look at the issues involved in a bit more detail.

6.2 What is ethnicity?

One of the things that's very clear from the instances just cited is that people made different assumptions about what ethnic group I belonged to. For some, this seemed to be based on my skin colour and/or my apparent 'race' classification, or on the place (they thought) I was from. Indeed, these various interpretations of ethnicity are not unusual: my students, for example, when asked to define *ethnic* and *ethnicity*, consistently produce statements such as 'to be ethnic is to be Black', or 'ethnicity is to do with your roots, or your culture', or 'ethnicity means race'. Importantly, these all contain a kernel of truth, since *ethnic* is ultimately derived from the Greek *ethnos* or 'nation'; and a nation is defined as a community which has a common history, cultural tradition and language. Since we each have cultural, historical and linguistic affiliations, we each also have an ethnic identity, in terms of which we can be (and often are) labelled. However, an individual can have more than one ethnic label, ranging from those they choose to those that are decided for them, again, as is evident in the examples I have just given.

It is noteworthy that discussions about ethnicity often make use of the concepts *ethnic majority* and *minority*. In contexts where ethnic majorities and minorities co-exist, the former term typically refers to a group which shares a socially dominant culture and the latter, to a group which shares ethnic affiliations that are socially marginalised. In many contemporary settings, the ethnic majority has been established for a longer period of time and the minority groups are the more recent products of migration, although it must be noted that this is not always the case. In the histories of Australia, the United States and Britain for example, settled Aboriginal, Native American and Celtic peoples (and their cultures) respectively became displaced and marginalised by later European migrants. In addition, majorities and minorities do not necessarily entail a significant numerical difference. In the sixteenth to nineteenth centuries, for instance, many European powers colonised West Indian islands, setting up sugar plantations cultivated by imported African slaves. Each island had a few large plantations, each home to a European planter, who had perhaps been accompanied by his immediate family, and about fifty to sixty slaves. Thus, in most islands, African slaves actually outnumbered their European masters: in Barbados (an island colonised by Britain) in 1684, for example, there were 19,508 British but 62,136 African slaves (Watts 1987: 311). However, this numerically larger group of slaves was, socially and politically, an ethnic minority.

The one thing that all instances of co-existing majorities and minorities have in common however, is the fact that the socio-cultural dominance of the former group establishes their ideologies, or 'assumptions, beliefs and value-systems' (Simpson 1993: 3, see Chapter 2), as norms which, it is typically assumed, 'everyone' shares. Thus, it has not been uncommon to hear or read statements such as 'England is a White Anglo-Saxon Protestant country', or that 'everybody speaks English here [in Britain]'. Statements such as these are often presented, and taken, as 'common sense': they represent a 'normal' state of affairs. In actuality however, they represent, and in so doing enforce, a perception of the racial, cultural and linguistic characteristics of one group as primary and typical. In such discourses, the ethnic affiliations of other, minority groups are rendered invisible (because they are not talked about), or are marked as 'different' at best, or 'deviant' at worst, by comparison. Thus, in our example, those who are not English-speaking WASPs (White Anglo-Saxon Protestants) can be represented as outsiders to the norm: an approach which is explicitly taken by certain groups who profess to be the mouthpiece of an ethnic majority, as we shall see in section 6.3.

The association between certain ethnic characteristics and difference from the norm therefore means that terms such as *ethnic* have come to denote anything perceived as racially and/or culturally distinct from the mainstream. For example, when an American Airlines flight crashed en route to the Dominican Republic in November 2001, an airport spokesman stated 'We know it was a very *ethnic* flight' (*The Guardian*, 13 November 2001). Hugh Massingberd, in his review of *British Food* by Colin Spencer (*The Daily Telegraph*, 14 December 2002), comments on the fact that the most popular '*ethnic* sauce' of the past fifty years is sweet and sour, and that modern Britain loves 'spicy *ethnic* food'. Sukhdev Sandhu, in another book review (*Goth: Identity, Style and Subculture*, *The Daily Telegraph*, 7 September 2002), observes that the fashion industry is no longer taken with the Goths, who generally tend to be middle-class and White. Instead, they prefer '"street", urban, *ethnic*'.

So far, we have been assuming that defining ethnicity, or ethnic identity, is fairly straightforward: it is something we all have, and it is either part of mainstream norms or marked as distinct from those norms. However, because ethnicity includes so many different characteristics, it can sometimes be much more multilayered. For example, in modern Britain, it is possible to distinguish four major long-established ethnic groups: the English, the Welsh, the Scots and the Irish. Members of all four groups share a 'British' identity, but might also choose to identify themselves as Welsh, Scots, English or Irish respectively, since each denotes a distinct group with a particular history, cultural practices and even linguistic affiliations. Some members may also have, and acknowledge, other ethnic associations at the same time, such as an Asian, African or Chinese heritage. Labels such as *British Asian* and *Black British* go some way towards encoding such ethnic multidimensionality.

BBC Radio 1 effectively illustrated this multilayering of ethnic identity in 1997, with an advertisement for a helpline for victims of racial harassment. It began with two men, one English; the other Scottish, arguing and trading insults based on the other's ethnicity. A third man, with an Indian accent, then intervened, causing the Englishman and Scotsman to claim solidarity as 'real' British, and turn on him as a member of a migrant minority group. A Frenchman then joined in, which caused the Englishman, Scotsman and British Asian to claim solidarity as 'British' and to carry on a well-established tradition of hostility with France. An American then stepped in, causing the Frenchman and the 'British' to merge into 'Europeans'. The sketch ended with the appearance of a Martian, which then united the rest as 'Earth humans'.

Thus, the fact that ethnic identity can incorporate many different characteristics means that its definition is neither clear-cut nor uniform. In addition, as we have seen, certain (perceived) characteristics may be given priority over others in the formulation of ethnic labels. To return to the personal experiences cited at the beginning of this chapter, I choose to label myself *Asian-Caribbean*, which acknowledges what I consider to be the two major strands in my ethnic heritage. However, some people class me as *Afro-Caribbean*, which recognises one element of my ethnicity (*Caribbean*) as distinctive, but negates my Asian affiliations by placing me in a category that seems to mean 'non-White' (*Afro*). And the person who shouted the offensive *nigger* at me had clearly prioritised physical characteristics (primarily again, that category of 'non-White') in choosing that particular label.

Such labels all feed into the different 'angles of telling' (Simpson 1993, see Chapter 2) that can be adopted in representing and reinforcing perceptions of ethnicity. In particular, the angles on ethnic minority groups which are 'told' by majority groups can have a powerful effect on perception, since they are disseminated through the mainstream, 'norm-upholding' branches of institutions such as the media and educational systems. We turn to examples of such 'angles' in Section 6.3.

ACTIVITY 6.1

The *London Metro* (17 March 2003) reported that a documentary to be screened in April 2003 would name David Beckham, a White British-born footballer, 'Britain's most famous black [*sic*] man'. On what grounds could such an ethnic classification be made? In other words, what are the attributes that might qualify someone for 'Black ethnicity', or any other for that matter? Consider this with a group and compare your answers. Do you think that they are adequate to qualify someone for 're-classification', or does ethnic affiliation have a dimension that we need to be 'born into'?

6.3 The language of prejudice

I stated in the last section that the ideologies of ethnic majority groups become established as norms, and that everything that does not conform is represented, and perceived, as different and peripheral. This also holds true in the context of representations and perceptions of ethnicity: that of the majority group comes to be seen, and talked about, as the norm, and that of minority groups as 'other'. This is typically achieved in discourse by explicitly creating an opposition between *us* and *them*, and making use of negative labelling and stereotyping. These are not discrete processes, as we shall see below.

6.3.1 Marking *us* and *them*

One of the assumptions on which the 1997 Radio 1 advertisement mentioned in section 6.2 was predicated was that, in 'angles of telling' on ethnicity, there is often a separation into what can be referred to as *us* and *them*. When the Englishman insults the Scotsman on his nationality, he is expressing assumptions on behalf of his group: *we* English who hate *them*, the Scots. The same goes for the Scotsman's insults to the English. As the different characters enter and affiliations change, so do the *us* and *them* groups; from *we* the 'real' British versus the *them* of the Asian immigrant community, to *we* of Earth versus the *them* of another planet.

Real-life, explicit instances of this kind of ideological division can be found in the discourses of political groups who present themselves as the mouthpiece of an ethnic majority, such as the British National Party (BNP). Some of their literature, such as that available on their website,[1] reflects (and, no doubt, hopes to perpetuate) their opposition to the immigration of certain ethnic groups into the UK. The discourse is therefore structured towards a particular 'angle of telling': the relevant ethnic minority groups are portrayed as a somewhat dangerous 'other', a *them* who threaten the well-being and security of *us*, a group which is assumed to include visitors to the website.

For example, the introductory address states that the BNP's aim is to nurture a 'feeling of national and cultural unity among *our* people', and makes reference to '*our* ancestors' whose efforts have made Britain '*our* country'. '*Our* innovations and ideas' are hailed as the foundation of the modern world. The reader, who is addressed explicitly as *you*, and who, importantly, is assumed to share *our* beliefs and *our* (White British) ethnicity, is asked 'Isn't it time *we* put *our* own people first? Like *you*, *we* say "yes".' The threat to *us* is constructed as being posed by immigrants who threaten *your* job, and take away the benefits of *your* taxes and *your* wages. Graphs and statements are included which indicate 'the speed with which *we're* losing *our* country' as 'flood[s] of immigrants and bogus "asylum seekers" [pour] into Britain'. The BNP therefore propose, as a solution to what they call 'the immigration problem', that all 'non-white [*sic*] immigration' into Britain be stopped, and a system of voluntary resettlement put in place whereby already resident non-Whites 'would be encouraged to return to their lands of origin'. Otherwise, the 'British people' will become a minority in *'our* own land'.

One of the many interesting things about such an angle of telling is the assumptions about ethnic groupings on which it is predicated. As mentioned above, the constant address of the reader as *you*, interspersed with comments about *our* heritage and country, suggests that the intended audience not only belongs to a White, British majority but also, very importantly, shares the same beliefs and attitudes. However, the notion of 'the British people' is less clear-cut: this grouping would seem to be based more on 'being White', and less on being born in Britain, since there are certainly generations of non-White, British-born people who are clearly excluded. This is underlined by the fact that 'British people' are threatened by 'non-White immigration', which implies that migration of other 'White' groups is acceptable. 'Non-White' migrants are labelled consistently as 'bogus asylum seekers', a phrase which has contemporary currency in certain UK newspapers, and which reflects and perpetuates a belief that many, if not all, migrants enter the country under false pretences.

It is noteworthy that such clearly explicit divisions between *us* and an alien *them* are now to be found mainly in the discourses of those who are themselves generally considered to be on the fringe of the mainstream. For example, the BNP put themselves forward as a representative of 'the British people', but the sector of the population who consider their views extreme appears to outnumber their supporters. This is not to say that notions of *us* and *them* no longer have general, mainstream currency. Indeed, in some areas of the British press, for example, the ethnic 'other' (and the associated 'immigration problem') seems to have become fused with fears about terrorism. *The Sun* newspaper (16 January 2003), for example, opens its editorial comment on the death of Stephen Oake (referred to in Chapter 2) with a sentence that links the event with immigration: 'If Britain wasn't such a soft touch, Steve Oake would be alive today'.

Like the BNP, *The Sun* assumes that the reader shares the value system it expresses here. It also assumes that the reader understands the associations of *soft touch*, a phrase commonly used in Britain in derogatory descriptions of the country's supposedly lax immigration policy. However, to make the connection between high numbers of immigrants and Stephen Oake's death, the reader must also make a perceptual link, as the article does, between migrants and the notion of the threatening 'other'. Once this is done, the dangerousness of *them* is reinforced by its correlation with the actual, physical death of one of *us*. The article goes on to state that Stephen Oake had been sent to arrest a 'bogus asylum seeker' who allegedly belonged to an al-Qa'ida cell; that there are unknown numbers of 'terrorists' in the country, living off the system while plotting to overthrow it, and that such 'extremists' should not be allowed in. It is arguable that the combination of such labels, which have highly negative associations, works to reflect and reinforce a strong perception of the dangerous outsider.

The consistent and repeated use of such negative **collocations** can therefore play a significant part in the angles of telling adopted for ethnic minority groups. In the following section, we look at a related phenomenon, the use of negative labelling, in a bit more detail.

6.3.2 Negative labelling

The data from *The Sun* and the BNP website demonstrate how ethnic minority groups can be constructed, in certain types of discourse, into threatening social stereotypes through negative association with concepts that carry immediacy for many people: *they* take the benefit of *our* taxes and endanger not only *our* job security but even *our* lives. Such negative constructions can also be, and often are, aided or achieved through the use of 'labels of primary potency' (Allport 1990: 248).

When we are asked to describe someone, for example, there are all sorts of different characteristics that we can focus on – hair and eye colour, height, disposition, accent, and so on. However, Allport states, there are certain characteristics which seem to carry more perceptual potency than others, and these are the ones which signal difference from what is considered mainstream. Thus, if a person is perceived as ethnically distinctive or as physically incapacitated, for example, then these are the attributes we may notice, and name, first. Allport (1990: 248) argues that the resultant 'labels of primary potency . . . prevent alternative classification'. In other words, they direct our perception of the described person. He quotes an example from Irving Lee, in which a man who had lost the sight in both eyes was consistently labelled as a 'blind man'. For those to whom this characteristic was primary, his other attributes, such as being 'an expert typist, a conscientious worker, a good student, a careful listener, a man who wanted a job' went unrealised. Thus, he found it difficult to get a job typing telephone orders for a department store, because the personnel representative couldn't get beyond what he perceived to be a wholly debilitating disability: '"But you're a blind man" he [personnel representative] kept saying, and one could almost feel his silent assumption that

somehow the incapacity in one aspect made the man incapable in every other'
(Allport 1990: 248).

It is worth noting that, thirteen years on, such occurrences are arguably
less frequent. Many societies have adopted, at the very least, more outwardly
liberal perspectives which seek to prevent such discrimination. This is not to
say that certain characteristics have lost their 'potency' for everyone; indeed,
as we have seen so far in this chapter, this is certainly not the case when it
comes to ethnicity. However, it has become much more difficult in certain
public domains to talk explicitly and derogatorily about, and act upon,
perceived difference from the mainstream. Change in language use does not
mean immediate change in attitude, and for the time being, negative attitudes
to ethnic minority groups can be channelled into 'angles of telling' which
associate them with social threat and danger.

In terms of explicit negative ethnic labelling, it is still possible to hear
the use of racist terminology, which clearly signals the 'otherness' of the group
or person being named. It is a particularly potent form of abuse because it
leaves the addressee feeling powerless; that they have been arbitrarily dumped
into a morass of negative perceptions which allows no recognition of them as
acceptable individuals. Members of various ethnic minority groups have
attempted to 'take power back' by reclaiming such terminology, as we shall
see later in this section.

Another way in which groups can be negatively labelled is through the
constant use of identity terms which have come to encode negative social stereotypes. Andersen (1988), for instance, pointed out that the label 'Black' was often
linked in the British media with negative signs such as *hate, fight, riot*. Van
Dijk (1991), in a study of the British right-wing and popular press, stated that
the reporting of negative topics, such as crime, becomes 'over-ethnicised', but
the reporting of stories considered positive becomes 'de-ethnicised', as the
following excerpt from a letter to the press indicates:

> Can you explain why black Englishmen and women who win Olympic
> medals or excel at games are described as 'English' while those who
> riot and throw petrol bombs are almost inevitably 'West Indian'?
>
> (reproduced in van Dijk 1991: 212)

In modern Britain, labels such as *Jamaican* and *Muslim* are particularly
potent for some speakers. The former has featured heavily in discussions of
illegal drugs entering the country, and the latter in post-9/11 debates. It is
worth noting that every speech community around the world has its own negative ethnic labels. For example, in Trinidad, the label *small islander* (which
refers to people who have migrated from poorer and smaller islands, such as

Grenada and St Vincent) is derogatory. No doubt *Trinidadian* is used equally negatively in speech communities in these areas! Again, however, the consistent use of ethnic labels which come to have derogatory associations can be just as potent as racist terminology – they simultaneously reinforce negative stereotypes of the group being named and disempower them.

This brings us to the phenomenon of reclamation mentioned earlier. Members of ethnic minorities sometimes attempt to reduce, or remove, the power of derogatory ethnic labelling by using those terms among themselves, as positive markers of group identity. For example, in my high school in Trinidad, one of our prefects with Afro-Caribbean ethnicity frequently addressed our class (comprising females mainly with Afro-Caribbean and Asian-Caribbean ethnicities) as *niggers*. In such a context, the term was not considered or treated as offensive to the majority, who could claim ethnic solidarity with her and each other as 'non-White'. However, our other prefect (of White British ethnicity) could not, and did not, use such a term, since to do so would have re-created an uneasy colonial relationship between a socio-politically powerful White majority and correspondingly powerless Black minority.

An interesting debate over the status of *nigger* as a reclaimed label surfaced with the release in 1997 of Quentin Tarantino's film *Jackie Brown*. Tarantino claimed that the dialogue of his Black characters from the ghetto needed to include the use of such terms if it was to be received as real and immediate:

> Ordell's [one of the main black characters] . . . a black guy who throws the word around a lot, it's part of the way he talks . . . that's just who he is and where he comes from . . . If you're writing a black dialect, there are certain words you need to make it musical, and 'nigger' is one of them.
>
> (James 1998: 8)

Tarantino's argument therefore seemed to be that he was capturing, and in a sense celebrating, the 'natural' cadences of a certain type of African-American speech, and the reclaimed ingroup use of once derogatory labels had become part of that. Director and producer Spike Lee however, criticised Tarantino's script, stating that since the Black characters are fictional, what is ultimately the source of the taboo term is Tarantino's White voice – one which, by virtue of its place in the majority group, cannot use such terminology in a positive way.

Such issues are not easily resolved but they do show that it is difficult to reclaim certain labels totally as positive markers of ethnic identity. Because they continue to be used as terms of ethnic abuse, and ultimately because ethnic prejudice continues to occur, they retain a certain measure of negative potency.

Reclamation of abusive or derogatory labels is not the only way in which ethnic minorities can claim solidarity and assert their ethnic individuality: they can, and often do, choose to do so through language use. This is, however, an undertaking that can also become fraught with difficulties, as we will see in the next section.

ACTIVITY 6.2

One way of discovering how a particular minority group is viewed by the majority is to look at the number of insult terms that exist for that group. Make a list of all the ethnically or racially marked insult terms that you can think of and group them according to the ethnic groups they refer to. Are there terms which seem particularly potent to you? Ask friends or family to do the same. Are your judgements similar? Consider, with a group, what kinds of factors can affect mainstream perspectives on minority groups, both favourably and unfavourably.

6.4 Language use as a marker of ethnic identity

A perception of, and angle of telling on, an ethnic group's 'otherness' creates, for some members of that group, a desire to acculturate to what is considered mainstream. This 'desire' is often fed by an association of mainstream cultural norms with social success. However, for many members of that group, the pull of the mainstream is not a straightforward affair – there is often a tension between acculturation to wider norms (both culturally and linguistically) and the maintenance of individual ethnic identity. Thus, members of ethnic minorities continue to participate in cultural, religious and linguistic practices which mark them as distinctive. In terms of language use, this can mean preserving or revitalising[2] a mother tongue different from that utilised and made official by the ethnic majority. Such choices are not always perceived favourably by members of majorities, who have the power to curtail and obstruct them. Language policy in the United States, to which we now turn, provides us with an effective case study. Since this is quite a huge subject area, the following section concentrates on a few salient developments.

6.4.1 Language policy in the United States

In 1990, the US government passed the Native American Languages Act, which would provide a framework for the promotion, protection and preservation of these minority languages. As a piece of legislation, this Act was pioneering: it was the first federal recognition of the rights of Americans to make use of, and promote, mother-tongue languages other than English.

The United States, at federal government level, has no official language policy, and no mention of language rights is made at all in the Constitution. Yet, as Schiffman (1996) points out, the dominant, current ideology is that 'everybody speaks English'. The historical lack of a formal language policy may be partly due to the fact that the majority of early settlers shared a common language (English), but Heath (quoted in Mertz 1982: 3) points out that the founding fathers recognised a close affiliation between 'language and religious/cultural freedoms' for the early settlers. Since freedom from religious persecution or oppression was a defining factor in the formulation of the new country's Constitution, the right to use one's native language could not therefore be legally restricted. In addition, Heath (in Mertz, ibid.) also emphasises the fact that the dominant ideology of late eighteenth- and early nineteenth-century America viewed multilingualism positively. Indeed, knowledge of a range of languages was considered an essential element of intellectual development.

Thus, different languages thrived in various communities as mother tongues: German in Pennsylvania, Dutch in New York, French in Louisiana and Spanish in California. However, by the mid to late nineteenth century, the earlier embracing of multilingualism had begun to give way to the promotion of monolingualism, namely, in English. The state of California, for example, stopped Spanish-medium education in 1855, and declared in its Constitution that all legal and official proceedings and documentation were to be conducted and published solely in English. As this period saw mass migration into the country from diverse ethnic groups, it is likely that a perceived need to define the basis of a 'true' citizen of the country began to grow. One of the social markers of 'real' integration may have been seen as the use of a common language. In fact, there have been similar parallels to this reasoning recently in Britain. In 2001, the Home Secretary David Blunkett, in the wake of race riots in the northern English towns Burnley and Oldham, stated that ethnic minority groups in such areas needed to become integrated into, and feel part of, 'British social values and norms of acceptability' (quoted in *The Daily Telegraph*, 10 December 2001). One of the ways in which this could be achieved, he proposed, was through the learning of English. We shall return to this issue of learning the ethnic majority's language, and what it signifies, later in this section.

In terms of the United States, legal restrictions on language use such as that passed in California were made in some states. However, no official proposal to declare English the national language has ever been legally ratified. This is not to say that such proposals have never been made. The US Congress considered the first one in 1923: a proposal to declare 'American' (as opposed to English) the national language. Though the Bill failed in committee, it was adopted later that year by the State of Illinois. In 1981, an amendment to the Constitution to make English the official tongue was put forward. The proposal has been before Congress several times (most recently in 2001), but has not yet been put to a vote. As we shall see later, organisations which support such proposals continue to be active in attempts to influence language policy.

Schiffman (1996: 211) has pointed out that since the United States at the moment has no explicit, federal policy with regard to language use, it is often assumed that it is 'neutral' with regard to English or any other language. However, this totally ignores the deeply ingrained, 'commonsense' assumption of English as the language of America. A very clear example of this can be seen in developments in twentieth-century educational policies. For instance, in 1923, a suit was brought against the state of Nebraska by German Lutherans, after it had legislated that only English could be used in its schools (Meyer *v.* Nebraska). Meyer was a teacher who taught German to children outside of school hours, but had nevertheless been accused of breaking the law. The Supreme Court ruled that the Nebraska law violated the Fourteenth Amendment (which forbids state-imposed discrimination on the basis of race), but maintained that the bulk of instruction in schools should be in English, and tuition in other languages should be considered ancillary in the curriculum.

Another landmark case took place in 1974, when the parents of approximately three thousand Chinese pupils took the San Francisco Unified School District to court (Lau *v.* Nichols). In a clear subscription to the dominant ideology of English as primary, the plaintiffs argued that approximately two-thirds of students from this ethnic group received no extra special tuition in English, which violated not only the Fourteenth Amendment but also Title VI of the 1964 Civil Rights Act, which prohibits ethnic discrimination in federally assisted education programmes. The Supreme Court found in their favour, ruling that simply providing all students with the same learning and teaching resources did not guarantee equality of treatment, since those whose English skills were limited would suffer a disadvantage from the start. In 1975, a series of guidelines for combating such inequalities, the 'Lau Remedies' (later the 'Lau Regulations'), was put forward by the US Commissioner of Education for adoption in schools across the country. However, they were never legally ratified.

Generally, since the mid-1980s, the promotion of English both inside and outside schools has taken on impetus. The *English Only* movement, formed in that era, promotes English as the language which unifies America and facilitates the social and cultural assimilation of ethnic minority groups into mainstream norms, much like David Blunkett's proposal referred to earlier. The policies of *English Only* are propagated mainly through two national groups, *English First* and *US English*. The former (founded in 1986) explicitly argues against potential policies which support multilingualism, which they view as costly and ineffective. The latter itself comprises two further organisations, the *US English Federation* and *US English, Inc.* The *US English Federation* is concerned primarily with the promotion of English in education where, again, it is assumed it will serve as an effective medium of integration among ethnically diverse peers with different mother tongues. It states that its goal is 'to ensure that English continues to serve as an integrating force among our nation's many ethnic groups and remains a vehicle of opportunity for new Americans' (US English 2002).[3]

US English, Inc. seeks to pass legislation making English the official language at state and federal levels. It, like its sister organisation, promotes fluency in English as a tool of social empowerment for ethnic minority immigrants with different mother tongues (US English 2002).

A more recent organisation, *English Plus*, has become the main policy alternative to the *English Only* movement. While it also advocates proficiency in English, it assumes that this should not be at the expense of other languages and cultures. An *English Plus* resolution expressing this principle (H. Con. Res. 9) has been introduced in the 107th Congress (2000–1) and similar measures have been introduced at the state level in New Mexico (1989), Oregon (1989), Washington (1989) and Rhode Island (1992). The support for these organisations promoting English is not insignificant. *US English Inc.* for example, boasts 1.7 million members worldwide. In addition, and very importantly, they explicitly express a 'commonsense' belief in the primacy of English as the language of America, which is even shared by communities with different native tongues (cf. Lau *v.* Nichols). A question we could reasonably ask at this juncture is, do they have a point? And also, how does promotion of English actually impact on speakers with different native languages?

There is no question that English is an important language in the United States or indeed, currently in the world. In places such as the United States, where English is the main language of everything from street signs to public addresses by the President, it is not surprising that many people come to see it as the 'only language' of the country, or that many feel that competence in it is necessary. Furthermore, the association of English with the mainstream, and the social opportunities present there, serves to make acquisition of the language even more attractive. Kloss (quoted in Schiffman 1996: 211) makes this point in his discussion of the 'absorbing power of the highly developed American society'. He argues that members of ethnic minority groups are drawn towards acculturating to mainstream social norms because 'the manifold opportunities for personal advancement and individual achievements which [American] society offer[s] [are] so attractive'. Thus, they voluntarily become subscribers to the ideology that adoption of mainstream norms, including language use, is not only necessary but a positive social step. Finally, we cannot discount the fact that the global growth of English only adds to belief in its primacy.

It is therefore arguable that there is no real need to legislate formally for giving English official status, since many people, including the minorities that the *English Only* movement seek to integrate, already believe in it as a first and only language. We could therefore justifiably question why such movements actively seek such legislation. Mertz (1982) states, and Schiffman (1996) implies, that an element of linguistic determinism (see Chapter 2) forms part of their motivation. Schiffman (1996: 247) for example, points out that any challenge to the primacy of English can be interpreted as subversive and unpatriotic: 'antipathy to any expanded role for "foreign" language [*sic*] in American life is strong . . . it does not wish to tolerate something that it sees as dangerous, untrustworthy . . . perhaps even un-American'.

In her examination of relevant case law materials, Mertz (1982) argues that the belief in language as a system which encodes and perpetuates a cultural value system is strongly held at a 'folk-theory' level. Thus, native-born Americans who learn English as a mother tongue 'naturally' also acquire the values of the country, and have a 'true' understanding of concepts such as *constitution* and *democracy*. In 1897, for example, the Supreme Court of Wyoming ruled that the requirement that all voters should be able to read the state's constitution meant that they had to be able to read it in English. An ability to read it in any other language was meaningless. The Court based its decision on an assumption of linguistic and cultural relativity (see Chapter 2): since direct translation between languages was practically impossible, given a lack of 'precise equivalents', then 'subjects of a despotic government' for example, would not truly be able to understand the concept of *constitution* and could not therefore subscribe to it in the same way as a native English-speaking American citizen could (Supreme Court of Wyoming, quoted in Mertz 1982: 4).

Those who had a different native tongue, therefore, had also had a 'natural' acculturation into a different value system, and the latter could potentially be politically dangerous. Mertz (1982) cites several interesting instances of this 'Whorfian folk-theory' at work. She quotes, for example, one of the arguments made in support of Nebraska's regulation in Meyer *v.* Nebraska:

> The object of this legislation . . . was to create an enlightened American citizenship in sympathy with the principles and ideals of this country, and to prevent children reared and educated in America from being trained and educated in foreign languages and foreign ideals before they have had an opportunity to learn the English language and observe American ideals. It is a well-known fact that the language first learned by a child remains his mother tongue and the language of his heart.
>
> (US Supreme Court, quoted in Mertz 1982: 4)

Similarly, the Supreme Court of Iowa (quoted in Mertz 1982), upholding a conviction against another schoolteacher who taught German to pupils, ruled that:

> if foreign languages are to be taught for 'cultural effect' it shall only be after the child has been 'rooted and grounded' in the recognized language of our country. The harmful effects of non-American ideas, inculcated through the teaching of foreign languages, might . . . be avoided by limiting teaching below the eighth grade to the medium of English.

It is arguable that this belief in the link between language use and cultural values is still a potent basis for the push to make English the official language of the United States. Mertz (1982: 6) also cites cases where immigrant adults from ethnic minority groups with different mother tongues had to demonstrate proficiency in English, not simply 'the ability to mumble a few . . . words and banal expressions' in order to be considered a 'true' citizen.

The link between language and culture certainly seems to have informed, in Britain, David Blunkett's comments about members of Asian communities 'needing' to learn English: integration into 'norms of acceptability' and 'core values' of Britishness would allegedly deter events such as race riots which threaten the mainstream. However, many of Blunkett's critics have argued that his focus on language detracted attention from wider social problems, such as poverty and racism, a criticism underlined by the fact that many of those involved in the riots were English-speaking British-born Asians. Indeed, Lee Jasper[4] pointed out that bringing the issue of language into discussions of the tension between ethnic minorities and majorities in Britain, shifted the 'blame' for social unrest on to the minorities' 'refusal' to integrate. Essentially, Blunkett's stance became predicated on an argument about *them* acculturating to *us* and *our* way of life: 'we have norms of acceptability and those who come into our home . . . should accept those norms just as we would have to do if we went elsewhere' (quoted in *The Daily Telegraph*, 10 December 2001).

It is important to note as well that the perceived link between language and culture is also one of the reasons why members of ethnic minorities with native tongues different from those of the majority sometimes strongly resent and resist the adoption of the latter group's language(s). Circumstances vary from context to context, but typically, younger generations of ethnic minority groups tend to be more willing, as Kloss (quoted in Schiffman 1996: 211) states, to 'voluntarily integrate' themselves into the culture of mainstream society; sometimes wholly, and sometimes maintaining a compromise between majority and minority norms. Older generations, on the other hand, may worry about the potential loss of their culture if their offspring become increasingly attracted to mainstream norms, including those of language use. For example, in the United States, the 1990 Act mentioned at the beginning of this section gives some financial teeth to attempts in the various Native American communities to revitalise their native languages among younger generations. However, federal grants are only part of the solution – the bigger problems lie in making the learning of these languages, and the cultural values they encode, attractive to young potential speakers, so that they will not only be encouraged to learn them but will also pass them on to their own children, thus ensuring cultural continuity. At the Fourth Annual Stabilizing Indigenous Languages Symposium (1997), one of the speakers, Richard Littlebear, commented on the fact that, if no attempts to save Native American languages are made, then tribal worldviews (such as those pertaining to tribal relationships and connections with the land), rituals and ceremonies will also be lost. And the fact that younger generations do not learn these languages means, importantly, that they do not learn about a cultural system in which they are valued. Instead, their attempts to integrate into a mainstream which still views them as 'other', contributes to a sense of alienation and frustration, which is in turn linked to increasing gang culture, alcoholism and high mortality rates.[5]

There is no easy solution to any of these issues. Language issues often become integrated into deeper social tensions between majority and minority groups and can become a focus of conflict. This is very likely, because, as Mertz (1982) implies, language use is typically interpreted as an outwardly significant marker of cultural similarity or difference. And similarity in cultural outlook is generally taken to be quite important: metaphors such as *we're speaking the same language*, meaning we see things the same way, are testimony to this. It would seem that difference, particularly in relation to ethnicity, is sometimes seen as threatening to the majority, but important to the minority. However, since the former group typically have the social power to enforce their position, the maintenance of cultural and linguistic distinctiveness for the latter group remains a difficulty.

6.5 Summary

We can conclude that language use in the construction of ethnic identity involves issues which are far from straightforward or easily resolved. The terms 'ethnic' and 'ethnic identity' comprise characteristics that we consider important when defining who we and others are, both as individuals and as part of larger groups. Despite the fact that everyone has an ethnic identity, it tends to be emphasised mainly for minority groups, who are treated largely as outsiders to the majority norm. The 'alien' identity of ethnic minorities is accentuated by the ways in which they are represented by the majority. The effect of this is that the distinctive nature of minority groups is constantly reflected through labels of primary potency. This representation in turn reinforces the perception of these groups as different and, sometimes, as threateningly distinct from the norm. To diminish the threat, accommodation to the norm on every practical level, including language use, is therefore encouraged or imposed by the majority. At the same time, however, minority groups do try to maintain their distinctiveness from a norm which ostracises them, and to express positive ingroup solidarity. One of the ways in which they do this is through language use: in attempting to reclaim abusive terminology and in preserving their native tongues in the face of opposition, they are rejecting the labels and norms imposed by the majority and 'taking power back' (Andersen 1988: 224).

Notes

1   The internet address is http://www.bnp.org.uk/. The data used for this chapter were accessed October 2001.
2   *Revitalisation* is a term used in the field of language obsolescence which, among other things, looks at the attempts made to save languages which are losing native speakers. In this context, revitalising a language refers to the attempts made to encourage its wider use in a speech community, particularly by younger speakers who, literally, carry its future in their hands.
3   US English (2002).
4   Lee, Jasper, 'Open Letter to David Blunkett'.
5   Littlebear (1999).

Suggestions for further reading

Lippi-Green, Rosina (1997) *English with an Accent: Language, Ideology and Discrimination in the United States*, London: Routledge. An accessible and engaging exploration of the creation and maintenance of social tensions between ethnic majority and minority groups in the United States.

Schiffman, Harold F. (1996) *Linguistic Culture and Language Policy*, London and New York: Routledge. Chapters 8 and 9 provide a detailed case study of language policy in the United States.

Van Dijk, T. A. (1987) *Communicating Racism: Ethnic Prejudice in Talk and Thought*, London: Sage. An interesting and useful text. Chapter 3 provides an interesting discussion of how social prejudice against minority groups is manifested in institutional set-ups and particularly in media discourse.

Chapter 7

Language and age

Jean Stilwell Peccei

7.1 Introduction: what has age got to do with language?

How would you describe yourself? Usually, quite a few possibilities come to mind. For example, I am a woman, an American who has lived in England for thirty years, a fifty-six-year-old 'baby boomer' and a university lecturer (just to name a few of my 'identities'). And, just as I have a variety of identities, I also have a variety of ways of speaking. Although in all cases I am speaking English, the language I use when talking informally to friends of my own generation can be quite different from the one I use when giving a lecture in London or the one I used when talking with my grandmother in California. The way I talk to my husband is not the same way I talk to my grown sons. And the way I talk to my sons now is quite different from the way I talked to them when they were toddlers.

As Hudson (1980) has pointed out, we make a very subtle use of the language variability that is available to us. It allows us as speakers to locate ourselves in a multidimensional society and as hearers to locate others in that society as well. Age, like gender, profession, social class and geographic or ethnic origin, has often been studied as one of the factors that locates us in society and causes language variation. One of the ways that I described myself was by my age and generation – a fifty-six-year-old 'baby boomer' – and one of the factors that influences the way I talk in a given situation is the age of my conversational partner. To see how the ages of the speakers can give conversations a characteristic 'flavour', look at the three conversations below. Which one involves two teenage girls, which one involves an adult and a toddler, and which one involves an elderly person and a younger adult?

> (1) A: what – what are these pictures doing here?
>   B: careful of them, darling. Gangan [grandmother] painted them.
>   A: me like a little one best.
>   B: do you?
>   A: which one do you like first? a big one or a little one?
>   B: I like that white one.
>
> (Fletcher 1988: 545)

(2) A: it's your cheque, love. [2 second pause] yeah.

B: [4 second pause] how much for?

A: God! [2 second pause] shall I just read what it says to you? [3 second pause] dear sir or madam you are entitled to supplementary benefit of a hundred-and-fifty pounds for the articles listed overleaf.

B: oh

A: for a cooker. [stove in American English] so you've got a hundred-and fifty pounds for a new cooker. er from Social. Social Security because you're on supplementary benefit all right? [. . .] so you've got a hundred-and-fifty pounds. and that is to get a cooker with my love, all right? [1.5 second pause] aren't you lucky? eh? didn't we do well?

> (adapted from data collected by Karen Atkinson)

(3) A: Anna's so weird

B: pardon? [laughter]

A: Anna. sometimes kind of hyper hyper

B: and sometimes kind of lowper lowper

A: no and [laughter] sometimes kind of 'We should care for the animals of this world', you know

> (Coates 1996)

Apart from the topics of the conversations, you probably used certain features of the language to give you clues about the ages of the speakers. In extract (1), A is three years old and B is her mother. We notice that the toddler has a serviceable but somewhat 'imperfect command' of her native language and that her mother appears to be using a slightly simpler and clearer form of the language than you would expect to be used with another adult. We also notice the mother's use of a 'pet name' *darling* when speaking to the child and a 'baby-talk' word for *grandmother*. In extract (2), A is a home help and B is her elderly client. You perhaps noticed that the conversation contains long pauses between the turns, making it seem that B is having a hard time 'taking in' what is being said to her and then making a response. Did you notice that A seems to have assumed this since she sometimes does not wait for B's answer to a question, repeats what she says several times and 'translates' the contents of the letter for B? Interestingly, like the mother speaking to her child in extract (1), the home help uses 'pet names' with her client: *love*, and *my love*. In extract (3), A and B are both fifteen years old. In contrast to extract (2), we notice that their conversation seems quite fluent. Each speaker comes in quite rapidly after the previous speaker's turn has ended. In contrast to extract 1, the structure of their sentences appears quite 'adult'. There are no sentences like *me like a little one best*. What might also give the game away is some of the vocabulary used by the girls: *weird* and *hyper hyper*.

Our everyday experience yields many examples of vocabulary used by teenagers and young adults which often appear to need 'translations' for older age groups. My twenty-year-old British students added a new meaning for *pants* (as in underpants) to my vocabulary. They said it was roughly equivalent to *terrible* as in *That was a pants exam*. Age-related differences in vocabulary are often the ones most easily noticed by people, but there are other slightly less obvious linguistic differences between age groups as well. For example, the sociolinguist Labov (1972a), found that older New Yorkers were less likely to pronounce the 'r' in words such as *fourth* and *floor* than were younger speakers, while Chambers and Trudgill (1980) found that in Norwich, England, the pronunciation of the 'e' in words like *bell* and *tell* varied according to the age of the speaker. (See also Chapter 8.) Suzuki (2002) has proposed that Japanese young people's interest in American and European popular culture as well as their greater use of the internet and text-messaging (as compared to older Japanese) has resulted not only in an increase of foreign loanwords entering Japanese but also in potentially permanent changes to the writing system, with a decrease in the use of Chinese characters and greater use of the western alphabet.[1]

ACTIVITY 7.1

Make a collection of current slang words used by children and teenagers. Ask people of different ages if they can give you a definition for those words. Do people of different age groups have differing perceptions of what those words mean and how they are used?

So far, we have touched on some of the ways in which the ages of speakers (and their conversational partners) will cause variations in the particular form of the language being used. However, there is another aspect to the language and age issue. Language is a fundamental human activity through which we communicate our particular representation of the world. It is primarily through language that cultural values and beliefs are transmitted from one member of a society to another and from one generation to the next. Thus, we can often see within the structure of a language reflections of the way that a particular culture views the world, and the kinds of distinctions that are held to be important. Age distinctions are frequently reflected in the world's languages. For example, in Italian, as in many languages, the use of certain pronouns is partly governed by the ages of the speaker and the hearer. Comanche, an Amerindian language spoken in the southern Plains region of the United States, had a special version with its own pronunciation patterns and vocabulary which was used with children under five years old (see Casagrande 1948). Closer to home, look at the opening sentences in these two newspaper articles:

(4) Senior citizen Tom Ackles risked his own life to save a drowning dog – a beloved neighborhood pet that had fallen through the ice on a frozen lake. The 66-year-old retired college janitor got a frantic call from a neighbour that a large dog was drowning in a nearby lake.

(National Enquirer, 24 February, 1998)

(5) Lifeguards had to intervene to separate two brawling pensioners during an early morning swimming session . . . Their dispute spilled out on to the pool side with both men clambering out of the water and squaring up to each other.

(The Daily Telegraph, 14 November 1997)

Did you notice that at the very beginning of each article a special term which refers to age group is used to describe the men: *senior citizen* in the American extract and *pensioner* in the British extract? We will return to this issue in the next section, where we will look more closely at how different age groups are represented in English.

In this chapter, we will be concentrating on language issues at the two ends of the lifespan: children under five, and the 'elderly', whom we will provisionally define as people over sixty-five. Two factors make these groups particularly useful for exploring the relationship between language, society and power. Firstly, children and the elderly have a high degree of cultural salience in most societies. That is, they are clearly differentiated from the rest of society not only by their special social, economic and legal status but also by the language which is used to describe and categorise them. Secondly, there are aspects of the communicative abilities of these two groups which can some-times be quite different from that of the 'middle segment' of the lifespan. By looking at these factors, we can explore the relationship between the way we talk to children and the elderly and the more general attitudes of our society towards the status of its youngest and oldest members.

7.2 How can a language reflect the status of children and older people?

In this section we look at the importance of age as a cultural category and the way that our language might reflect a special status for the young and the old.

7.2.1 Age as an important cultural category

How often have you filled in a form where you were asked for your date of birth? It would be hard to imagine a culture which did not use age as a social category and as a means for determining duties, rights and privileges. Your age can determine whether you can attend school, marry, drink alcohol, vote, draw a pension, or get into the movies at half price. To see just how important age labels can be, unscramble the words in (a) to (d) below, and put them into the order which seems most 'natural' to you.

(a)	intelligent woman the old	(c)	dishonest man young the
(b)	singer the teenage attractive	(d)	middle-aged the nurse kind

Most people produce the following:

(a)	the intelligent old woman	(c)	the dishonest young man
(b)	the attractive teenage singer	(d)	the kind middle-aged nurse

In every case, the age description is placed closer to the 'the person' than the other description. There is a very strong tendency in English to place the adjective expressing the most 'defining' characteristic closest to the noun. What might seem to be a 'natural' word order for these phrases is really a reflection of which of the two characteristics we consider to be more important for classifying people. Even though intelligence, honesty, physical attractiveness and kindness are all important to us, they somehow seem to be secondary to a person's age. As Turner (1973) has pointed out, a word order such as *the old intelligent woman* can seem a bit odd not because it violates any rule of grammar but because it does not reflect our habitual way of thinking.

Collect a series of articles about people of different ages. Take a look to see how many explicitly age-related terms appear. In extracts (4) and (5), we saw that the participants' advanced age seemed particularly newsworthy. Would a minor fight between two younger people at a local swimming pool make it into the pages of a national newspaper? Do you notice any other age groups receiving this kind of treatment in your collection? If so, in what sorts of situations?

7.2.2 Labelling age groups

Write down all the labels you can think of which can be used for people under five; between twenty and sixty; and over sixty-five, for example *baby*, *woman*, *person*. (For now, omit any derogatory expressions.) Below are some of the most common terms.

Under 5	20–60	Over 65
person	person	person
child	adult	adult
youngster	grown-up	grown-up
girl	mature person	mature person
boy	woman	woman
minor	man	man
newborn	lady	lady
kid/kiddy	gentleman	gentleman
tot		aged (as in *the aged*)
neonate		oldster
infant		elderly person
baby		elder
toddler		senior citizen
		retired person
		pensioner
		OAP (old age pensioner)

Even with today's life expectancy, the under-fives and over-sixty-fives account for only about a quarter of the lifespan, yet they seem to have a disproportionately large number of specialised age group labels. Did you notice that, even though all the expressions used to label the twenty-to-sixty group could have been used just as accurately for the people over sixty-five, it might not have occurred to you to use them? The first words that come to mind are often those which specifically single out the over-sixty-fives as having a special status, such as *elderly person, senior citizen, pensioner.* If you did use some of the same terms that you listed for the twenty-to sixty group, you may have added *old* or *elderly.* Explicit age marking also occurs with expressions for the very young, although for this group size is also used as an age marker: *little/young child, tiny/young tot.*

7.2.3 Talking about age groups: underlying evaluations of early childhood and old age

Have you ever noticed that some adjectives seem to 'belong' to a particular age group? Words such as *wise, dignified, cantankerous, sprightly, frail* for the elderly and *bouncing, cute, bratty, misbehaved* for young children are a few examples. On the other hand, have you also noticed that there seem to be several adjectives, both positive and negative, such as *little, dear, sweet, fussy, cranky, stubborn, foolish* that are used very frequently to describe both these groups? Expressions such as *second childhood* for old age make this cultural equation between children and the elderly quite explicit.

(6) It is important to recall that the term 'child' was initially used to describe anyone of low status, without regard for their age. Being a child continues to express more about power relationships than chronology, although the two are intimately intertwined. Children's powerlessness reflects their limited access to economic resources, their exclusion from political participation and the corresponding cultural image of childhood as a state of weakness, dependency and incompetence.

(Franklin 1995: 9)

(7) Elderly woman, Morocco: I have no liberty. It is simply that my children have taken me in their charge.

(Tout 1993: 25)

(8) Woman who cares for her elderly mother, USA: I 'listen' to her requests but do what I think best.

(Coupland and Nussbaum 1993: 233)

(9) Virginia Magrath, a retired nurse, waits with her husband, John, who suffers from Alzheimer's and must undergo surgery to remove a blood clot in his brain. She says the doctors ignore her, despite

her medical training, speaking to her daughters instead. 'When you're old, people treat you like you're invisible.'

(Winokur 2001)

Childhood and old age are often viewed as particularly problematic and vulnerable life stages, requiring special attention from the rest of society. There are the terms *paediatrician* and *geriatrician* for doctors who specialise in treating children and the elderly, but no special term for doctors who concentrate on twenty-to-sixty-year-olds. We have *Save the Children* and *Help the Aged*, but a charity called *Save the Adults* or *Help the Grown-Ups* sounds quite odd and would be unlikely to collect many donations. Aid to Dependent Children and Medicare in the United States and Child Benefit and Old Age Pension in Britain are just a few examples of economic resources that governments target specifically to these age groups. We also find special legal institutions designed to protect them. Children are in the care of their parents or guardians and are extremely limited by law in the choices they can make. You may even have left *person* off the list of terms for the under-fives. The legal term *minor* makes direct reference to this aspect of childhood. Although elderly people who become too mentally or physically frail to manage their own affairs may have guardians appointed for them, the over-sixty-fives, as a group, have far more legal independence than children. However, there is one restriction which can have quite far-reaching consequences for their status in society. In most occupations, they are normally required to retire at the age of sixty-five.

(10) Elderly man, Morocco: Nobody bothers with me. When I had means they were all here, but now that I have nothing, nobody knows me.

(Tout 1993: 24)

(11) Nurse at a day hospital for the elderly, UK: All they've got to give is their memories. And that's why you find old people are always going on about the past ... because that's all they've got to give to say thank you.

(Coupland and Nussbaum 1993: 68)

Very young children are financially dependent on their parents, and even those who inherit or earn money in their childhood are not free to spend it as they wish until they 'come of age'. The physical limitations that sometimes accompany the ageing process as well as retirement norms mean that the majority of people over sixty-five are no longer 'earning a living'. Some of the labels for the over-sixty-fives make specific reference to this aspect of their identity: *retired person*, *pensioner* and *OAP*. Lack of financial independence can be particularly problematic for the elderly. While it is assumed that children will one day become 'productive' members of society, people over sixty-five are often seen (and see themselves) as no longer capable of contributing to the general prosperity of their families or of the wider society, a potential 'burden' rather than an 'investment'. Another factor which has been proposed as contributing to ageism, at least in Western societies, is the fear of death. As death is feared, old age, the 'final' stage before death, is also feared. Butler (1969: 243) has suggested that 'Ageism reflects a deep seated uneasiness on the part of the young and middle-aged – a personal revulsion to and distaste for growing old, disease, disability; and a fear of powerlessness, "uselessness", and death.'

One way of seeing whether particular groups have a low, or at least problematic, status is to look specifically at the number of negative, demeaning or insulting terms in the language which are exclusive to that group (see also Chapters 5 and 6 for negative terms related to gender and ethnicity.) The loss of status resulting from physical and economic dependence can be seen in a thesaurus. You will find that there are virtually no insulting or demeaning terms that are exclusive to the middle of the lifespan, but there are several for children, often accompanied by young or little. Examples are *brat, punk, whelp, whippersnapper*. When we look at demeaning or insulting terms for older people, the choice is, unfortunately, vast. The terms *fogy, hag, biddy, fossil, geezer, codger, crone, duffer, bag, wrinklies* (a term that appeared in Britain in the 1990s), are just a few examples. Most of these words can be made even more derogatory when preceded by *old*. Perhaps because of this, many people over sixty-five reject the label *old* entirely as a way of describing their age group, finding that it focuses too much on the negative aspects of ageing. In an American study described in Coupland, Coupland and Giles (1991), the researchers found that the expressions *senior citizen* and *retired person* had positive connotations of 'active', 'strong', 'progressive' and 'happy', while *aged, elderly* and *old* person were much more negatively evaluated. The researchers had three age groups carry out the rating task (seventeen to fort-four; forty-five to sixty-four; sixty-five plus) and found that all three groups tended to agree on the evaluations. However, more recent research using focus groups of people over sixty-five by Wooden (2000) suggests that older Americans harbour 'a profound anger at being labeled anything – they hate being labeled as *retired*'.

This raises some interesting questions about the complex relationship between language and thought, a subject which was the focus of Chapter 2. Our language might reflect underlying attitudes to children and the elderly, but does it also shape them? If so, would getting rid of ageist language also get rid of ageist attitudes? Would the use of more 'positive' words change our negative perceptions of old age? Or might it be the case that new socio-economic circumstances will lead to changed attitudes towards older people and then to a change in the way we talk about them?

In the United States, a 'baby boomer' turns fifty every 7.6 seconds, and by the middle of the twenty-first century old people will outnumber young people for the first time in history. There are now serious proposals both in the United States and in Britain to raise the retirement age to provide sufficient pension cover for this group. The population bulge resulting from the 'baby boom' makes this generation a powerful voting bloc. Postwar prosperity, smaller families and increased career opportunities for women mean that when they retire, this generation will have considerably more economic power than their predecessors. There are already signs that the advertising and marketing industries are rethinking their strategies to adapt to the new economic reality.

> (12) John F. Zweig, CEO of the advertising form, WPP Group-USA addressing a conference at the International Longevity Center in New York City in November 2001: 'It's not lost on these people that this 25% of the population [55 or older] controls 70% of the purchasing power. Yet, despite this there are countless examples of ageist or just plain stupid exclusions of this incredibly important market' (quoted in Kleyman 2001).

Medical advances allowing many more people to have a healthy and active old age could also change our perceptions of what it is to be 'old'. However, not all 'baby boomers' are relying solely on changing socio-economic circumstances to solve the problem. In *Declining to Decline: Cultural Combat and the Politics of Midlife* (1997), Margaret Gullette places a very strong emphasis on ageing as a socially constructed process and urges that 'we who are in our forties and beyond, older and wiser than we once were, must write our own age-positive autobiographies' (quoted in Breines 1997: 29).

ACTIVITY 7.3

Ask ten people to write down the first four words that come to mind for three different ages: three, twenty-three, and eighty-three. Compare the age groups in terms of the proportion of words that refer to:

- positive and negative qualities
- physical qualities; mental or emotional qualities; legal or socio-economic status
- age itself, e.g., youthful, elderly, etc.

7.3 Talking to young children and the elderly

In this section we turn from looking at the way the very young and the very old are talked about, and look at the way these groups are talked to.

7.3.1 Language characteristics of the under-fives and over-sixty-fives

Very young children's language takes its characteristic 'style' from the fact they are apprentice speakers. During the first five years of life, children are still in the process of acquiring the grammar of their native language and a 'working' vocabulary. Young children's speech also has a characteristic 'sound'. Firstly, the pitch of their voice is quite high relative to that of adults. Secondly, their early pronunciations of words can be quite different from the adult versions.

Unlike young children, the over-sixty-fives are experienced language users. However many people believe that old age inevitably results in a decline of communicative ability. Although there is evidence to suggest that older people may require slightly longer processing time to produce and understand complex sentences, numerous studies have shown that the normal ageing process in itself does not result in a significant loss of verbal skill unless serious medical conditions, such as a stroke or Alzheimer's disease, intervene. In some types of discourse, such as complex storytelling, elderly speakers generally outperform younger speakers. However, hearing often becomes less acute as people get older, and this can lead to a reduced understanding of rapid or whispered speech, or speech in a noisy environment. The 'elderly' voice, like a young child's, is instantly recognisable. The normal ageing of the vocal cords and muscles controlling breathing and facial movement results in slower speech and a voice which has a higher pitch and weaker volume and resonance than that of younger adults.

It is important to remember, however, that the way a person sounds is quite separate from what that person is actually saying. The problem for elderly speakers is that people do not always make that distinction. Just as different accents can lead hearers to make all sorts of stereotyped and often inaccurate judgements about everything from the honesty to the education level of the speaker (see Chapter 11), the sound of an elderly person's voice can immediately link the hearer into a whole set of beliefs about old age which may or may not be true of that particular person.

You and I speak. Children babble and chatter. Old people drone and witter. Or do they? Chapters 5, 6, 10 and 11 show how the talk of people in other 'low-status' groups is often devalued or described in negative terms. See whether this holds true for young children and the elderly by examining descriptions of their talk in literature, in the media and in your own conversations.

7.3.2 Child Directed Language

Child Directed Language (CDL), sometimes called 'Baby Talk' or 'Motherese', is a special style used in speech to young children and has been extensively studied over the past thirty years. It has several characteristics, some of which were illustrated in extract 1:

- calling the child by name, often using a 'pet' name or term of endearment
- shorter, grammatically simpler sentences
- more repetition
- more use of questions or question tags ('That's nice, *isn't it?*')
- use of 'baby-talk' words
- expanding on and/or finishing a child's utterance.

CDL also has a characteristic 'sound':

- higher pitch
- slower speed
- more pauses, particularly between phrases.
- clearer, more 'distinct' pronunciation
- exaggerated intonation (some words in the sentence heavily emphasised, and a very prominent rising tone used for questions).

Observational studies of parents' conversations with their children have also highlighted several common features in the way the interaction proceeds. Young children are usually perceived to be incompetent turn-takers, with older speakers having expectations that their contributions will be irrelevant or delayed. The younger the child, the more likely their attempts to initiate a new topic will be ignored by older speakers and the more likely they are to be interrupted or overlapped (two speakers talking simultaneously). There is a relatively high proportion of 'directive' and 'instructive' talk from adults, either by blunt commands – *be careful, don't do that* – or by 'talking over' (talking about people in their presence and referring to them as *we, she* or *he*). Here is an example:

> (13) c 5 Child, T.; m 5 Mother. C wants to turn on the lawn sprinklers. A researcher is present.
> c: Mommy.
> m: T. has a little problem with patience. We're working on patience. What is patience, T.?
> c: Nothing.
> m: Come on.
> c: I want to turn them_._._. M: (at the same time) What is_._._.
> c: on now.
> m: patience? Can you remember?
>
> (Ervin-Tripp 1979: 402)

7.3.3 Similarities between Child Directed Language and 'Elder Directed' Language

In section 7.1 we noted that there seemed to be several parallels between the speech style used by the home help to her elderly client and that of the mother talking to her child. Coupland, N., Coupland, J. and Giles, H. (1991) review several studies which confirm the similarity between CDL and the speech style which is often used with the elderly, particularly by their caregivers. These similarities involve both the content of the talk – simpler sentences, more questions and repetitions, use of pet names, etc. – and the sound of the talk – slower, louder, higher pitch, exaggerated intonation, etc. As the next extract illustrates, there can also be similarities in the ways speakers interact with young children and the elderly, interrupting and overlapping them, treating the person's contribution as irrelevant to the conversation, and using directive language, especially 'talking over'.

> (14) [–] indicates unintelligible syllable(s); HH 5 home help; CL 5 elderly client; D 5 Relative of CL.
> HH: How are you today?
> CL: Oh I [–] I've
> CL: – got a [–] D: (at the same time) She's a bit down today because we're leaving
> HH: I guessed that's what it would be today

Later discussing cakes which have been left for CL who is still
present

D: – They're in there and I'm hoping. They're in the fridge you
see. I'm hoping she will go in there and take them and eat
them.

HH: That's right yeah don't waste . . .

(adapted from data collected by Karen Atkinson)

7.3.4 Why might these similarities occur?

One of the original explanations for the use of CDL was that parents used it
as a language-teaching tool. And, indeed, there are some aspects of CDL which
could potentially be of help to novice speakers. The problem is that variations
in the amount of CDL which children receive do not seem to affect significantly their progress in acquiring their native language. And, as Ochs (1991)
points out, not all cultures use this type of talk with young children. So, if
CDL is not primarily a teaching tool, why is it used in some cultures?

One proposal is that one of CDL's primary uses is to ensure understanding in someone who is not believed to be a fully competent language
user. This might account for the considerable similarities between CDL and
the language used with the elderly. Its use could therefore be closely connected
to cultural expectations and stereotypes about people in these groups. Matched
guise experiments have shown that speakers with an 'elderly' voice tend to
be rated as vulnerable, forgetful and incompetent more often than speakers
with younger voices (see Chapter 11 for an explanation of matched guise
techniques). The low expectations of the elderly resulting from cultural stereotyping of old age as an inevitable decline in physical and mental capacity is
illustrated in the following extract between a home help (HH) and her elderly
client (CL):

(15) cl: Well I don't know your name anyway
    hh: Ann.
    cl: Ann_._._.
    cl: mmm hh: (at the same time) Right.
    cl: I don't need to know your surname do I?
    hh: – (2 second pause) Well you can know it. It's Campbell, but I
don't think you'll remember it, will you. (laughs)
    cl: – (2 second pause, sounds annoyed) What do you mean I
won't remember it? I'm not dim.

(adapted from Atkinson and Coupland 1988)

Another proposed explanation for the use of CDL is that it asserts the power of the caregiver in relation to the child, establishing the caregiver's right to command compliance. When young children are taught the socially appropriate way to 'ask', the message is often that adults can make demands of children but children must make polite requests of adults.

(16) mother: I beg your pardon?
    child: What?
    mother: Are you ordering me to do it?
    child: Mmm, I don't know, Momma.
    mother: Can't you say 'Mommy, would you please make me some?'

(Becker 1988: 178)

The emphasis on unequal power relations between adult and child fits in with our observations about conversational interaction between children and the elderly on the one hand and their caregivers on the other, where the more powerful speaker tends to use interruption, overlapping and 'talking over'. While the use of questions and question tags by caregivers can help elicit conversation, it also allows them to 'direct' the responses of their conversational partners. Tag questions can be especially controlling because they explicitly seek agreement with the speaker.

Atkinson and Coupland (1988) have suggested that using CDL with the elderly can reflect not only a cultural equation between these two groups which is potentially demeaning to elderly people but also a deliberate strategy to constrain and marginalise them, particularly in institutional settings. However, there is another dimension to the use of CDL which is seemingly in contradiction to this proposal. That is, some aspects of CDL might reflect an attitude of affection and nurturance toward the recipient and a willingness to accommodate to their needs. Cromer (1991) has pointed out that affectionate talk to lovers and pets is also characterised by higher pitch, exaggerated intonation, pet names and baby-talk words. And, while no one is likely to appreciate being interrupted or talked over, a negative reaction by the elderly to pet names and repetition accompanied by slower, louder and simpler speech cannot be taken for granted. Coupland, J., Nussbaum, J. and Coupland, N.'s (1991) review of studies involving elderly people's evaluations of this style of talk showed that some found it patronising or demeaning and negatively evaluated caregivers who used it. Others, particularly those who were very frail or suffering from deafness or short-term memory loss, found it nurturing and 'encouraging' and a help in understanding and participating in the conversation. The American Speech-Language-Hearing Association (ASHA) estimates that, in nursing homes, 60 to 90 per cent of residents may actually have communication disabilities.

(17) Speech-language pathologists from the ASHA, Martin Shulman and Ellen Mandel, on how family members and caregivers can make communication with older people easier:

1 Before you begin your conversation, reduce background noises that may be distracting (turn off the radio or TV, close the door, move to a quieter place).

2 Begin the conversation with casual topics (the weather, what the person had for lunch). Avoid crucial messages at the beginning.

3 Continue conversation with familiar subjects such as family members and special interests of the person.

4 Stick to a topic for a while. Avoid quick shifts from topic to topic.

5 Keep your sentences and questions short.

6 Give the older person a chance to reminisce. Their memories are important to them.

7 Allow extra time for responding. As people age, they function better at a slower tempo. Don't hurry them.

8 Give the person choices to ease decision-making ('Do you want tea or coffee?' rather than 'What do you want to drink?')

9 Be an active listener. If you're not sure what is being said, look for hints from eye gaze and gestures. Then, take a guess ('Are you talking about the TV news? Yes? Tell me more. I didn't see it.')

10 After your visit, tell others who visit (relatives, physicians, nurses, aides) what you've learned to improve communication with the older person.

(www.asha.org/speech/development/
communicating-better-with-older-people.cfm)

7.4 Conclusion

At the beginning of this chapter, I asked you to identify the approximate ages of the speakers in three conversations. We will end with the same sort of task.

(18)   A: what have you been eating?

       B: eating

       A: you haven't been eating that spinach have you

       B: (laughs) spin

       a: you know what Pop_._._._happens to Popeye when he eats his spinach

                            (adapted from data collected by Karen Atkinson)

(19) I'm CUTE and SMART and have a GREAT sense of humor. Look like an animated Q-Tip with curves in ALL the right places. Not over-weight, clinging, needy, whiney, or psycho. And if I was ever fed ugly-pills, they DID NOT work!

                                        (www.match.com)

(20) Dominic, I'm putting some people in the bus. Now drive off. Down to the end . . . Drive off down to the village, darling . . . Now are you going to do that?

                                (Harris and Coltheart 1986: 79)

(21) I remember love – the beauty, the ecstasy!

      Then – how it hurt!

      Forgetting helped time dissolve the hurt and pain

      of defeated expectation.

                          (Thorsheim and Roberts 1990: 123)

Extract 18 is a conversation between a home help, A, and her elderly client, B. Extract 19 was written by a seventy-year-old subscriber to an internet singles site. The speaker in extract 20 is four years old and is explaining how to play a game to her two-year-old brother. Extract 21 was written by an eighty-year-old retirement home resident in the United States. If you were surprised by the ages of some of the speakers in these extracts, it simply shows that there is a very complex relationship between physical, mental and social factors in determining a person's use of language and how others perceive and react to that language.

7.5 Summary

In this chapter we have seen that age is an important cultural category, an identity marker and a factor in producing language variation within a speech community. The way we talk about young children and the elderly reflects their special status in our society, a status which is partly determined by the amount of social and economic power which these groups possess. There are parallels between talk addressed to young children and talk to the elderly. These parallels cannot be explained entirely by physical and mental immaturity in the case of young children or by physical and mental decline in the case of the elderly. The status of young children and the elderly in our society, and culturally determined beliefs and stereotypes about their communicative abilities, can play a significant role in producing these parallels.

As a final thought, the following excerpt is from a somewhat tongue-in-cheek review of a television documentary about au pairs. Analyse the language, looking particularly at any references to children's socio-economic status, the 'characteristic' attributes of young children which have been highlighted and the degree to which the piece reflects cultural attitudes towards childhood (or turns them on their head).

> Say what you like about Paul Newman, I regard him as the acceptable face of capitalism. His physiognomy may be prominently displayed on the side of every jar of his high-priced spaghetti sauces, but that's okay by me because he gives 100 per cent of his profits to a children's charity. Lloyd Grossman, who also sticks his face on his pasta sauce bottles, ensures that his profits go to an equally deserving cause (Lloyd's bank), and I'm planning to follow suit by marketing Vic's own brand of olive oil, made from freshly pressed olives. No, on second thoughts, I think I'll market Vic's baby oil instead, made from freshly-pressed babies. Mmmm, great on salads.
>
> I doubt if anyone who watched last night's Cutting Edge would need much persuading to operate the baby crusher. We all know that children are little, noisy, stupid people who don't pay rent but, worse still, here were dozens of precocious and over-indulged American brats, all fed on rocket fuel and all screeching 'mommy' through voice boxes seemingly powered by the windchest of a Harrison & Harrison cathedral organ.
>
> (Victor Lewis-Smith, 'Days of whine, not roses', *Evening Standard*, 4 March 1998)

Note

1   Japanese has a very complex writing system. There are three types of script, which are all used at the same time: *kanji* (Chinese characters for words of Chinese origin), *hiragana* (a rounded script based on syllables) and *katkaana* (a square-shaped script also based on syllables but used for words borrowed from languages other than Chinese).

Suggestions for further reading

Maxim, J. and Bryan, K. (1994) *Language of the Elderly*, London: Whurr. This advanced undergraduate-level book is clearly written and explains the relevant linguistic terminology before applying it to the analysis of elderly people's language. It provides a wealth of information on both the normal ageing process and age-related illnesses and their effects on communication with the elderly. It also discusses wider social issues related to the ageing process, including attitudes to old age and the effects of social isolation on the elderly.

Gleason, J. (ed.) (2000) *The Development of Language* (5th edition), Boston: Allyn & Bacon. This undergraduate textbook provides a series of accessible and well-illustrated articles on all aspects of children's language development. The article 'Language in Social Contexts' is particularly useful for pursuing some of the issues raised in this chapter.

Coupland, N. and Nussbaum, J. (eds) (1993) *Discourse and Lifespan Identity*, London: Sage. This advanced undergraduate book contains a series of very interesting articles on the relationship between language, self-identity and social interaction throughout the lifespan. The discussions are supported by a wide range of data from speakers of all ages.

Schieffelin, B. and Ochs, E. (eds) (1987) *Language Socialization across Cultures*, Cambridge: Cambridge University Press, A collection of classic articles on the role of language in socialising children into a variety of cultures around the world.

Chapter 8

Language and class

Jason Jones

8.1 Introduction

A given language is never used in exactly the same way by every one of its speakers, as we have already explored in Chapters 5, 6 and 7. Speakers vary considerably in their use of language, and this variation can be caused by a number of things. One of these things is class, and this chapter explores the connection between a person's social class and the **linguistic variety** that they use: in other words, the way in which their social background affects the way they speak.

The chapter begins by considering **accent** and **dialect** and the relationship between regional and social variation and social position. We then highlight some of the issues involved in defining social class, before considering some of the methods that have been used by sociolinguists to determine the social class of different groups of people in their studies of **linguistic variation**. The chapter concludes by discussing the findings of these studies and what they suggest about the influences of social class on linguistic behaviour.

8.2 Linguistic variation and social class

8.2.1 Accent and dialect: regional and social variation

All speakers have both an accent and a dialect. The term 'accent' refers to pronunciation. To speak with a regional accent, for instance, is to pronounce your words in a manner associated with a certain geographical area. For example, in the south-east of England the vowel sound in the word *bath* would usually be pronounced 'ahh' like the 'a' in *car*, but in most parts of the north of England it would sound like the 'a' in *cat*. In many of the southern states of America, *bath* would be pronounced with a vowel sound that is more like the second syllable of player (i.e. 'bay-uth').

'Dialect', on the other hand, refers to grammar and vocabulary (or lexis). For example, according to which region of Britain or the United States you come from, you might use a sentence such as *I didn't do nothing* as opposed to *I didn't do anything*, or *I might could do it* instead of *I might be able to do it*. These are grammatical variations. In terms of vocabulary, speakers in certain regions of Britain might use the word *bairn* as opposed to *child*, while American speakers of English are likely to use *diaper* where a British speaker would use *nappy*. (For more examples of dialect differences see Trudgill 1990.)

In spoken language, a dialect is often associated with a particular accent, so a speaker who uses a regional dialect will also be more than likely to have the corresponding regional accent. This does not always work the other way around though. While it is rare for someone who uses regional grammar and vocabulary to do so without a regional accent, it is very common for a speaker to have a regional accent but use grammar and lexis that are not associated with a particular geographical area, as not all dialects and accents are regional. Both Britain and the United States have standard varieties of English and these varieties are also dialects, albeit prestigious ones. As prestigious dialects they are social rather than regional; that is they are preferred by particular (usually higher) social groups, and in particular (usually more formal) social situations. Standard English is often equated with 'correct English' and in Britain is also known by terms which reflect its status, such as 'Queen's English' or '**BBC** English'. (See Chapter 10 for a discussion of standard English.) Although there is a standard dialect, there is not a standard pronunciation of English in the UK. There are, however prestige norms, the most prestigious accent being known as **RP (Received Pronunciation)** which, like standard English, has a social rather than regional distribution. Probably the most widely recognised prestige form of pronunciation in Britain is that associated with formal broad-casting, such as the BBC national news. In the United States it is speakers from the midwest who provide a widely recognised norm.

However, in practice, it is not possible to separate regional and social linguistic varieties so clearly: regional dialects are usually social dialects too. Speakers of the variety of a given geographical area tend also to be associated with a certain position on the social scale. In the example above, we would probably assume that the speaker who uses the form *I didn't do nothing* is not a member of the higher social classes, because this is a grammatical form which is considered to be non-standard. In the absence of any other evidence, most people tend to evaluate a speaker's social position on the basis of their accent and dialect. So, in Britain, a speaker with the accent associated with Merseyside or the West Midlands might be judged as being working-class, while those with accents linked with the 'Home Counties' or Edinburgh might be placed at a higher position on the social scale. Although such language attitudes (see also Chapter 11) are based to some extent on social stereotypes, there is often an element of truth in stereotypes! Two people may come from the same geographical area or region, but how they talk will also depend on their social position. For example, although she comes from London, Queen Elizabeth does not speak in the same way as a London cab driver.

Because we associate features of speech with particular social groups, we also expect members of these groups to behave in linguistically appropriate ways. Consider this extract from a reader's letter to *The Sunday Telegraph* (21 December 1997):

> Many teachers have not known how to speak properly for years and I'm sure this partly explains the lack of esteem in which they are now held. I recently heard a bank manager telling someone that they should 'fink' seriously about something or other – this would have been unheard of some years ago. On television the other day there was a vicar[1] holding forth in a raging Cockney accent – for God's sake!

'Fink' is an example of a form of pronunciation typical of London and the south-east of England (though also spreading to other urban centres). The 'th' in words such as *three, think, Kath* or *Arthur* is pronounced as 'f', giving *free, fink, Kaff, Arfer*. It is a highly stigmatised form of pronunciation in the UK. 'Cockney' is the name given to the accent and dialect of the East End area of London, which also has, among other things, the *fink* pronunciation and which is also highly stigmatised. People who are classed as 'professionals', such as teachers, bank managers and vicars, are usually considered to occupy comparatively high positions on the social scale and are not expected to use such stigmatised forms. The extract above demonstrates how it is assumed that such people will (or should) automatically speak the **prestige variety**, the variety which society associates with education and high social standing. In Britain, this means speaking standard English with an RP accent, whatever region or area you might come from.

Television soap operas and situation comedies, which tend to deal largely in social stereotypes like those we are discussing, show how widely held these assumptions about accent and dialect can be. For example, in 2001 the popular British soap opera *EastEnders*, which is set in a predominantly working-class suburb of London, introduced two new characters: a medical doctor and his brother, a former small-time criminal. In spite of supposedly having been brought up by the same parents in the same home in the same part of Britain, the two characters had surprisingly different accents and dialects. Dr Anthony Truman, a stereotypical 'pillar of the community', spoke standard English with a near-RP accent, while his brother Paul, a somewhat less savoury character, spoke with the much less prestigious Cockney accent and dialect that is associated with the area in which the soap is set.

The social stigma attributed to a regional accent is also illustrated in an article which appeared in the *Washington Post* (16 December 1997) on speakers with a New York accent, labelled 'Noo Yawkese'. The report explains that such speakers have an extra 'uncharted and rather unappetizing vowel' in words like *bad* (pronounced '*bayuhd*'), which, it is claimed, is: 'to the ears of a great many Americans, part and parcel of a regional accent that sounds like hell. Outsiders associate the New York accent with someone who is fast-talking, sleazy, hucksterish and low-brow'. According to a speech pathologist interviewed for the article, 'Noo Yawkese has a whole quality of sound that is abrasive to the ears', and the accent is described by a Bronx-born aspiring actress as being 'quite limiting', having 'soured countless auditions' she has attended.

Of course, there is nothing inherent in any given variety that makes it 'bad' or 'good'; it is very often the case that the stereotypical view of a geographical area and the people within it causes the associated linguistic variety to be seen in the same light. Urban areas and accents are often stigmatised and this is why people might feel that there is something wrong with a vicar or a doctor (both positively viewed occupations) speaking with a Cockney (a negatively viewed) accent, or why all speakers with a New York accent tend to be viewed in negative terms. (See Chapter 11 for a discussion of attitudes to language use.)

8.2.2 Accent and dialect: a clue to social information

The expectation that we can gain social information from accent and dialect is widespread. You only have to look at some of the canonical literature to see how the social position of a given character is often indicated by the type of accent or dialect they use. Shakespeare, for example, is well known for his use of language as a means of signifying a character's position in society. In the famous graveyard scene from *Hamlet*, Shakespeare makes some clear linguistic distinctions between the lowly gravediggers (here called 'clowns') and Prince Hamlet:

1	CLOWN:	Is she to be buried in Christian burial, that wilfully seeks her own salvation?
2	CLOWN:	I tell thee, she is: and therefore make her grave straight: the crowner hath sat on her, and finds it Christian burial.
1	CLOWN:	How can that be, unless she drowned herself in her own defence?
2	CLOWN:	Why, 'tis found so.
1	CLOWN:	It must be se offendendo; it cannot be else. For here lies the point: if I drown myself wittingly, it argues an act, and an act hath three branches: it is to act, to do, and to perform: argal, she drowned herself wittingly.

(Act 5 Scene 1 lines 1–13)

These gravediggers, members of the lower social classes, speak in prose (that is, ordinary speech), rather than in the verse which is spoken by the characters of higher social standing throughout the play. Compare their speech patterns with those of Hamlet in the example below, an extract from his most famous soliloquy earlier in the play:

> To be, or not to be, that is the question:–
> Whether 'tis nobler in the mind, to suffer
> The slings and arrows of outrageous fortune;
> Or to take arms against a sea of troubles,
> And by opposing end them? – To die, – to sleep,
> No more: – and, by a sleep, to say we end
> The heart-ache, and the thousand natural shocks
> That flesh is heir to, – 'tis a consummation
> Devoutly to be wish'd . . .

Hamlet's speech is much more poetic than that of the gravediggers. Such poetic language was seen to be more formal than ordinary prose, therefore suggesting a character's educated background and socially superior position. In addition to this, by using distinctive spellings for certain words, Shakespeare also suggests that the gravediggers pronounce these words with regional accents. The first gravedigger uses the word *argal*, which is a written approximation of the Latin word *ergo* (meaning 'therefore') pronounced with an accent associated with the south-west of Britain (in Bristol, for example, speakers are traditionally known for adding an 'l' sound to certain words that end in vowels, although research suggests that this feature is dying out now). *Coroner* is also written *crowner*, which again approximates a south-western pronunciation of the word. Finally, the second gravedigger uses the second person singular pronoun form *thee*, which was a more informal version of *you* at the time. Shakespeare's characters tend to use *you* mainly in formal contexts.

Shakespeare is not the only famous writer to have used language to indicate social class. For example, one of the central themes of many of Charles Dickens's novels is that of society and the social class divisions that separate the rich from the poor. Many of Dickens's characters are portrayed as archetypal members of either the rich and privileged classes or the poor, working classes. Their membership of one or other of these groups is usually reflected in the way they speak.

The literary use of linguistic variation to highlight social class divisions is made explicit in D. H. Lawrence's novel *Lady Chatterley's Lover* (1928). Here, the working-class background of the gamekeeper Mellors is mirrored by his broad East Midlands[2] speech, while Lady Chatterley's use of a standard linguistic variety indicates her elevated social position. This is implicit in the speech of each of these characters throughout the novel, but in the following extract Lawrence draws greater attention to the social distance between the two lovers by emphasising the specific differences between their respective uses of language:

> 'Tha mun come one naight ter th' cottage, afore tha goos; sholl ter?' he asked, lifting his eyebrows as he looked at her, his hands dangling between his knees.
> 'Sholl ter?' she echoed, teasing.
> He smiled.
> 'Ay, sholl ter?' he repeated.
> 'Ay!' she said, imitating the dialect sound.
> 'Yi!' he said.
> 'Yi!' she repeated.
> 'An' slaip wi' me,' he said. 'It needs that. When sholt come?'
> 'When sholl I?' she said.
> 'Nay,' he said, 'tha canna do't. When sholt come then?'
> He laughed. Her attempts at the dialect were so ludicrous, somehow.
> ''Coom then, tha mun goo!' he said.
> 'Mun I?' she said.
> 'Maun Ah!' he corrected.
> 'Why should I say maun when you say mun?' she protested. 'You're not playing fair'.
>
> (Lawrence 1961: 184–5)

In this extract, Lawrence's characters are explicitly aware of the social distance between them, and also of the fact that their different ways of speaking reflect this distance.

The reason that these characterisations are used to communicate information about social position and class division is that we, the readers, are expected to share a common attitude towards linguistic varieties, a popular perception of which varieties are 'high' and which are 'low'. Lawrence is distinguishing between **unmarked** and **marked** varieties (varieties which are considered to be the norm and those which are seen as deviating from that norm), and he shows this in the spelling system he adopts.

Lady Chatterley's speech (except when she is imitating Mellors) is represented with standard **orthography** (spelling conventions), while Mellors's speech is consistently written in spelling which attempts to approximate his accent: *slaip* for *sleep*, *coom* for *come*, *goo* for *go* and so on. It is Mellors's accent that is marked here; Lawrence writes Mellors's *shall* as *sholl* to reflect that character's pronunciation, and yet Lady Chatterley's *should* is not an exact phonetic representation of the way she speaks. Check your pronunciation of this word. Lady Chatterley is likely to have pronounced should as *shud*, not pronouncing the 'o' or the 'l'. Lawrence sees no need to attempt to approximate his spelling to Lady Chatterley's prestige variety, even though standard orthography does not, in reality, represent such pronunciation. So, in deciding not to follow standard spelling conventions in representing Mellors's way of speaking, Lawrence is marking Mellors's accent as being different from the norm. In so doing, Lawrence is drawing attention to Mellors's social position, and is exploiting the relationship between linguistic variety and social class. We can see this technique being used much more recently in J. K. Rowling's *Harry Potter and the Philosopher's Stone* where the language used by Rubeus Hagrid, essentially a working-class character who is a bit 'rough around the edges', is represented through unconventional spelling. On the other hand, Vernon Dursely, a company director who lives in middle-class suburbia, speaks in a very formal manner.

ACTIVITY 8.1

Find two examples of an author using unconventional spelling and/or non-standard language as a means of indicating the social class of her or his characters. You might like to compare an earlier and a more modern work of literature. Is it always the characters from the lower social classes whose speech is marked in this way?

8.3 Does social class really affect language?

We have seen that we have expectations that people in certain social positions will speak in certain ways, but is it the case that social class affects language in reality, not just in our expectations or in literature? In other words, is it really true that the higher a person is on the social scale, the more their speech will reflect prestige norms?

Well, it seems that the answer to this is 'yes'. Those of you who live in Britain may have observed that people who belong to the highest social classes tend not to have a particularly 'broad' regional accent and dialect, or, at least, they don't have a variety that can be easily identified as belonging to a particular region. Standard linguistic forms are used throughout Britain, with little variation. As we move further down the social scale, we find greater regional variation. This situation is illustrated by the two 'cone' diagrams below. Figure 8.1 represents social and regional variation in dialects (grammar and lexis only), while Figure 8.2 represents social and regional variation in accents (pronunciation). Both diagrams emphasise the point that it is impossible to separate regional and social variation: they are two sides of the same coin.

In Figure 8.1, the most prestigious variety is standard English, and in Figure 8.2 Received Pronunciation has the most prestige. Figure 8.1 shows that speakers at the top of the social scale (i.e. at the top of the 'cone') speak standard English with very little regional variation; any variation that is apparent will usually occur between two (or more) equally standard forms. For example, *he's a man who likes his beer* or *he's a man that likes his beer* are both acceptable forms in standard English, and it is quite likely that it will be speakers' regional backgrounds that dictate which form they use. But the further down the social scale we go, the greater the regional variation, so that we encounter additional forms such as *he's a man at likes his beer, he's a man as likes his beer, he's a man what likes his beer, he's a man he likes his beer* and *he's a man likes his beer* (after Trudgill 1983a: 29–30). Each of these is a non-standard form and each belongs to a different regional variety. The same pattern of variation can be seen in lexical items. *WC, lavatory* and *toilet* are all acceptable in standard English, and all refer to the same thing. But *bog, lav, privy, dunny* and *john* are all non-standard words for the same

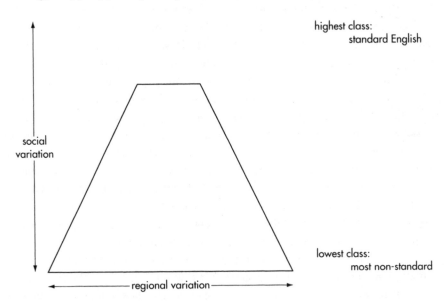

highest class:
standard English

social
variation

lowest class:
most non-standard

regional variation

Figure 8.1 Social and regional variation in dialects
Source: Trudgill (1983a: 29–30)

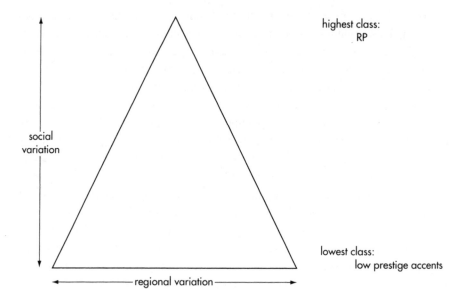

highest class:
RP

social
variation

lowest class:
low prestige accents

regional variation

Figure 8.2 Social and regional variation in accents
Source: Trudgill (1983a: 29–30)

object, and are not only features of lower social varieties but can also be categorised in terms of regional usage.

Figure 8.2 represents variation in pronunciation. The main difference between the two diagrams is that there is no regional variation in the accent used by the speakers of the highest social class. This is why we see a point at the top of the 'cone', rather than a plateau. This means that speakers at the top of the social scale tend to pronounce their words with the same accent (i.e. RP) regardless of their regional background. But, as with dialect varia-tion, the further we move down the social class scale, the greater spread of regional pronunciation we find. You might want to think about the kind of hierarchical language conventionally used to describe class – *upper, lower, top of the scale,* etc – and the degree to which it serves to perpetuate notions of superiority and inferiority, of some people being better or of greater value or worth than others. Since these qualities are not in themselves inherent in the kinds of differences which these classifications are used to describe, do they therefore serve to reinforce stratification and social control?

It is important to point out that these diagrams are representative of the situation in Britain only: in other countries where English is spoken, it is more likely that people who belong to the higher social classes will speak with at least a regional accent. It is also important to bear in mind that, even with reference to Britain, these two diagrams are generalised representations of regional and social variation, and that different combinations of social class and linguistic variety are possible. For example, it is entirely possible for a person from any other position on the social scale to speak standard English or use RP and they may well do so on appropriate occasions (see also Chapters 10 and 11). It is also possible to speak standard English without having an RP accent. Nevertheless, these two diagrams give a useful illustration of the way the relationship between prestige, social class and linguistic variety works in Britain.

It is also important to note that these observations of the relationship between social class and linguistic variation are based on 'consensus' views of social class: that is, that members of a society as a whole agree on norms of behaviour and (usually) aspire to prestige norms. However, there are other explanations for linguistic variation, such as the influence of social networks, which can often encourage situations where the maintenance of stigmatised forms is viewed as a positive marker of group membership and non-acceptance of the norms of more prestigious social groups (see also Chapters 6, 9 and 10). In other words, speakers who belong to a close-knit social network – that is, a group of individuals in which all or most of the members know each other well and interact in a number of social contexts – might aspire (consciously or otherwise) towards stigmatised linguistic features as a way of 'fitting in' with the group. This has been observed in adolescent speakers, for whom language is one among many tools for constructing identity, often in opposition to social norms (see Cheshire 1982 and Eckert 1988). Milroy (1987) also observed the influence of close-knit social networks on the linguistic behaviour of adult speakers in three areas of Belfast, Northern Ireland. She noted that the extent to which speakers in these working-class communities maintained the stigmatised pronunciation features of their regional linguistics variety correlated closely with the strength of the networks to which these speakers belonged. Milroy found that the stronger the bond was between the members of social networks, the more likely those speakers were to use vernacular forms. This led Milroy to conclude that social networks act as 'norm-enforcement mechanisms', and included among these norms is linguistic behaviour.

However, the use of covert prestige forms is not restricted to speakers who belong to less prestigious social groups. In 1984 David Rosewarne, a British sociolinguist, identified the increasing geographical dominance of a variety of English which he dubbed 'Estuary English'. This linguistic variety is a mixture of non-regional and south-eastern English pronunciation, vocabulary and grammar, which many linguists believe to have originated around the banks of the River Thames and its estuary (hence the name). Features of Estuary English include the glottalisation (replacing 't' with a **glottal stop,** as in *butter* pronounced as 'buh-uh'), pronunciation of 'th' as 'f' or 'v' as in *mouth* pronounced as 'mouf' and *mother* pronounced as 'muvver', the use of multiple negation, as in *I ain't never done nothing*, and the use of the non-standard *them books* instead of *those books*. Rosewarne and other linguists have observed the gradual spreading of Estuary English across many parts of Britain, reflecting the ever-increasing influence, both linguistic and cultural, of London on the rest of the country. The geographical spreading of Estuary English is an example of a phenomenon known as **dialect levelling**. This is a process whereby differences between regional varieties are reduced, features which make varieties distinctive disappear and new features appear and are adopted by speakers over a wide geographical area.

The extent of the influence of Estuary English can be seen in the British media, where many radio and television programmes which would, until relatively recently, have employed only speakers with RP accents, now boast presenters whose accents share many of the features of Estuary English. Even Tony Blair, the British Prime Minister since 1997, has been heard to use **glottal stops** and 'dropped *gs*', although not without criticism from some quarters! This clearly suggests that Estuary English is not a class-based variety, which, as Rosewarne points out, is one of the main reasons why people adopt it so readily. It 'obscures sociolinguistic origins'.

8.4 The problem of defining social class

Up to now we have used the term 'social class' as if we all have a common idea of what it actually is. But trying to define precisely what social class is, and exactly what criteria you would base an assessment of someone's social class on, is actually quite hard. Social class is a difficult concept to pin down.

When we talk about being 'higher' or 'lower' on the social scale, or about 'higher' and 'lower' social classes, we are making the assumption that society can be stratified according to class. Stratification means dividing something into hierarchical layers so that one layer is above or higher up than another one. People on each layer have similarities with each other and are considered equals, but they are different from, and not equal to, the people on the other layers. In the case of social class, we commonly talk of 'upper', 'middle' and 'lower' or 'working' class stratification. But the question of defining what it is that differentiates members of one social class from those of another still remains. As Wolfram and Schilling-Estes (1998: 152) put it:

> We would hardly mistake a chief executive officer of a major corporation who resides in a spacious house in a special part of town for an

uneducated, unskilled labourer from the 'wrong side of the tracks'. The reality of social stratification seems obvious, but identifying the unique set of traits that correlate with social status differences in a reliable way is not always that simple.

Before we look at other people's definitions of social class, check your own intuitions by making a list of the major factors which you feel combine to determine a person's social class, indicating their order of importance. How many factors did you come up with? Compare your list with a friend's. Did you differ in terms of which factors you felt were the most important? Did one of you come up with anything that the other one didn't?

It's quite likely that your lists have much in common: you might have mentioned things such as parentage, education, occupation and economic means. But you might also find that there are differences in both the content of your lists and the order of importance you gave them.

Surveys can emphasise or focus on specific social factors as well. For example, a survey conducted in 1997 in London, England (*THES*, 18 April 1997), revealed that people living in certain areas of London have a statistically much greater chance of entering higher education[3] at the age of eighteen than people living in certain other areas of London. It is generally agreed that participation in higher education in Britain is still very much class-based, with greater numbers of students from middle-class backgrounds than from working-class backgrounds. This being the case, in suggesting that there is a direct link between the area you come from (defined by postal (zip) code) and your chances of going to college or university, this report assumes that a person's social class can be predicted, and partially defined, by the area they live in. Further links have been drawn between social class and the availability of higher education in the wake of the British government's announcement in January 2003 that, in future, students will have to pay up to £3000 per year in extra university fees. Many people have commented that this new policy will serve only to increase the imbalance between middle- and working-class students in higher education. Clearly, people with this opinion are equating social class with money. But does this connection always hold?

ACTIVITY 8.3

Rank the following occupations in order of social class, from highest to lowest. Do this once for each of the following criteria:

1   Income
2   Education or training
3   Responsibility

Used car salesperson	Bank manager
Bank teller	Nurse
Unemployed graduate	Student in higher education
Judge	Police officer
Doctor	Nurse
Office cleaner	Teacher
Factory worker	Plumber
Sixteen-year-old job seeker	Solicitor/lawyer on permanent maternity leave

Was the order in which you placed the occupations any different each time? The main problem with equating social class with money in this way is that it is not only (or always) the middle classes that have money. If we define social class on the basis of something other than money (for example, education or training), then it is entirely possible that an individual who is middle-class (for example, a nurse) might not earn more than an average amount of money.

A report published in 1997 proposed a new classification scheme for social class divisions in Britain. Like traditional classification schemes, this new scheme defined social class solely on occupation. Unlike previous schemes, it also officially recognised the existence of an 'underclass': the permanently unemployed. The new class divisions proposed were:

Class 1   Professionals and senior managers: doctors, lawyers, teachers, fund managers, executive directors, professors, editors, managers (with more than twenty-five staff under them), top civil servants.

Class 2   Associate professionals and junior managers: nurses, social workers, estate agents, lab technicians, supervisors, managers with fewer than twenty-five staff under them, journalists, entertainers, actors.

Class 3   Intermediate occupations: sales managers, secretaries, nursery nurses, computer operators, stage hands.

Take a risk today – tell someone you love them. Or run with scissors.

LANGUAGE AND CLASS

Class 4   Self-employed non-professionals: driving instructors, builders.
Class 5   Other supervisors, craft jobs: charge hands,[4] plumbers, telephone fitters.
Class 6   Routine jobs: truck drivers, assembly line workers.
Class 7   Elementary jobs: labourers, waiters, cleaners.
Class 8   Unemployed.

(David Walker, *The Independent*, 15 December 1997)

One of the things you might have noticed about the groups of jobs in each of these eight categories is that the further down the scale you go, the less well paid the jobs seem to be. So, on first sight, what this classification seems to say is that the more money a person earns, the higher up the social scale they are. But some of the jobs included in the lower divisions can actually provide a fairly high income. A plumber, defined solely by her or his occupation, would fall into one of the lower social classes, but plumbers can have a comparatively high income. Equally, some of the occupations listed in some of the higher class divisions, such as teaching or social work, are not always the most well paid. So, if we take economic means as the main factor in defining social class, a conflict of factors emerges. This report acknowledges this conflict and bases its evaluation of social class on the level of responsibility a particular job entails, on whether people 'give orders or take them', rather than the income attached to it. A model based on occupation can also be applied to social class in the United States.

Class 1   Major professionals: executives of large concerns
Class 2   Lesser professionals: executives of medium-sized concerns
Class 3   Semi-professionals: administrators of small businesses
Class 4   Technicians: owners of very small businesses
Class 5   Skilled workers
Class 6   Semi-skilled workers
Class 7   Unskilled workers

(Wolfram and Schilling-Estes 1998: 152)

Again, people are ranked according to the job they do and there are similarities between the levels proposed here and those proposed for occupations in Britain.

Although there are difficulties in relying on any one feature in isolation to determine social class, you will probably have realised that those we have considered are not unconnected. For instance, housing (or the area in which you live) relates to income, as does occupation. Occupation also relates to education, which is another factor often considered in defining social class.

And all these factors relate in different ways to gender and ethnicity. So, researchers who are interested in language and social class tend to use defined formulas for quantifying social class based on the analysis of a combination of characteristics and factors.

> Ultimately, social class distinctions seem to be based upon status and power, where, roughly speaking, status refers to the amount of respect and deference accorded to a person and power refers to the social and material resources a person can command, as well as the ability to make decisions and influence events.
>
> (Wolfram and Schilling-Estes 1998: 152)

In the next section you will see how sociolinguists interested in explaining the connection between social class and linguistic variation have approached the task of determining the social class of their informants.

8.5 Research into the relationship between language and social class

Different sociolinguistic studies have used combinations of factors in calculating social class. For instance, Labov's (1966) major study of linguistic variation in New York City calculated social class according to the criteria of education, occupation and income, resulting in categories of lower class, working class, lower middle class and upper middle class. Shuy *et al.*'s (1968) study in Detroit used education, occupation and residence to distinguish upper and lower middle class, and upper and lower working class. In Britain, Trudgill (1974) used income, education, housing, locality and father's occupation to classify his informants. In the following sections we will look in more detail at Trudgill's study and at Labov's 'department store' study in New York City. It is important to note, though, that these now 'classic' studies of linguistic variation are based on the 'consensus' views of social class that we discussed at the end of section 8.3. We will also look at a more recent study carried out by Williams and Kerswill (1999), who focused on the language of working- and middle-class adolescents in the British towns of Hull, Reading and Milton Keynes.

8.5.1 William Labov: the social stratification of 'r' in New York City department stores

In 1962, the American sociolinguist William Labov conducted a survey of the relationship between social class and linguistic variation in New York City

(Labov 1966; 1972b). He wanted to find out whether the presence or absence of a pronounced 'r' in words such as *mother*, *bird* and *sugar* was determined by a speaker's social class. In New York City (NYC), the prestige variety has pronounced 'r' (known as **post-vocalic** 'r'), and lack of this feature is stigmatised. Note that the NYC situation is the reverse of that in Britain, where the prestige variety is 'r'-less (that is, *mother* is pronounced 'muthuh' and so on) and only a small number of non-prestige varieties have postvocalic 'r'.

Labov believed that the higher the social class of the speaker, the more instances of post-vocalic 'r' he would record from them. In order to test this hypothesis, he carried out a study of speakers in three NYC department stores. These three stores were carefully chosen so as to present an accurate cross-section of society. Labov assumed that, by selecting stores from 'the top, middle and bottom of the price and fashion scale' (Labov 1972b: 45), he could expect firstly that the customers would be socially stratified, and secondly that the sales people in each of the department stores would reflect this in their speech styles. He supported this second assumption by citing C. Wright Mills, who 'points out that salesgirls [*sic*][5] in large department stores tend to borrow prestige from their customers, or at least make an effort in that direction'. So they would 'borrow' the prestige speech style; postvocalic 'r'.

The three stores chosen by Labov were Saks Fifth Avenue (highest social ranking), Macy's (middle social ranking) and S. Klein (lowest social ranking). Labov's main criteria for judging the social status of these three stores were the kinds of products they sold, the price of their products and, very importantly, the newspapers in which they advertised:

> Perhaps no other element of class behaviour is so sharply differentiated in New York City as that of the newspaper which people read; many surveys have shown that the *Daily News* is the paper read first and foremost by working class people, while the *New York Times* draws its readership from the middle class.
>
> (Labov 1972b: 47)

In terms of prices, Saks' were the highest, followed by those in Macy's, and then by S. Klein's. As far as advertising was concerned, Labov found that Saks only ever advertised in the *New York Times* (a 'quality' newspaper); Macy's advertised mainly in the *Daily News* (a 'popular' newspaper) but sometimes in the *New York Times*; and S. Klein advertised almost exclusively in the *Daily News*.

The location of the department store was also an important factor on which the evaluation of social position was based. So, although one of Labov's indicators was economic wealth, he also used a combination of other factors as a means of determining social class.

Labov's method of observation was to approach sales assistants in each store and ask the location of a particular department, to which he already knew the answer would be 'fourth floor' (in which, as the spelling indicates, there are two places where it is possible to pronounce post-vocalic 'r'). Labov also believed that speakers tend to shift towards the prestige variety when paying more attention to their speech, and in order to test this, he pretended that he had not heard the informant's response the first time, and asked them to repeat it. In this way, Labov hoped to elicit a more 'careful' style of speech, in addition to the 'casual' style of the first response. Figure 8.3 shows a simplified version of the results of the investigation.

Figure 8.3 shows the pronunciation of post-vocalic 'r' as a percentage of the number of times it could have been pronounced. The horizontal axis shows the two occasions on which 'fourth floor' was produced. Speakers from Klein's pronounced the 'r' infrequently, with a very small increase on each occasion they had the opportunity to pronounce the 'r'. Speakers from Saks and Macy's pronounced the 'r' in a similar pattern of frequency to each other although informants in Sak's pronounced the 'r' more often. Speakers in all three stores showed a tendency to increase their pronunciation of 'r' when they repeated 'fourth floor': that is, when, according to Labov, they were being more 'careful' with their speech. It is clear that, according to Labov's results, the presence or absence of post-vocalic 'r' was indeed related to social class, such that the pronunciation of 'r' in words like *mother* and *bird* was more common for speakers wishing to project a higher social position. Interestingly, when Joy Fowler replicated Labov's study in 1986,[6] she found almost exactly

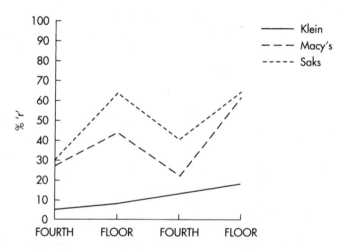

Figure 8.3 Simplified version of Labov's results
Source: Labov (1972b: 52)

the same pattern of social stratification. Thus, we can say that the presence of postvocalic 'r' in the accents of NYC speakers is socially stratified.

8.5.2 Peter Trudgill: the social differentiation of English in Norwich

Another famous large-scale sociolinguistic investigation was conducted by the British sociolinguist Peter Trudgill in Norwich, England, in the late 1960s and early 1970s (Trudgill 1974). Trudgill's primary interest was to find out whether social factors played a part in the way the people of Norwich spoke, his basic assumption being that the higher a person's social class, the closer to the prestige variety their speech would be. To test this hypothesis, Trudgill took a sample of sixty speakers randomly selected from the electoral register, in equal numbers from four separate areas of Norwich. These areas were carefully chosen to reflect a wide variety of housing and an accurate cross-section of the population. Trudgill used a detailed method of calculating each individual's social class, which he called the Social Index Scale. This was a six-point scale, according to which each individual informant was given a score ranging from 0 to 5 for each of the following: occupation (type of employment); income; education; housing; locality; and father's occupation. On the basis of the total scores he categorised social class as follows:

19 and over	middle middle class	(MMC)
15–18	lower middle class	(LMC)
11–14	upper working class	(UWC)
7–10	middle working class	(MWC)
3–6	lower working class	(LWC)

None of Trudgill's informants was classified as anything higher than middle middle class; this is simply because it was unusual to find anyone of a higher social class living in the areas of Norwich in which Trudgill was working. There is, of course, no reason why a score on the Social Index Scale could not be assigned to such groups of people if they were present in an investigator's sample area.

Creating situations of varying formality, Trudgill then elicited linguistic data from each of the informants. The procedure consisted of eliciting four 'styles' of speech: 'word list style' (WLS), the most formal style, in which the informant read words from a list in front of them; 'reading passage style' (RPS), slightly less formal than WLS, requiring the informant to read a passage of prose containing a number of the words included in the word list; 'formal style' (FS), less formal again, which comprised the main part of the interview; 'casual style' (CS), the least formal style, for which informants were asked to recount a funny story. Trudgill's four styles assumed a 'scale of formality', working on the assumption that the more formal the style was, the more attention the speaker would pay to their speech. As in Labov's study, the resultant 'careful' speech would be closer to the prestige variety.

One of the linguistic features Trudgill was interested in was the way in which speakers pronounced '-ing' at the end of words such as *running*, *singing* and *raining*. He believed that the higher the social class of the speaker, the more likely they were to say, for example, *running* rather than *runnin'*, while the further down the social scale the informant was, the greater the likelihood of them saying *runnin'* rather than *running*.

In Figure 8.4 each social group's score is given for this feature, the number of times they said *-in'* rather than *-ing* as a percentage of the number of times a word with this ending occurred. Thus, a score of 0 indicates exclusive use of *-ing* (as in the prestige variety), while a score of 100 signifies exclusive use of *-in'*. Figure 8.4 shows that, for the pronunciation of *-ing*, the higher the social class of the speakers, the closer their speech is to the prestige variety. The assumption that speech also moves closer to the prestige variety in direct proportion to an increase in formality (and thus attention to speech) is also borne out. In fact, the middle middle class use exclusively *-ing* in the two most formal styles (WLS and RPS), while the lower working

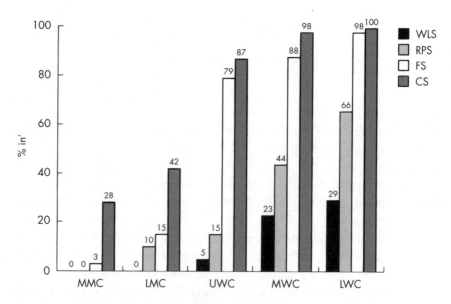

Figure 8.4 Results of Trudgill's sociolinguistic survey, Norwich
Source: Trudgill (1974: 92)

class use only *-in'* in casual style, when they are assumed to be the least 'careful' with their speech. This pattern was also apparent for other linguistic features that Trudgill investigated.

Like Labov's in NYC, Trudgill's research in Norwich illustrates that the higher a person's position on the social scale, the closer their linguistic variety is to prestige norms. Another interesting point suggested by both investigations is that, when they wish to, people can change the way they speak in accordance with the demands of the situation. You can see this if you look at the way in which the speech of Trudgill's informants moved closer to the prestige variety in line with the steady increase in the 'formality' of the situation, as did the speech style of Labov's informants when repeating the words *fourth floor*.

8.5.3 Williams and Kerswill: dialect levelling in three British towns

The central concern of this investigation, the results of which were published in 1999, was to analyse the extent to which the accents of adolescent speakers in three English towns, Reading, Milton Keynes and Hull, are converging – that is, levelling or becoming more alike. The towns were chosen as research sites on the basis of similarity of size but distinct differences in terms of geographical location and social composition.

Williams and Kerswill collected linguistic data from a total of ninety-six speakers aged fourteen or fifteen, interviewing equal numbers of speakers of both sexes and from both the middle and working classes. They collected their data using three elicitation techniques:

- individual interviews with the speakers, including a wordlist reading
- a discussion with pairs of speakers
- a group discussion with four to six speakers in a single-sex group, guided by the fieldworker

In addition, four elderly working-class speakers (two male, two female) were recorded in each town, so that the researchers could chart any changes in pronunciation patterns over time. As a means of corroborating any observations made on this basis, material from the Survey of English Dialects (SED) was also used for comparison of traditional and modern pronunciation patterns.

On the surface, Williams and Kerswill found that the accents of the three towns were, indeed, converging. However, the situation was quite complex, with some marked differences between them, especially when Hull (a seaport in the north of England) was compared with the two southern towns, Reading and Milton Keynes. One of the phonological variables investigated by Williams and Kerswill was the vowel sound in words such as *bite* and *bride*. In Reading, the predominant pronunciation of this vowel among the elderly speakers and the SED informants was as in the RP pronunciation of these words. This remained unchanged among the adolescent speakers. However, this continuity was not present in Milton Keynes, where there had been a great deal of in-migration and the newer inhabitants had little connection with the old people of the area.

In Milton Keynes, the predominant pronunciation of this vowel among the older speakers was as in the RP pronunciation of *boy*, giving 'boit' and 'broid', whereas the adolescent speakers tended to favour the vowel used in Reading. In the traditional dialect of Hull, the vowel is pronounced differently depending on the other sounds in the word. For example in *bite* where it is followed by a voiceless consonant 't' it is pronounced as it is the RP accent. However in words such as *bride* where it is followed by a voiced consonant 'd', it is pronounced like the 'a' in *ah*, giving 'brahd'. Today, this distinction in Hull is class-based. The working-class adolescents there still observe this rule categorically, but the middle-class adolescents use the more southern pronunciation in all contexts.

Further class-based differences were observed in the shift to the conso-nant patterns of Estuary English: the glottalisation of 't' in *butter*, and the replacement of 'th' sounds with 'f' or 'v' (see section 8.3). While in general the adolescents in all three towns were increasingly adopting these features, the trend was much more pronounced in working-class adolescents, including those in Hull, even though they had resisted the shift to the southern model for vowel pronunciation.

8.6 Summary

This chapter has looked at the relationship between regional and social varia-tion and the connection that holds between a linguistic variety and social class. This connection might be perceived (based on prevailing attitudes regarding linguistic norms) or based on a more reliable assessment of a speaker's social class, calculated by a variety of different means. We have looked at the diffi-culties in objectively determining the social class of speakers and at the way in which linguists have approached this problem in their investigations into linguistic variation. The results of such investigations suggest that the higher a person's social class, the closer their linguistic variety is to prestige norms. In addition, speakers change their speech, adopting more or less prestigious styles, in accordance with the perceived demands of a given situation.

Notes

1   In the Church of England (the Anglican Church), the vicar is the priest in charge of a parish. Vicars have a relatively high social status in Britain.

2   The East Midlands is the area in central England around the city of Nottingham.

3   In Britain, 'higher education' refers to college or university level study.

4   A charge hand is a supervisor who ranks slightly lower than a foreman.

5   The use of the Latin term *sic* indicates a correct transcription of the original, even though this may not be a term the present writer would use or condone. In this case, a non-gender-marked term would be preferred, such as 'sales personnel' or 'sales staff'.

6   Fowler's study of the social stratification of 'r' in NYC department stores replicated Labov's survey in every detail but one: she had to substitute May's for Klein's, as Klein's was no longer in business. A detailed summary of Fowler's findings may be found in Labov (1994).

Suggestions for further reading

Coupland, Nikolas and Jaworski, Adam (eds) (1997) *Sociolinguistics: A Reader and Coursebook*, London: Macmillan. In addition to both Labov's article on the social stratification of 'r' in New York and Trudgill's on the social differentiation of English in Norwich, this reader has a wealth of articles that are relevant to many of the chapters in *Language, Society and Power*.

Wardhaugh, Ronald (1997) *Introduction to Sociolinguistics*, Oxford: Blackwell. The chapter on regional and social variation gives good coverage of the sociolinguistic findings in this area.

Williams, A. and Kerswill, P. (1999) 'Dialect levelling: change and continuity in Milton Keynes, Reading and Hull' in P. Foulkes and G. Docherty (eds), *Urban Vocies*, London: Arnold. This article discusses Williams and Kerswill's research in depth and also highlights some of the other social variables, including gender, that are at play in the process of dialect levelling.

Chapter 9

Language and identity

Joanna Thornborrow

9.1 Introduction

One of the most fundamental ways we have of establishing our identity, and of shaping other people's views of who we are, is through our use of language. This chapter continues the theme established in Chapters 5, 6, 7 and 8 about how people use language to construct a social identity (or identities) for themselves, and also about how social groups and communities use language as a means of identifying their members, and of establishing their boundaries.

Because language is so important in the construction of individual and social identities, it can also be a powerful means of exercising social control. Identifying yourself as belonging to a particular group or community often means adopting the linguistic conventions of that group, and this is not just in relation to the words you use, but also in relation to the way that you say them. The way those conventions are defined and maintained is usually controlled by the group rather than the individual. In this chapter we will also look briefly at how language relates to national and political identities.

9.2 What do we mean by linguistic identity?

How you talk, along with other kinds of social codes such as how you dress or how you behave, is an important way of displaying who you are; in other words, of indicating your social identity. This question of identity, who we are, how we perceive ourselves and how others perceive us, is not defined simply by factors such as where we were born and brought up, who our parents are or were, and which socio-economic group we happen to belong to. Identity, whether it is on an individual, social or institutional level, is something which we are constantly building and negotiating all our lives through our interaction with others. Identity is also multifaceted: people switch into different roles at different times in different situations, and each of those contexts may require a shift into different, sometimes conflicting, identities for the people involved. One of the ways in which we accomplish and display this shift is through the language we use.

How can language indicate this kind of information? Various factors come into play here. First of all, on the individual level, where you grew up, where you went to school, how wealthy (or not) your family were, will to some extent be displayed through the **variety** of the language that you speak. Often the most immediately obvious difference in the way that people speak is in their **accent** (the **phonological** level of language), but there are also grammatical **variations** between speakers (see also Chapters 8 and 10) and, in Britain at least, someone's accent and **dialect** always carries a great deal of information about them. They can indicate not only their regional origin but also their social class and, to some extent, the kind of education they had.

It is often the case that children change the way they talk if they move from one region of Britain to another, sometimes even from one school to another. As a personal example, I was born and brought up in Cumbria, in the north-west of England, in a middle-class family. I attended a small private school until the age of eleven, when I went to the local secondary school, and then my accent changed. From fairly mainstream **RP**, I began to sound much more regionally marked as a Cumbrian. When I was fourteen years old, my parents moved to the Midlands, my accent changed again and I began to sound less Cumbrian and more mainstream RP again. After leaving school I went to a northern university, and shifted back into using some of the sounds I had left behind in Cumbria.

The way that I spoke was also commented on by people in the places where I lived. In the Midlands, new friends referred to me as a 'primitive northerner'; when back visiting old friends in the north, they said I talked like a southerner. Later, while at university, I visited my sister in the south of England where her friends commented on how different I sounded from her. In order to fit into a new community, one of the most powerful resources I had at my disposal to show that I was just like the new group of young people I was spending my time with was the way I spoke. Significantly, this was not the same way either my parents or my sister spoke. So within the same family, even within the same generation, there can be a very wide diversity in the way different family members sound.

The importance of accent as a label of identity is evident in so far as this is the aspect of their language that speakers most frequently change, either to disguise their membership of, or distance themselves from, a particular social or regional group, or to move closer to another group they want to belong to. However, linguistic identity is not just a matter of using one dialect or **code** (the term sociolinguists use to refer to language varieties as systems of communication) rather than another, or one accent rather than another. It is also a matter of how we use language with others; in other words, how we communicate and interact with others through talk.

9.3 Language and the construction of personal identities

In this section we look first at how personal identities are socially constructed through the use of names, naming practices and rituals. We also look at systems of address, i.e. the way you refer to someone when you are talking to them directly, and how speakers use language to classify and identify each other through these systems.

9.3.1 Names and naming practices

One of the most obvious linguistic means of establishing people's identity is through the giving and using of names. We are distinguished from other members of a group by our name, which sets us apart as an individual, as different from others, even though we might share other attributes, such as belonging to the same family, or the same school class. In Britain and the United States, Western cultures distinguish between given (first) name and family (last) name, the given name being chosen, the family name being traditionally the father's family name. In some cultures, for example in Russia, people are identified further by names which designate them as 'son of x' or 'daughter of y'. These names are called patronymics. In Icelandic, it is the patronymic name that is used as the family name, so this changes from generation to generation.

Names can sometimes carry important meanings for individual identity, as expressed by Zambian writer Felly Nkweto Simmonds:

> Friends ask me why I don't just drop my non-African names. It would be a good idea, but not a practical one. In reality, my reason has nothing to do with practicality, it has to do with my own identity. For better, for worse, my names locate me in time and space. It gives me a sense of my own history that I not only share specifically with a generation of people in Africa but also with all Africans in the Diaspora.
>
> I belong to a time. The twentieth century. A time of fragmentation, a time of rebirth. I need to understand and know myself from that position. It is the only position I have, wherever I am. In both my private and my public life. I'm also lucky. Naming myself differently to suit the occasion allows me the space to experience all my subjective realities and identities (we all have many) in a way that does not imply fragmentation, but coherence.
>
> (Nkweto Simmonds 1998: 36)

The naming practices and rituals of social groups are often similarly important ceremonies, and vary from culture to culture. The following passage describes the Hindu practice of choosing a child's name:

> Later that same day the priest was called, and he was known to be a good man and a holy one; and one, moreover, who could read the patra, the astrological almanac, and cast a horoscope and tell in a minute the luck of a child; what it should guard against as it grew up and the name it should have in consonance with its horoscope.
>
> (Naipaul 1976: 26)

In the Hindu religion as practised in Trinidad up until about thirty years ago, a child was given two names. One, called the 'rasi' name, was determined by reading the 'patra', which gives the astrological positions of the stars at the time of the birth of the child. The function of this name was to give the child strength, but it was not used to address them, as anyone who knew your 'rasi' name could possess or manipulate you if they wished. A second name was also given to address the child by, also based on the 'patra', and its function was to protect the child and give them as much good fortune as possible according to their predicted horoscope. Both names were conferred at a naming ceremony at the first full moon after birth.

The giving of a name can also be part of the acceptance of an individual into a particular culture or religion, establishing individual identity but also simultaneously a religious identity (for example the bar/bat mitzvah in the Jewish religion, or the giving of a saint's name at confirmation in the Roman Catholic faith).

The attribution of names is only part of the story, however. Once you have your name, how people use it becomes very important. The way names are used in interaction is central to the process of constructing individual identities within a group. In one of his lectures, the American sociologist Harvey Sacks (1995) describes the relevance of how names are used in introduction sequences for establishing not only who people are but what they can call each other. Introductions can be symmetrical, in so far as speakers can choose to introduce people as being of the same type and status, or belonging to the same group, for example by using both first names as in:

Jim, this is Alice

or as **asymmetrical**, i.e. being of a different type, as in:

Jim, this is Dr Jones

This choice of names by the person doing the introducing can have an effect on how the rest of the conversation proceeds, and Sacks suggests that, when you put people 'into a state of talk' by introducing them, you are not just giving them a name to use but 'the choice of a name is already informative to them of more that they can use in conducting their conversation' (1995: Lecture 6).

What you get called is not necessarily a matter of personal choice, though. Names can cause problems, particularly if they don't fit in with the conventions of a community. Children's playground practice of 'calling someone names' is also a powerful resource for a dominant group to enforce their dominance and marginalise others. Nkweto Simmonds again comments that:

> In public, at conferences, for example, I insist that my full name appears on my name tag. In a society that cannot accommodate names that come from 'other' cultures, this can be a frustrating exercise. It is no wonder that many Black children will Anglicise their names to avoid playground taunts . . . and much worse.
>
> (Nkweto Simmonds 1998)

ACTIVITY 9.1

What kind of identity does your name give you? How do you feel if someone uses it wrongly? Think of all the different ways people can name you (e.g. nickname or pet name, title plus full name) and how these construct different identities for you in different contexts.

9.3.2 Systems of address

It is not only the name you have, but the way that people use it in different contexts which helps to establish your identity within that context. The way that other speakers refer to you can depend on the degree of formality, of intimacy and of relative status of all the participants involved in the interaction. Think of the people you know and how you have to address them; for example, by first name (Mary), by title and last name (Ms A, Mr B, Dr C), by some kind of deferential form (sir, ma'am). These systems of address are culturally determined. For example, it is customary in France to address members of the legal profession as *maître*, whereas in Britain there is no equivalent professional label to use when directly addressing a lawyer – but there is if you are addressing a judge: *your honour* or *m'lord* or *m'lady*. To disregard the rules can lead to some form of disapproval or sanction, or, at worst, be interpreted as an insult.

The way that address terms are used can have important implications and effects on the participants in a conversational exchange. In her study of American address terms, Susan Ervin-Tripp describes a famous triple insult based on the choice of address terms by a white American policeman in addressing a black American doctor:

> 'What's your name, boy?'
> 'Dr Poussaint. I'm a physician.'
> 'What's your first name, boy?'
> 'Alvin.'

> (Ervin-Tripp 1980: 22)

She shows how, by using the address term 'boy', the policeman is deliberately insulting the doctor by not acknowledging his age, rank or status. Poussaint responds by giving his title and last name, and in doing so he indicates that he is not complying with the white policeman's use of an address term that places him in a socially inferior position. The policeman's next question shows that he does not consider the response 'Dr Poussaint' from a black adult male as a suitable answer to his question. In asking for his first name and again addressing him inappropriately as 'boy', the policeman is repeating his earlier insult and assigning the doctor to the rank of 'child' or 'inferior'. In his choice of address terms, he is signalling his refusal to recognise the doctor's adult status and professional rank. The effect of this sequence was experienced and recorded by Dr Poussaint as 'profound humiliation' (Ervin-Tripp 1980: 18).

The way that the **second person pronoun** (you) is used in many languages can also be a linguistic indicator of social identity, used to construct social relations of solidarity, intimacy or distance (see Crystal 1987). The so-called T/V distinction (based on the French **pronoun** system where *tu* is the familiar form of address, and *vous* the formal, polite form) in second person pronouns has now been lost in English, where social relations are no longer encoded in the pronoun system. But in many other European languages speakers have a choice between addressing someone with the informal, intimate second person pronoun (*tu/du* in Spanish and German), or the formal, distancing second person pronoun (*Usted/Sie*). Age can also determine the use of these pronouns. For example, in French it is acceptable for a child to address adults using the *tu* form, whereas if one adult addressed another they did not know very well using *tu*, it would be noticeable, and, as with the absence of a particular title, in some cases may be taken as an insult.

In a language with complex **honorific** markers, such as Japanese, a speaker must learn the social hierarchy of respect and condescension, and their place within that hierarchy, in order to produce grammatically correct pronoun forms (Mühlhäusler and Harré 1990). For example, the **first person pronoun** *watashi* ('I') is used by men to mark formal status, but by women to mark neutral status (Crystal 1987). In Russian, the choice of address pronoun is governed by a range of complex individual and social considerations; group membership is indicated by the use of the familiar *ty* form between speakers, for example between people who come from the same village, while individual emotional states of closeness, anger, respect and love can also be signalled by switching to *ty* rather than *vy*, the more formal, distancing form.

So the words you choose to address people by are important ways of showing how you situate yourself in relation to others, of creating social distance or intimacy, of marking deference, condescension or insult through the conventions of the address system of a language.

9.4 Language and the construction of group identities

We next examine how people can construct their social identity by categorising themselves (or being categorised by others) as belonging to a social group through particular types of **representation**. We also look at how speakers' choice of linguistic code, or variety, plays an important role in establishing their group identity. We'll illustrate these ideas with some of the findings of research on the relationship between language and group identity, looking at such aspects as shared **linguistic norms** within a group, the role of **speech communities** (this term refers to social groupings which can range in size from a whole region to a city street, to a teenage gang) and the definition of social categories and group boundaries.

9.4.1 Identity and representation

In places where there is social conflict there will often be linguistic conflict too, about whose words are used, and about which terms are used by which group of people to identify themselves and their opponents. People often have to work to establish their own identity categories, to name their particular social group, and stake their claim in owning their representations of themselves. In a discussion of these kinds of categories, Sacks (1995) analyses the case of teenage groups in the United States during the 1960s who used the term 'hotrodders' to describe themselves, and makes the following observation:

If a kid is driving, he's seen as a teenager driving, and he's seen via the category 'teenager,' compared to the variety of things he could be categorised as. His problem, then, initially, is that he is in fact going to be typed; where for one, the category 'teenager' is a category owned by adults.

(Sacks 1995: Lecture 7)

The point Sacks is making here is that social categories, or labels of identity, are frequently imposed on some groups by others, who may be in a more powerful position than they are, or may be using the label to make some kind of social judgement about them. We do not always control the categories people use to define our identity, or the cultural assumptions that accompany them. In Sacks's example above, the important thing for this group was to be in a position to own their own category, 'hotrodder', rather than have one imposed upon them by another group. Sacks suggests that one of the ways in which kids work towards establishing independence from adults, and also exert some form of control over who gets to be a member of a particular group, is to develop their own set of categories rather than be defined by terms used by others, whose values they do not share.

9.4.2 Ingroups and outgroups

Your social identity is not something you can always determine on your own; it is also bound up with how others perceive you. In fact, it would be difficult to conceive of identity as a purely individual matter. Your perception of yourself as an individual can only be in relation to others, and your status within a social group. This status can be constructed through language use in various ways.

As with other kinds of social codes which people use to display membership of a social group, like dress codes, certain kinds of linguistic behaviour also signal your identity in relation to a group, as well as your position within it. Being able to show that you can use linguistic terms appropriately according to the norms associated with a particular group helps to establish your membership of it, both to other members of the group, the **ingroup**, and those outside it, the **outgroup**. Furthermore, adhering to the linguistic norms of one group may position you very clearly as showing that you do not belong to others.

In his study of the language used by members of street gangs in New York, William Labov (1972c) found that the core members of groups shared the most linguistic similarities. Although all the members of these gangs were perceived as speaking the non-standard 'Black English Vernacular' (BEV), it was those boys who were at the centre of the group, and who were perceived by the other boys as its core members, whose speech showed the strongest and most consistent use of the **vernacular**. Labov also found that the more integrated a boy was into the 'vernacular' culture of the gang, the more his use of language would be consistent with the vernacular, non-standard grammar used by those members at the core of the group. Those on the periphery of the gang culture, referred to by the gang's own category label of 'lames', would show a greater degree of distance from the vernacular. So membership of a group, and the position you hold within that group, either as a core member or as a peripheral member, is accomplished in considerable measure through the language that you use.

Often, language use fits in with other indicators of social identity and group membership, such as style of clothes, type of haircut and taste in music. In a study of high-school students in the Detroit suburbs in the 1980s, Penelope Eckert found that there were two social categories: students who participated in all school activities and who would go on to college were referred to and referred to themselves as 'jocks'; students whose lives were based outside school in the local area and who were destined for the blue-collar work-force were referred to, and referred to themselves, as 'burnouts'. These two categories were the defining identities of all the adolescents, boys and girls, within the school. Other students who did not see themselves as belonging to these two extremes of the school community nevertheless defined themselves in relation to them as 'in betweens' (Eckert 1997: 69). The linguistic patterns also mirrored this categorisation, with the burnout girls having the strongest local urban accent overall, and the jock girls having the strongest suburban accent.

The performance of identity through language can be also asserted in a positive way by minority groups who want to maintain their difference from other social groups. In a study of a group of high-school girls in California, Mary Bucholtz shows how they use language to negotiate gender and construct aspects of their identity as 'nerd girls':

> Nerds, like Jocks and Burnouts, to a great extent consciously choose and display their identities through language and other social practices. And where other scholars tend to equate nerdiness with social death, I propose that nerds in US high schools are not socially isolated misfits, but competent members of a distinctive and oppositionally defined community of practice.
>
> (Bucholtz 1999: 211)

This community is characterised linguistically through the girls' use of super-standard and hyper-correct accents and grammar, the use of formal lexical items, and an orientation to aspects of language form such as punning, parody and word-coinage (Bucholtz, 1999: 212).

Other investigations have also revealed that even slight variation can be significant enough to signal affiliation with one group and, correspondingly, disaffiliation with another. Beth Thomas (1988) found that, in a mining community in south Wales, women who lived on the same street used different sounds from each other according to whether they attended either the Congregational, Methodist or Baptist church locally. The variation was therefore linked to the particular religious community which the women belonged to and identified with. Labov (1972d), in his study of the island community in Martha's Vineyard, Massachusetts, also noted the variation between the speech patterns of those islanders who identified with the traditional fishing community, even among those who had left the island to go to college but had later returned to take up employment there, and the summer community of holidaymakers from the mainland. The sound changes he identified clearly functioned to establish the local inhabitants who identified with the island's traditional fishing industry as different from the visitors and those involved with them.

The process can also work the other way, when speakers adopt the speech patterns of a group they do not belong to, but which, for whatever reason, they see as prestigious, or they aspire to belong to. This can be a short-term strategy, where a speaker temporarily moves towards the speech of a group for a particular communicative effect, or a long-term one, where speakers gradually shift their patterns of speech to match those of the target group. The short-term occasional strategic use of the speech of another group has been termed **crossing** by Ben Rampton (1995) in his study of the use of **creole** in Britain by outgroup speakers (in this case adolescents whose ethnic backgrounds were white Anglo, Bangladeshi, Indian or Pakistani). He found that their perception of creole as tough and cool meant that its use was 'strongly tied to a sense of youth and class identity':

> **Informants** generally credited black adolescents with the leading role in the multiracial vernacular, introducing elements that others subsequently adopted. In this way, for example, 'innit' was analysed as being originally black, and young people most often ascribed Creole roots to new words in the local English vernacular.
>
> (Rampton 1995: 128)

Some varieties of language are more prestigious than others, and what counts as the prestige form can vary according to the context and type of linguistic activity. One example of this was in the early 1960s, when British pop singers often produced sounds (such as the **vowel** sounds in words such as *dance*, *girl*, *life* or *love*) with stereotypical American pronunciation. One explanation that has been suggested for this is that, because of long-standing American domination within the field of popular music, British singers were attempting 'to model their singing style on that of those who do it best and who one admires most' (Trudgill 1983b: 144). As the status of British pop music rose during the 1960s and early 1970s, this feature became less frequent, and, with the advent of punk rock music and 'new wave' bands in the mid-1970s, whose 'primary audience was British urban working-class youth' (Trudgill 1983b: 154), things changed again. The use of American features declined, while non-standard, low-prestige features associated with southern English pronunciation (such as a **glottal stop** in a word such as *better*) and non-standard grammatical forms (such as **multiple negation** in *I can't get no . . .*) became more frequent, as these bands moved towards adopting a British working-class identity. These non-standard, **covert prestige** forms have not replaced the American sounds in British pop music, but rather co-exist with them.

ACTIVITY 9.2

Think of any 'in' words or phrases which are used currently by your own peer group. What kind of words are they? Where do they come from? What happens if someone outside your peer group uses them? Why do you think this is the case?

9.5 Linguistic variation and the construction of identity

In this section we discuss how people can shift between different styles of speaking, varying the features of their accent and dialect which contribute to the construction of a particular social identity at different moments and in different situations.

9.5.1 Stylistic variation and language choice

Defining common systems of representation and adherence to ingroup linguistic norms are not the only means by which people display their affiliation to (or disaffiliation from) a social group. We also position ourselves in relation to others by the way that we talk in different kinds of interaction. People do not always talk in exactly the same way all the time: they don't always pronounce words the same way, and they don't always use the same grammatical forms (for example *you was* rather than *you were*). This kind of variation in speech is usually referred to as **style-shifting** (see also Chapter 8).

One of the theories explaining this variation in style is that speakers take into account whom they are talking to, and alter their speech style accordingly. This concept of **audience design** (Bell 1984) provides a theoretical account of the reasons why speakers change the way they talk depending on the situation and context they are talking in. This account is based on the premise that people are mainly seeking to show solidarity and approval in their dealings with others, and one way that speakers can do this is through linguistic **convergence**, i.e. by changing their patterns of speech to fit more closely with those of the person they happen to be talking to (Giles and Powesland 1975; Giles and Sinclair 1979).

Linguistic convergence can, however, backfire, as it can be perceived by the hearer as patronising, ingratiating or even mocking behaviour. This is particularly the case when standard speakers converge towards non-standard, low-prestige forms. The imitation of another person's speech can be interpreted as linguistic behaviour that is designed to insult, by emphasising the difference between speakers, rather than behaviour that is designed to display solidarity. In a study of young adolescents' use of creole in London, Roger Hewitt found that young black creole speakers were usually quite hostile to their white peers' use of creole, which was perceived not just as parody but as a display of power:

> white Creole use was regarded (a) as derisive parody, and hence as an assertion of white superiority, and (b) as a further white appropriation of one of the sources of power – 'it seems as if they are stealing our language'.
>
> (Hewitt 1986: 162)

There seems, then, to be a relationship between social questions of power and status, and the way in which speakers accommodate to each other in their use of language. Who converges with whom is an important issue in any speech situation where the participants have different social status.

In some situations, speakers may choose not to converge, but instead either to maintain their own variety (linguistic maintenance) or move to a more extreme variety of their dialect (linguistic **divergence**), in order to emphasise the difference between themselves and the person or people they are talking to. An example of this comes from Jenny Cheshire's (1982) study of the use of non-standard English in adolescent peer groups in Reading, England. Cheshire recorded her informants' speech both within the peer group and within the more formal setting of the classroom. In line with common practice, most of her informants produced more standard forms in school, converging with the standard norms of the institutional environment. One of her informants, however, increased his use of non-standard forms, diverging from the expected linguistic variety and thus emphasising his distance from and non-acceptance of the school's norms. Viv Edwards (1997) reports similar linguistic signals given by children who diverge from expected norms by using their variety of Black English in the classroom as an expression not only of solidarity with the black peer group but of distance from and exclusion of the outgroup (teachers and/or white children).

Speakers may wish to be identified with different groups at different times, and their linguistic patterns may produce a shift, whether between different varieties of a language or from one language to another. The question of group affiliation and identity can determine the choices a speaker makes about how to speak and, for bilinguals or multilinguals, which language to use.

When a choice is made between two different languages, the question of identity becomes even more marked, particularly when the choice is bound up with the national and political status of a language. Monica Heller (1982) describes how, in Quebec, speakers have to deal with the issue of which language to use before the business of the talk gets under way. In choosing French rather than English, or vice versa, speakers are always making a statement about how they align themselves in terms of national and political identities. Heller describes an instance of a call to a bilingual hospital where the conversation between the hospital clerk and the patient has been conducted in English, until the clerk reads out the patient's name (Robert Saint Pierre) in French. The caller corrects the clerk angrily, by repeating his name using the English pronunciation, thereby claiming his identity as an English speaker despite the 'Frenchness' of his name (Heller 1982: 118).

9.5.2 Power and linguistic imperialism

A sense of cultural identity is often centred on a particular language, and speakers' perceptions of the connection between the languages they use and that identity is well documented (see for example Gumperz 1982a; Alladina and Edwards 1991; Gal 1998). Language rights and recognition are often important issues in socio-political conflicts all around the world. Maintenance of a minority language within a majority culture (such as Spanish in the United

States, Gujerati in Britain) is often associated with the maintenance of a minority's values and with the continuation of its unique cultural identity (see Chapter 6). In Wales, bilingualism is actively maintained through policies such as teaching in Welsh-medium schools, a Welsh television channel (S4C) and the distribution of all official documents in both English and Welsh. Although not everyone in Wales speaks Welsh, this type of support for the Welsh language contributes to the strong sense of cultural and national identity of Welsh people. For younger people, the phrase 'cool Cymru' has also come to signify this sense of cultural identity through its association with the music of Welsh bands such as Catatonia and the Manic Street Preachers.

Loss of a language can also be associated with a loss of cultural identity. Languages can be lost for a variety of reasons. For example, speakers may choose to shift from one language to another as social conditions change, or one language may be imposed and another suppressed by a dominant power. In the fictional account below of the historical relationship between Denmark and Greenland, the principal character draws on the intricate relationship between language and identity and describes her feeling that in losing her ability to speak her mother tongue, she is also losing her Greenlandic identity:

> When we moved from the village school to Qaanaaq, we had teachers who didn't know one word of Greenlandic, nor did they have any plans to learn it. They told us that, for those who excelled, there would be an admission ticket to Denmark and a degree and a way out of the Arctic misery. This golden ascent would take place in Danish. This was when the foundation was being laid for the politics of the sixties. Which led to Greenland officially becoming 'Denmark's northernmost county', and the Inuit were officially supposed to be called 'Northern Danes' and 'be educated to the same rights as all other Danes', as the prime minister put it. That's how the foundation is laid. Then you arrive in Denmark and six months pass and it feels as if you will never forget your mother tongue. It's the language you think in, they way you remember your past. Then you meet a Greenlander on the street. You exchange a few words. And suddenly you have to search for a completely ordinary word. Another six months pass. A girlfriend takes you along to the Greenlanders' House on Lov Lane. That's where you discover that your own Greenlandic can be picked apart with a fingernail.
>
> (Høeg 1996: 105)

The passage also illustrates the implications that language use has for wider issues of social, ethnic and national identities. The reference here to the passage to Danish education as 'the golden ascent' which 'would take place in Danish' shows how the ability to speak a language can either make possible or restrict access to social and institutional structures, privileging one community of speakers over another.

9.6 Summary

In this chapter we have looked at the construction of personal identities through the use of names and systems of address, and at the construction of group identity through types of representation and adherence to linguistic norms. We have seen how linguistic variation plays a part in the expression of solidarity with, or distance from, group norms, and how language is connected with cultural identity. In this way we have investigated linguistic identity from the point of view of the individual and the group, as well as the institutional and cultural practices of a community of speakers. As always, however useful these categories have been for the purposes of discussion, in practice they overlap and the boundaries between them are probably less clearly defined than is perhaps implied here. The relationship between language and identity will always involve a complex mix of individual, social and political factors which work to construct people as belonging to a social group, or to exclude them from it.

Suggestions for further reading

The question of identity is a thread that runs through many studies in socio-linguistics. This is reflected to a large extent in many of the chapters in this book which have been concerned with identities of gender, age, ethnicity and social class, so much of the reading already suggested will be relevant here. However, one of the first collections bringing together a variety of work in this area is:

Gumperz, John (ed.) *Language and Social Identity*, Cambridge: Cambridge University Press, 1982.

If you want to read a concise and interesting critical account of research in language and social identity, try:

Ochs, Elinor (1993) 'Constructing social identity: a language socialisation perspective', *Research on Language and Social Interaction*, 26 (3): 287–306.

Chapter 10

The standard English debate

Linda Thomas

10.1 Introduction

Of the many different dialects of English both within Britain and beyond, the dialect known as standard English has special status. Standard English (whether British English, American English, etc.) is the dialect of institutions such as government and the law; it is the dialect of literacy and education; it is the dialect taught as 'English' to foreign learners; and it is the dialect of the higher social classes. It is therefore the prestige form of English. However, the word 'debate' in the title to this chapter indicates that the idea of a standard English is not a straightforward one, and we will investigate ideas about standard English, as well as ways in which to define it. We will also look at some of the problems involved in trying to get a clear linguistic definition of standard English based on its grammar, and at some social and ideological definitions of standard English. Part of the **ideology** of standard English is that it is the 'correct' form of the language and that other **varieties** are 'incorrect'. Some well-established English usages which don't happen to belong to the standard, such as **multiple negation** and the use of 'ain't' as in *I ain't got none*, are therefore stigmatised. The debate about standard English centres on such differences in grammar and the notion that that standard is linguistically superior to others. We will also look at the central role that standard English holds in the debate on English teaching within the school.

10.2 What is standard English?

10.2.1 Beginning a definition

It is important first of all to draw a distinction between the terms **dialect** and **accent**, as discussions about standard and non-standard English technically refer to the former and not the latter (see also Chapter 8). Linguistically, accent relates to pronunciation; dialect relates to words and grammar. In theory, and for the purposes of discussion, it's possible to separate accent and dialect, although in practice the two go together, at least in spoken English. It's not possible to talk without both an accent (pronunciation) and a dialect (words or **lexis**, and grammar), and traditional studies of regional dialects usually incorporate accent within their descriptions of a dialect area. In some accents of English, for example, words such as *bear* and *beer*, or *pier* and *pear* are **homophones** (meaning they sound the same), but in others they are pronounced differently. Different dialects, on the other hand, can use totally different words for the same thing, such as *autumn* and *fall*, or *wee* and *little*; or different grammatical constructions, such as *I ain't got none* as opposed to *I haven't got any* or *I don't have any*. Although dialect and accent are technically separate entities, they are often treated as the same thing because of their close connection. However, in our discussion, the terms 'standard English' and 'non-standard English' will refer to different dialects, not accents, of English.

The statement that standard English is a dialect is unfortunately the point where the easy part of any linguistic definition stops; there is no comprehensive linguistic description of standard English. Although there are plenty of grammar books which describe standard usage, standard English is, like other dialects, difficult to isolate and put linguistic boundaries around, and we'll come back to some reasons for this in due course. To make matters more complicated, there are also different varieties of standard English worldwide. The two main standard varieties, standard American English and standard English English, while sharing many similarities, also have their differences. Unless otherwise stated, the variety of standard English under discussion in the rest of this chapter is standard English English, although the notions of prestige to be developed here may apply equally to other varieties in other countries.

As it isn't easy to define what standard English is, it might be beneficial to start with trying to understand what it isn't. Let's take as an example the usage of multiple negation. We mentioned in the introduction that the use of more than one negative in an expression is not standard English. If you use this form in an utterance such as *I didn't say nothing*, you stand to be 'corrected' by someone who thinks they are in a position to judge your language use. So why is this the case when multiple negation is a form which so many people use? To begin to answer this, we need to turn to history and the time when grammarians were working on the **codification** (we'll come back to this term in section 10.2.2) of standard English. Milroy and Milroy (1985) point out that multiple negation was a normal feature of English up until the seventeenth century. However, by the end of the eighteenth century, grammarians had decided that this form was unacceptable. They had decided to suppress forms like *I didn't say nothing* and promote forms like *I didn't say anything* on the grounds that multiple negation was illogical; an argument that is still used today. Robert Lowth, the eighteenth-century grammarian who devised the rule, believed that the mathematical logic which states that two negatives make a positive had a wider, more general application, including to language use. Thus, *I didn't say nothing* would really mean *I said something*.

However, given that this is one of the most widespread non-standard forms of English in Britain today, it seems that the 'logical' interpretation is not one that speakers readily employ. Despite the mathematical evidence, speakers understand *I didn't say nothing* and *I didn't say anything* to mean the same thing (and we have yet to meet anyone who interprets *you ain't seen nothing yet* in the so-called logical way). Milroy and Milroy (1985) also point out that multiple negation remains an acceptable feature in the standard forms of many other languages, so it seems that the kind of logic which applies to mathematical relations doesn't apply quite so readily to linguistic ones.

Although the appeal to logic doesn't quite work, multiple negation remains a stigmatised form and this is also partly because it is, like many non-standard forms, a socially distributed form. This means that speakers from one social class are less likely to use it than speakers from another social class. The higher up the social scale you go, the less likely you are to use non-standard forms such as multiple negation, and the more likely you are to be a standard English speaker. It is no coincidence that standard English is the dialect of the middle and upper classes and that its forms are socially prestigious. It is the dialect that attracts positive adjectives such as 'good', 'correct', 'pure' or 'proper' and similarly bestows upon its speakers terms such as 'articulate', 'educated' and 'intelligent'. Features of other dialects or varieties of English, social, regional, and sometimes national, tend to be judged negatively when compared to it, as in the case of multiple negation. These aspects of the definition of standard English are social ones, and we will keep returning to this social dimension in the rest of this chapter.

ACTIVITY 10.1

Different varieties of English use different words. Think about your own variety of English by deciding which word you would use to describe the following:

(a)   the place where pedestrians walk alongside the road
(b)   a sweet, crumbly, baked snack
(c)   the implement for attaching paper to a noticeboard
(d)   the elasticated straps worn over the shoulders and clipped on to the waist-band of lower-body clothing
(e)   a woollen garment worn on a chilly summer evening
(f)   discarded waste or unwanted or useless items
(g)   the item of clothing which is worn on the lower part of the body, encasing the legs
(h)   fuel for a car

(i)   the hinged part of the car that gives access to the engine

(j)   the separate compartment with storage space at the back of the car

Your answers to this exercise may include the following:

(a)	pavement	sidewalk
(b)	biscuit	cookie
(c)	drawing pin	thumbtack
(d)	braces	suspenders
(e)	jumper	sweater
(f)	rubbish	garbage
(g)	trousers	pants
(h)	petrol	gas
(i)	bonnet	hood
(j)	boot	trunk

The list on the left reflects British English usage and that on the right American English usage. Do your own replies seem to be more in line with British or American vocabulary? You may find your answers have words from both lists (*sweater* for example is used in both varieties). If you have words that don't appear here, do you think they are words in local or general use? Check your list with your friends.

10.2.2 Standard English, history and society

The development of a standard form of a language is tied up with the development of a national and cultural identity, and a national standardised language becomes a symbol of that identity. When English began to rise to prominence in England, replacing French and Latin as prestige languages, it became necessary to choose one variety of that language to develop as a standard. There is not space here to detail the history of standard English, but writers who have done show how the selection and development of the standard variety was often based on social and political, rather than linguistic, choices (see Milroy and Milroy 1985; Crowley 1989; Leith 1992). For instance, the variety which was chosen for promotion was one based on that of the south-east Midlands[1] area. This was a variety already achieving social prominence, not on linguistic grounds but because of the region's role as the centre of learning, politics and commerce. If the political, social and commercial heart of England had been elsewhere, the current standard form of the language would look different, since it would have been based on a different English variety.

Once a variety is selected, the standardisation process continues with codification. Codification means that scholars and academics analyse and write down the vocabulary and grammatical patterns and structures of the selected variety in dictionaries and grammar books. For English, much of this codification work took place in the eighteenth century. The patterns and structures that are written down then become grammatical 'rules'.

Standardisation and codification involve what Milroy and Milroy (1985: 8) call 'the suppression of optional variability'. This means that where there are two or more forms in use, two or more ways of saying the same thing, only one is selected as standard. We saw an example of this with multiple negation. Another example they give is the choice of *from*, in the expression *different from*, as opposed to *different to* or *different than*. Milroy and Milroy suggest that although there are reasonable arguments to support the choice of any of the three candidates, the decision to choose *different from* as the standard form was entirely arbitrary in linguistic terms. It rested instead on 'the observed usage of the "best people" at that time' (ibid. 1985: 17); in other words, it was a socially determined decision. Incidentally, *different than* is the standard form in the English of the United states, which just shows how arbitrary a decision can be, and it is still a feature of British English.

Once codification takes place, the dictionaries and grammar books become 'authorities' which people can consult to find out what standard usage, which readily becomes associated with 'correct' or 'good' usage, is. Thus one form, the now standard form, becomes dominant. The alternative forms that are not adopted as the standard do not disappear, but, as in the examples we have looked at, remain in use. However, as standard forms become 'correct', the forms designated non-standard become 'incorrect' and are stigmatised. Instead of being able to opt for one form or another, only one has recognition as 'proper English' and so takes precedence, while the other is suppressed. Grammar books, instead of being descriptions of what speakers do with their language, are made to become prescriptions on what they should do, and non-standard forms, despite a long history, and continued use, are seen as sub-standard forms. It then becomes difficult to remember that the selection of one dialect and its forms over others for promotion as the standard is only a result of historical accident, not linguistic superiority.

However, the idea that there can be only one variety of English is an idealised notion. As we saw in Chapters 6 and 9, cultural and social identity is complex, and the language variety you use is, as Cheshire and Milroy (1993: 18) explain, a linguistic 'badge' of your identity, indicating who you are, where you come from and whom you share social and cultural links with. There are many such linguistic 'badges' or varieties of English. Standard English itself is the badge of identity of particular social groups in the same way that non-standard varieties are. So even though standard English is considered to be the correct form of English, it is not an easy prospect simply to adopt it as your own if you come from a different social group. Changing your language variety and conforming to the **norms** of another social group means changing the badge of your identity (as discussed in Chapter 9).

There is, however, a tension between standard and non-standard usage. Milroy and Milroy (1985) point out that, even if the universal adoption of the standard has failed, promotion of the ideology of a standard has been very successful. There is a belief among many people in Britain that there is a correct way of using English even if they don't use it that way themselves. And it is still the language habits of the 'best people' which are used, both in Britain and the United States, to provide the examples of 'proper' English and 'correctness' which constitute the standard. But, as Rosina Lippi-Green (1997) points out, whilst reasons may be put forward for using prestige groups to dictate usage, there is nothing objective about doing so. The choice of models for standard English is not a neutral one, and standard English is not, there-fore, a neutral variety. Because it belongs to a social group, it is defined by that group and is still determined less by what it is than by who speaks it.

ACTIVITY 10.2

Think about your own speech. Have you ever been corrected by someone on your language use? What kinds of things have they objected to? They may have objected to features of your pronunciation (such as saying *bu'er* not *butter*, or *gonna* not *going to*) or they may have objected to features of your grammar (such as saying *I don't know nobody* instead of *I don't know anybody*, or *we was* instead of *we were*). Check with the generation older and/or younger than you. Were they or are they corrected by other people, and was it or is it for the same kinds of features that you have been corrected for, or for different ones?

10.3 The linguistic definition of standard English

10.3.1 Linguistic variation

One of the reasons it is difficult to give an exact linguistic definition of stan-dard English is that language varies in its use. This means that you choose different kinds of words and put them together in different kinds of ways according to the situation or context. Most people are aware that they use different styles of spoken language during a typical day depending on the situations they find themselves in. Social contexts are infinitely varied but can include: where you are (at home, in the office, in the pub or bar); whom you are talking to, for instance in terms of status (your boss), age (your grandmother) or intimacy (your best friend); what you are talking about (the state of the nation's economy, your opinion of a work of art, last night's date). Written language also varies according to its purpose and audience, so a note to your friend looks nothing like a novel, a newspaper editorial or an academic textbook. To a large extent the style of language you use depends on the formality of the context and the amount of planning that is involved. For example, a casual conversation between you and a close friend is an informal event which won't be planned in advance. What you say, and how you say it, will occur spontaneously as the conversation develops. On the other hand, in a more formal situation, such as giving a speech or lecture, you will plan what you say, and the way you say it, more carefully. Written language tends to occur in more formal contexts than spoken language, so it usually requires more planning. In most cases, written English will be in standard English.[2]

There are many grammar books, dictionaries and guides to English usage which describe and give advice on the standard English that appears in writing. When you are writing you can refer to them to check your own usage, although such reference books don't always agree with each other, and, as Mackinnon (1996: 356) illustrates, sometimes their judgements are based on nothing more substantial than the prevailing attitude to a particular construction, rather than on grammar.[3] Disagreements aside, these books are widely used for guidance on what constitutes standard English. However, there is often also a tendency to apply these judgements, which are about written English, to spoken English. But the norms of spoken and written language are not the same; people don't talk like books even in the most formal of situations or contexts. If you can't refer to a written norm to describe spoken language, then, as we have seen, you base your judgements on the speech of the 'best people', the 'educated' or higher social classes. But basing your judgements on the usage of the educated is not without its difficulties. Speakers, even educated ones, use a variety of different forms. Quirk and Stein (1990: 117) give the following as examples of **variation** within spoken standard English:

> Who/whom did they elect to speak for them?
> His sister is younger than him/he
> The data is/are just not available
> Neither of them were/was present

So which of each pair is correct? Quirk and Stein suggest that the assessment of correctness in English can depend on 'style and personal judgement', saying that, although in each of these examples the second alternative is 'preferable in certain circumstances (such as formal writing), all of these are used freely by educated people and must be regarded as acceptable within Standard English. But we should be prepared for honest disagreement in such matters' (1990: 117). So it seems that variation is acceptable within standard English, but only on the authority of educated speakers who themselves may not always be in agreement.

However, another, perhaps more controversial, example comes from Cheshire *et al.* (1993), who investigated the use of *sat* in expressions such as *she was sat there*, where the standard English of the grammar books would advocate *she was sitting there*. The usage *was sat* is now widespread in English English, and Cheshire *et al.* report that it also appears in educated spoken and written English. The fact that educated speakers are using this construction should make it standard English, but purists, whom Milroy and Milroy (1985) call language 'guardians',[4] would remain reluctant to accept it as such, regardless of its 'educated backing'. Such guardians might even claim, along with John Honey, that 'misuse of the language was so prevalent that even "educated" people were unable to speak correctly' (*The Observer*, 3 August 1997). So it would seem that the authority of educated speakers is not total, in which case, you might be tempted to ask the unanswerable question 'whose is?'.

The notion of 'educated speakers' is, in any case, a problematic one. The people who make up this group are different in different countries and produce different norms. So standard Englishes in different parts of the world contain features that make them different from one another. Trudgill and Hannah (1994: 77) exemplify such differences with the following:

I haven't bought one yet.
I didn't buy one yet.
Have you read it already?
Did you read it already?

The second sentence of each pair would be acceptable to speakers of standard US English, but not to speakers of standard English English. While such differences may seem trivial, and standard Englishes may have more similarities than they have differences, it does highlight the fact that there is no universal consensus on which constructions are 'correct' and by extension, that such decisions are not linguistically but socially based, making them continuously open to controversy and debate.

It should also be pointed out that standard and non-standard varieties of English are not separate linguistic systems either. There are large areas of overlap between standard and non-standard grammars, although linguists describing different varieties of English, and prescriptivists complaining about usage, concentrate on the differences, which may give them a greater emphasis than they deserve. Speakers typically use both standard and non-standard features to a greater or lesser degree, but not exclusively. It is a question of choice, although not necessarily a conscious choice. Speakers and listeners are not typically aware of the variation that takes place in their spontaneous spoken language, but will choose forms that are appropriate to the contexts they are in. It is important to note that such variation is not random, but is subject to a variety of different factors, some related to linguistic contexts and some to real-world contexts; it is a normal part of everyday language use.

ACTIVITY 10.3

Which of the following sentences would you consider to be 'correct' English? Which would be 'bad', and why?

That's the girl he gave the bracelet to
Buffy the Vampire Slayer is dead cool
I want you to quietly leave the room
My old man gave me a set of wheels for my birthday
The guy that works in the bar is really nice
Who did you see?
I don't like him doing that

Check your answers with the generation older or younger than you – do your intuitions tally? Now check your answers in a reference grammar such as Fowler's *Modern English Usage*. Do you have a sense that notions of what is 'correct' and what is not are in fact subject to change?

10.3.2 Logic and correctness

As we have seen, one of the claims which is made for standard English is that it is 'correct'. Other varieties are therefore by definition 'incorrect'. Sometimes the basis for the notion of correctness is that the standard variety is 'logical', or that it is systematic and rule-governed (i.e. it has grammatical rules), whereas non-standard varieties are not. Linguists resist these notions, arguing instead that standard English is no more 'correct' or systematic than any other dialect. It may be desirable to know and be able to use standard English when necessary (especially in writing), but this does not make standard English 'better' or more 'correct' than any other variety. So let's have a closer look at the basis for these arguments.

We saw in the example of multiple negation (see section 10.2.1) that applying logic to English is not always successful, but this doesn't stop people from trying. In an article in the *Evening Standard* on 17 November 1988, John Rae[5] criticised linguists and educationists who argue that the form *we was* is a dialect form and therefore not incorrect:

> You could have fooled me. I thought it was correct to write 'we were' and incorrect to write 'we was'. I did not realise it was just a question of dialect; I thought it was a question of grammar or, if you do not like that word, of logic. You cannot use the singular form of the verb with a **plural pronoun**.

I don't think many (or any) linguists or educationists would support the use of *we was* in formal writing, and neither did the report which this article criticises (the Cox Report). The point that the report was trying to make was that, although the standard English form *we were* is appropriate for writing, this doesn't make the corresponding non-standard *we was* incorrect, just not appropriate. The same argument would apply to spoken English: spoken standard English is more appropriate in some contexts than non-standard English. But (putting the reasons why one is more 'appropriate' than the other aside) can Rae's claim for 'correctness' and 'logic' be upheld? To answer this question we need to look at the way verbs in English work. In standard English, the past tense of verbs is typically formed by the addition of *-ed*, regardless of the subject:

Singular	*Plural*
I loved	we loved
you loved	you loved
s/he loved	they loved

Verbs which follow this pattern are called regular verbs. However, there are also irregular verbs which behave differently:

Singular	*Plural*
I saw	we saw
you saw	you saw

s/he saw	they saw
I went	we went
you went	you went
s/he went	they went

In both sets of verbs, regular and irregular, you can see that the form doesn't change between singular and plural; in fact it doesn't change at all throughout the paradigm. The verb *be*, however, behaves in a different fashion from other verbs:

Singular	*Plural*
I was	we were
you were	you were
s/he was	they were

If we look at the different patterns which standard English verbs have, it's difficult to apply the notion of 'logic' to one which behaves in a totally idio-syncratic manner. The verb *be* is alone in its distinction between singular and plural, and could be considered quite 'illogical'. For many non-standard vari-eties of English, however, this illogical distinction doesn't exist; they simply have *be* with one past tense form, like all the other verbs:

Singular	*Plural*
I was	we was
you was	you was
s/he was	they was

This is no less systematic than the standard and in fact, could be seen to be more logical.

Rae's point about using singular forms of the verb with plural pronouns doesn't even stand much scrutiny within the standard itself. You can see that there is no distinction in standard English between the form of *be* with singular *you* (*you were*) and plural *you* (*you were*), although there is a distinction between the forms used with the other singular and plural pronouns. This doesn't seem 'logical' either.

The use of *we was* is every bit as systematic and rule-governed as the standard, and there are many other examples of non-standard forms for which the same claim can be made; it's just that the systems and rules are different (for examples see Trudgill and Chambers 1991; Milroy and Milroy 1993; Thomas 1996).

10.3.3 So what is standard English?

We have shown that historically the standard dialect of English is based on linguistic forms that were selected from among many competing forms that were in general use. It is bound up politically with notions of national identity and it is connected socially with the middle and upper classes and consequently with education, correctness and prestige. As a linguistic system, the grammar of standard English has similarities with and differences from the grammars of other varieties of English.

ACTIVITY 10.4

The following appeared in a column in a British newspaper:

They said it
'I'm talking to you slightly differently than I would if I was buying tomatoes' – Two solecisms in one sentence addressed to Melvyn Bragg by Jean Aitchison, Rupert Murdoch Professor of Language and Communication at Oxford.

'solecism – 1a) the non-standard use of a grammatical construction; 1b) any mistake, incongruity, absurdity. 2. a violation of good manners' (*Collins Dictionary*).

What is the nature of the journalist's objection? Use a reference grammar to check, then try this exercise on your friends. Consider whether you think the objection is justified and why (not).

10.4 Standard English and education

10.4.1 Standard English in the school

The debate about standard English in England often centres on education and education standards. This brings us to a problem with terminology. The word 'standard' has at least two meanings. It can mean a 'unified form' or 'consistency' (as in 'standard' measures) and this is probably what the term is meant to convey in relation to 'standard' English. But the term 'standard' also refers to levels of attainment, as in 'standards of excellence' or 'falling standards' and it is easy to confuse the two meanings. Once standard English is the 'standard of excellence' rather than the 'unified form', 'non-standard' is reinforced as synonymous with 'sub-standard'.

In the discussion about education we have, once again, to separate ideas about written and spoken language. Teaching literacy, and therefore written standard English, is one of the main functions of the school, but the state-imposed national curriculum in England and Wales also made it a requirement that children should be taught to speak in standard English when appropriate. 'Appropriate' contexts tend to be both public and towards the formal end of the spectrum; in other words, prestigious contexts, although why standard English is appropriate in these contexts is not examined. At the same time, the same orders try to support dialects other than the standard, the dialects that most children coming into school speak, by talking of the 'richness' and 'integrity' of non-standard varieties. Teachers are encouraged to aim for the 'high standards of excellence' in spoken language that only standard English is said to bring, without undermining the validity of the non-standard varieties spoken by the children in their classes. Similar sentiments are uttered in the United States. In her discussion of English in the education system, Lippi-Green (1997: 109) notes a statement by the National Council of Teachers of English which claims to 'respect diversity in spoken and written English' while arguing for the imposition of a standard form. It is difficult to see how teachers might maintain the validity of non-standard varieties, or respect for diversity, given the status and prestige of the standard, the constant confusion of 'non-standard' with 'sub-standard' and the explicit message that nothing else counts, both inside and outside the school. As we saw above, *we was* is recognised not as a form of English, with appropriate occasions for usage, but as an incorrect form, not to be used at all.

The motivation for making children speak standard English in school is explicitly given as the need to communicate effectively. Apparently, those who don't speak the standard (and that constitutes the majority of the population of Britain) have communication problems. While there are undoubtedly contexts where standard English is designated as appropriate, does this really mean that non-standard Englishes don't work as forms of communication? Some people in Britain and the United States think so. In 1995 the then British government launched the 'Better English Campaign', whose aim was to improve standards of spoken English around the country; in other words, to encourage spoken standard English. The committee included prominent public figures and its mission was to 'declare war on communication by grunt'. The Secretary of State for Education, Gillian Shephard, in promoting the campaign, claimed that 'grunts and slack language were impoverishing children'. By 'grunts and slack language' she meant non-standard English. Compare this with a statement made in the early part of the twentieth century:

> Come into a London elementary school and see what it is that the children need most. You will notice, first of all, that in a human sense, our boys and girls are almost inarticulate. They can make noises, but they cannot speak.
>
> (quoted in Crowley 1989: 242)

Crowley comments that these children lacked the ability to speak standard English, not the ability to speak. Lippi-Green records a similar comment about non-standard speakers from a teacher in the United States in the late twentieth century:

> These poor kids come to school speaking a hodge podge. They are all mixed up and don't know any language well. As a result, they can't even think clearly. That's why they don't learn. It's our job to make up for their deficiency.
>
> (1997: 111)

10.4.2 Standard English and social equality

The debate about standard English tends to centre not on written but on spoken English; who should speak it, where and when. Those who view standard English as the only really 'correct' form of English argue that speaking it brings increased personal power and social equality for everyone. John Honey (1997) for example, argues that to encourage the maintenance of non-standard varieties is to deny social equality to the speakers of those varieties. In this argument, non-standard speakers are trapped by their language in the lower social orders. Others agree. John Rae, for example, links standard English to economic survival and success:

> nothing more effectively condemns an individual to his class or ethnic ghetto than an inability to communicate clearly and logically in English. It is not a question of teaching children to 'talk posh'. It is just a question of giving them the essential tool for survival in our society.
>
> (*Evening Standard*, 17 November 1988)

Notice again the reference to 'logic' and the suggestion that non-standard English speakers cannot communicate clearly.

Again, there is a comparison to be made with the situation in the United States, where speakers of a non-standard variety of English known as African American Vernacular English (AAVE) may suffer discrimination at the hands of teachers and employers. Although it is politic in the United States to make statements to the effect that standard and non-standard varieties are equally valid, AAVE is seen as sub-standard and the onus is firmly placed on its speakers to change. The argument for this is summarised as follows:

> FACT: Language A [standard] and Language B [non-standard] are equal in linguistic and cultural terms.
>
> ⇩
>
> FACT: Language B is rejected by teachers and employers.
>
> ⇩
>
> FACT: Rejection has a negative effect on the speakers of Language B.
>
> ⇩
>
> CONCLUSION: Language B must be discarded in favour of Language A.
>
> The teachers writing this essay never even discuss an alternate conclusion: *Teachers and employers must learn to accept Language B.*
>
> (Lippi-Green 1997: 113)

Standard English is therefore seen as the appropriate dialect in the job market, and indeed in Britain, Gillian Shephard went so far as to suggest that 'those who have not mastered "our marvellous language" should not expect to be able to get a job' (*Daily Mail*, 14 October 1994). Again, there is a clear onus on non-standard speakers to change if they wish to keep their rights as citizens to take up employment.

Many employers set great store by their employees' ability to speak standard English when appropriate in the work environment, and they have a reasonable expectation that their employees should be literate in standard English. It is misleading, however, to suggest that the only bar to full employment is a lack of ability to speak the standard. Equality or inequality of opportunity may be linked to language, but language is not the sole contributor.

The linking of standard English with employment and on employers' expectations seldom focuses explicitly on why standard English is so important. We have already seen that standard English is related to education and, in an extension of that debate, standard English is also equated with society's rules. In Britain, there is a link between standard English, or what is seen as correct grammar, and the morality of a well-ordered world. This link tends to be made in the context of education and English teaching, and can be seen in the language of prominent public figures at both ends of the twentieth century:

The great difficulty of teachers in Elementary schools in many districts is that they have to fight against the powerful influences of evil habits of speech contracted in home and street. The teachers' struggle is thus not with ignorance but with a perverted power. (Newbolt Report 1921)[7]

If you allow standards to slip to the stage where good English is no better than bad English, where people turn up filthy at school ... all these things tend to cause people to have no standards at all, and once you lose standards then there's no imperative to stay out of crime. (Norman Tebbitt, MP, 1985)

Attention to the rules of grammar and care in the choice of words encourages punctiliousness in other matters ... As nice points of grammar were mockingly dismissed as pedantic and irrelevant, so was punctiliousness in such matters as honesty, responsibility, property, gratitude, apology and so on. (John Rae, *The Observer*, 7 February 1982)

(all quoted in Cameron 1995: 94–6)

Thus we have a 'perverted power' working against authority and morality and causing the social order to break down. Watts (2002) suggests that the link between standard English and 'positive' social behaviour (and, by default, between non-standard forms and 'negative' social behaviour) really took shape in eighteenth-century England, in the framework of an 'ideology of politeness'. 'Polite' behaviour was held to be that of the gentry, who were the social stratum that ambitious members of the middle class modelled themselves on. Certain attributes, such as 'decorum, grace, beauty, symmetry and order' were held up as innately characteristic of this 'polite' class in all things – their manners, morality and of course their language, standard English. Thus, to use the standard English of the gentry, was to demonstrate an affiliation to, and engagement with, a certain set of values which signalled sophistication and gentility. The use of non-standard forms then, by default, came to symbolise a lack of integration into socially esteemed attitudes and behaviours. Thus, standard English is equated with authority, discipline and a traditional social and moral order and its speakers are consequently seen both as educated and as having respect for society's standards or norms. Those who do not conform, or who conform to a different set of rules, have attributed to them a kind of 'perverted power' which undermines the authority of those who seek to impose their rules, the socially powerful people. Standard English on the other hand supports that power and is promoted as being able to give access to it. This is because the contexts in which it is used are institutional ones such as education, law, government; public arenas where large-scale social decisions are taken. Its use in these prestige contexts means that its status is reinforced. It also means that, to take part in the higher order functions, you must use standard English. The link between standard English and power is well recognised. Honey's book, for example, equates language with power in its title (*Language Is Power: The Story of Standard English and its Enemies*) and Trevor Macdonald, the chair of the Better English Campaign, also expressed his wish, 'I want every young person in the country to understand that language is a source of power' (quoted in *The Sunday Times*, 21 April 1996). In both cases 'language' means standard English. Speaking standard English should then in theory enable us all to become part of the socially powerful group. It is, however, doubtful to suppose that, if everyone really did speak standard English, then we would all achieve the social equality which Honey and Rae suggest is denied us simply because of a dialect of English. In any case, even if we could all become members and adopt the norms of high status social groups, it's unlikely that we would all want to.

Rather than impose standard English, there are those who support the genuine acceptance of non-standard dialects of English and who maintain that it is possible to have the best of both worlds. Access to the standard should not come at the expense of a home dialect, which is neither illogical nor incomprehensible, but as an addition to it. Accepting the usefulness of standard English, or society's general high regard for it, should not invalidate other varieties, nor promote intolerance of them. There are many complex social reasons for the dominance of standard English and its use in the important public and institutional arenas of social and political life and we should be aware of these, rather than simply accepting the notion that standard English is inherently a linguistically superior form.

10.5 Summary

In this chapter we have considered the difficulties in defining standard English and have looked at its historical, social and linguistic foundations. We have seen how notions of 'logic' and 'correctness' cannot be applied linguistically to standard English, but how these ideas are connected with social and political values, and with the maintenance of moral, social and institutional order. We have discussed the fundamental role of standard English in education as giving access to literacy and to wider communication, but we have argued that promotion of the standard should not invalidate non-standard varieties, and that access to, and acquisition of, the standard does not have to be at the expense of a home dialect.

Notes

1   The south-east Midlands is the area in central to south-east England which includes the capital, London, and the cities of Oxford and Cambridge, the homes of England's two oldest and most prestigious universities.

2   There are occasions when written language is less formal, such as when you write a note to a friend. There are also occasions when non-standard English is deliberately used in print, for example in magazines which are aimed at younger audiences and try for an air of informality and intimacy, or in novels. It isn't possible to define language use by strict categories as people are very creative and varied in the way they use it. So ideas about contexts which relate to formality and planning and their corresponding linguistic forms are referring to tendencies rather than absolutes.

3   Mackinnon gives an example of a change in accepted use by comparing the entry on *due to* in Fowler's 1926 *Dictionary of Modern English Usage* with that of the 1983 *Oxford Guide to English Usage*. Fowler claimed that *due to* was 'impossible' in sentences like 'The old trade union movement is a dead horse, largely due to the incompetency of the leaders' while the *Oxford Guide* puts the same construction among its accepted usages.

4   In Britain it is common for individual people to take it upon themselves to comment on English usage by way of letters to newspapers or complaints to broadcasters, setting out to prescribe what everyone else should do with their language. The people who make such comments act as 'guardians' of the language and are part of what Milroy and Milroy (1985) call the 'complaint tradition' serving an unofficial but none the less prescriptive function.

5   John Rae is the former head of Westminster School, one of England's leading public schools. In England the term 'public school' is used to refer to a small number of high-status private schools. Schools maintained from the public purse, and which the majority of children go to, are referred to as state schools.

6   Examples taken from 'Children's use of spoken standard English', SCAA Discussion Papers: No. 1, February 1995.

7   This was a government report on the teaching of English.

Suggestions for further reading

Cameron, Deborah (1995) *Verbal Hygiene*, London: Routledge. Chapter 3 presents an interesting discussion of the issues involved in the standard English debate in Britain.

Leith, Dick (1992) *A Social History of English* (2nd edition), London: Routledge. A comprehensive and comprehensible account of the history of English, including coverage of standardisation processes.

Milroy, James and Milroy, Lesley (1985) *Authority in Language: Investigating Language Prescription and Standardisation*, London: Routledge & Kegan Paul. Examines notions of 'correctness' and issues of prescriptivism.

Bex, T. and R. Watts (eds) (1999) *Standard English: The Widening Debate*, London: Routledge. An interesting collection of papers which looks at the history and ideology of the standard in Britain, as well as its current development in the United States and continental Europe.

Chapter 11

Attitudes to language

Linda Thomas

11.1 Introduction

Attitudes towards language(s) and language use are commonplace throughout the world. People assign various attributes to language forms; they may feel that a language or **variety** of a language is 'elegant', 'expressive', 'vulgar', 'guttural' or 'musical', or that one language form is 'more polite' or more 'aesthetically pleasing or displeasing' than another one. All levels of language use are subject to such notions, and we invest some language forms with prestige while others are stigmatised. Prestige and stigma are connected with speakers of languages and have to do with social class and social or national identity, and with ideas about status, solidarity and unity. Popular evidence from the media and academic surveys of language attitudes reveal the same underlying and recurrent patterns of values and value judgements within a community about the languages and varieties of language within it, and such judgements affect our social and cultural lives in important and influential ways.

11.2 The evidence

Throughout this book we have shown that issues to do with language are far from peripheral, but are central to people's daily lives. Similarly opinions about or attitudes to language, while common, are not trivial; people hold their opinions very seriously. We can find evidence of positive and negative attitudes in relation to a wide range of linguistic issues, such as whole languages, varieties of a language, words and **discourse** practices, pronunciation and **accent**, or anything perceived as different, new or changing. Such attitudes are not themselves necessarily new, nor are they restricted to English, although here it is English we will be concentrating on, and attitudes to English in Britain and the United States.

Before we begin to consider the broad picture, jot down the kinds of features that you like and/or dislike in other people's (or your own) speech. These might include someone's accent, the words or expressions they use, the quality of their voice and so on. Try to figure out why you like or dislike the features you've noted and then check your opinions with your family or friends to see how much agreement exists between you.

11.2.1 Whole languages

Fasold (1984) gives a summary of the academic research into people's language attitudes around the world, showing, for example, how bilingual or multilingual speakers may regard one language as more suitable to a particular topic than another, or may regard one language as aesthetically more pleasing than another, or have clearly expressed feelings about their languages in relation to their social and cultural identities. In Britain, although many languages are in daily use, only English has official recognition. For the English especially, multilingualism is viewed with suspicion and as a threat to national unity. In a speech to a meeting at the Conservative Party Conference in October 1997, Lord Tebbitt, a prominent Conservative, called for national unity saying, 'we need common values, a common culture and a single language'. As stated in Chapter 6, David Blunkett, the Home Secretary, stated that all who consider themselves British should have mastery of English. A similar kind of idea is expressed by Beryl Goldsmith in *The Sunday Telegraph* (26 January 1997). She describes her irritation with the 'enterprising Asian couple' who own her local newsagent's shop when they speak to each other in their native tongue, rather than in the 'fluent English' that they use for their customers. Goldsmith regards this use of another language, and one which she doesn't understand, with suspicion: 'I am not comfortable with this [use of their native tongue]; are they making personal remarks?'. She also see it as evidence of lack of unity. 'Why', she asks, 'are they determined to establish a permanent kind of "separatism" from their fellow Brits?'. She goes on to say: 'Asian Britons no doubt do respect the country chosen by their parents or grandparents in which to settle, and to rear their families. But they should show it by using English, even at home'. So, for this writer, use of a language other than English is threatening and indicates lack of respect, not the valid maintenance of part of someone's cultural and personal identity (see also Chapters 6 and 9). Older indigenous languages don't escape this negativity either, and are seen not only as threatening but as inferior, as Jan Morris writing about Welsh (Cymraeg) in *The Times Weekend* (28 February 1998) illustrates:

> The English have always resented the very existence of Cymraeg – think of it, an apparently inextinguishable foreign language within the limits of their own island. They have always laughed at its spelling and jeered at its pronunciation.

Attitudes towards English in the United States have an association with national unity similar to that found in Britain – multilingualism is seen as threatening and subversive and opposed to images of the ideal society as a homogeneous one (see also Chapter 6). Homogeneity and national unity, therefore, mean getting rid of linguistic differences, as Rosina Lippi-Green points out: 'English, held up as the symbol of the successfully assimilated immigrant, is promoted as the one and only possible language of a unified and healthy nation' (1997: 217). The promotion of English, both in Britain and in the United States, leads to the marginalisation of the other languages which exist there. Popular attitudes may on the surface see them as less useful or expressive than English, even as unintelligible, as the Welsh example illustrates. On another level, minority languages and their speakers may be seen as divisive, even dangerous, and a threat to political, social or economic stability.

11.2.2 Varieties of a language

Attitudes towards languages and language use also focus on varieties of the same language. For example, Fasold (1984) describes how the French spoken in Europe is seen to be more prestigious than that spoken in Canada, even by native Canadian French speakers. Mackinnon (1996) reproduces letters of complaint about English usage in the Englishes of New Zealand and Singapore, and we saw in Chapters 8 and 10 the negative attitudes toward non-standard varieties of English in Britain, or towards American varieties such as African American Vernacular English (AAVE) in the United States.

Although there may be discrimination against anything other than the standard variety of American English in the United States, in Britain standard American English itself is a favourite for complaint and stigmatisation. Media style guides warn against the use of 'Americanisms', meaning any usage which is thought to be typical of the English of the United States, but not of varieties of British standard English. The American Bill Bryson recalls working for *The Times* in London when the editor would criticise him for using Americanisms:

He would say something to me along the lines of: 'Mr Bryson, I'm not sure what patois you spoke in Idaho or Ohio or wherever it was your misfortune to be born, but here at *The Times* we rather like to stay with the English.'

(reported in *The Sunday Times*, 22 May 1994)

Deborah Cameron (1995: 240) reports that *The Times* traditionally distinguished between 'English' and 'American' as two separate languages. The 1992 *Times* style guide similarly warns not to use Americanisms 'as alternatives to an English phrase'.

Bryson (1994) points to the long history of derision of American English by the British, despite the fact that many Americanisms have passed into common usage in British English without British speakers being aware of them. For example, words such as *reliable* and *influential* were originally Americanisms, as was the phrase *to keep a stiff upper lip*, traditionally regarded in Britain as a very British activity. He also explains how American English has preserved English words and phrases which have died out, or all but died out, in Britain. Perhaps the most well-known example is the word *fall*, in its meaning of a season.

Given that many Americanisms are no longer recognised as such on the British side of the Atlantic, it is not clear how to define an 'Americanism'. Current criticisms may be directed at usages which haven't made the transition (such as *visit with someone* for British English *visit someone*); at less well-known older British forms, such as *gotten*[1] which are still in use in the United States and which show evidence of 're-invading'; or at innovations, such as turning nouns into verbs. This method of making new words is one that is popularly criticised, as in this letter to *The Times*:

could we stop assuming that any noun can automatically be turned into a verb? 'To access' may be a battle already lost but I draw the line at 'to impact', heard last week. As for 'to outsource', words fail me.

(*The Times*, 1 January 1994)

The creation of verbs from nouns tends to feature more in American English than in varieties of British English (see Figure 11.1) and it receives positive acclaim from Bryson:

We turn nouns into verbs to give them inventiveness not seen in English since the Elizabethan age. The list of American verb formations is all but endless: to interview, to highlight, to package, to curb, to demean, to corner, to endorse, to engineer, to notice, to advocate. I could go on.

(*The Sunday Times*, 22 May 1994)

Figure 11.1 Turning nouns into verbs
Source: Calvin and Hobbes: Universal Press Syndicate, 1993

Again, these examples would no longer be recognised as Americanisms by most people, so the definition remains unclear. It seems, then, that charges of 'Americanism' are reserved for newer usages that are somehow seen as a threat to standards of British English, but which are equally likely to be absorbed into it.

What does seem clear is that the influential attitudes towards language varieties in both societies are determined by powerful groups (such as those who control newspapers or have access to them) or those in authority (such as those responsible for education). Mainstream US attitudes serve to marginalise and stigmatise non-mainstream varieties. Similar mainstream attitudes prevail in Britain towards its own non-standard varieties, and, in a hopeless attempt to preserve some kind of ideal embodied in the 'Queen's English', towards other varieties of English abroad.

11.2.3 Words and interaction

Words, the meanings ascribed to words, their usage and who gets to use them, are also the subject of comment and debate. We saw in Chapter 1 how Ofsted's decision to use the word *attainment* rather than *ability* in respect of pupils' assessment caused comment via a letter to *The Daily Telegraph*. Examples of such decisions on usage can also be found elsewhere. In 1997, the British Psychological Society decided to prohibit the use of the word *subjects* in its publications to refer to those taking part in psychological experiments. Such participants were to be referred to as *individuals, people, students* and so on. The letters to October 1997's edition of *The Psychologist* describe this decision as 'tosh' or 'trivial', and one which leaves the eminent writers of these letters 'baffled'. Most of the letter writers use 'political correctness' as a generally disparaging term for the Society's decision and to convey their dislike of what they see as interference with, or policing of, their use of language (see Chapters 1 and 3 for more on 'political correctness'). At a more general level, discussion of the use of the word *gay* to mean 'homosexual' still continues in the national press in Britain, with letters to *The Daily Telegraph* recording readers' attitudes as 'deploring the loss of that useful word', as being 'in mourning for dear old *gay*' or accusing those who use it of 'mis-use', 'destruction of the word' or 'misappropriation of the English language'. Arguments over meaning and who has the right to dictate or control it often centres on individual words.

Attitudes to words may be so negative that the words may be considered not suitable for use at all. We often invent **euphemisms** to cover such words so that, for example, instead of 'death' and 'dying' we might talk about 'passing away'. Some words are considered so unsuitable that they become totally taboo. In a discussion of four-letter or offensive words entitled 'The big C', *The Guardian* (3 March 1998) cites a forthcoming television play in which 'the most reviled single utterance in the English language' is to be used. The 'little four-letter word' is so taboo that, as *The Guardian* writer points out, many people feel incapable of writing it, let alone uttering it (see Figure 11.2). Taboo words of this kind are 'immensely powerful', as the scriptwriter says, and have the power to shock. The fact that its use on television warrants serious newspaper discussion is indicative of social attitudes towards such words and their public expression. When looking at taboo words we can see how our dislike (for whatever reason) of the thing a word refers to gets transferred to the word itself. Those who continue to use the word then take on the same stigma. The complex link between attitudes to words and attitudes to their users is a difficult one to unravel.

Figure 11.2 The power of taboo words
Source: Ros Asquith, *The Guardian*, 3 March 1998

Other expressions, such as *right, like, you know, see you later* also come in for negative treatment. Some of these expressions may be associated with certain groups and may function as identity markers, such as those discussed in Chapter 9. For example, *see you later*, meaning 'goodbye', first came to my immediate attention in the part of Surrey where I live as an expression used by young adults, such as my grown-up children and their friends. A friend of mine complained long and hard about this innovation, since those uttering it were not necessarily going to see her, or each other, later. Her objection, of course, ignored the fact that more acceptable expressions such as *Good morning* or *How do you do?* don't mean what they seem to on the surface either. The morning could be anything but good and you don't really want to know how someone 'does'. In reality, her complaint was only superficially about *see you later*; her real complaint was about the linguistic behaviour of the young, which, like other aspects of youth behaviour, is different from, and challenging to, the norms of the older generation. As *see you later* is now widespread, it would appear that her battle has in any case, predictably, been lost.

It's not only in the UK that negative attitudes to such terms are expressed. An investigation by Stubbe and Holmes (1995) into the use of phrases such as *you know* in New Zealand opens with a quotation from the *New Zealand Listener*:

> The phrase 'you know' is used with monotonous regularity when a person is being interviewed on TV or radio – to commence a sentence, be interspersed throughout, and even to conclude the same sentence. Let's hope 'you know' will soon die a natural death, although another exasperating expression will probably replace it – to ruin my listening enjoyment.
>
> (*New Zealand Listener*, 16–22 April 1994)

You know is a stigmatised form, as the quotation suggests, considered to be a 'marker of imprecise, uncertain or uneducated "lower class" speech'. Although its use was found in this survey to be frequent in both middle- and working-class groups, it is used more frequently by working-class speakers and this accounts for the stigma attached to it.

Linguistic features (such as *you know* or *see you later*) may be preferred, then, by different groups. People may also have opinions about preferred linguistic behaviour for different groups. It may be considered appropriate, for instance, for children to be 'seen but not heard'. Silence has also been seen as appropriate behaviour for women. When women do speak, attitudes towards their talk are often negative; women's talk is labelled as 'chatter' or 'gossip' about 'inconsequential' or 'trivial' topics (see also Chapter 5; for a summary of attitudes to women's language see Coates 1993).

Attitudes to linguistic behaviour can also vary cross-culturally. At the height of his career, the African-American boxer Muhammad Ali was noted for his brand of self-promotion, which consisted of boasting at length about his abilities. His bragging style alienated many people, although European-Americans typically had a more negative attitude towards it than African-Americans had. In a test to determine why this might be, Holtgraves and Dulin (1994) concluded that European-Americans and African-Americans may have different conversational rules:

> For European Americans, positive self-statements seem to violate a rule prescribing modesty, and this results in an overall negative evaluation of someone who brags . . . African American rules regarding positive self-statements are more complex . . . Boasts and truthful bragging are relatively acceptable and this results in a less overall negative evaluation of someone who brags truthfully.
>
> (Holtgraves and Dulin 1994: 282)

Cultural differences in attitudes towards linguistic behaviour like this one can therefore contribute to cross-cultural misunderstanding or even communication breakdown.

The attitudes we have explored in this section can relate to the power to ascribe meanings to words and to the power we invest in words themselves. Our attitudes can also be a reflection of the social groups we associate particular words or kinds of linguistic behaviour with; negative evaluations are often associated with stigmatised or less powerful groups.

11.2.4 Pronunciation and accent

The way in which something is said is often at least as influential for the message as what is said. The British press happily prints the numerous complaints from its readership on pronunciation and accent. These, and the many articles and comments on this issue that journalists themselves write, give ample illustration of the British obsession with the way people talk.

It also seems that we commonly have stereotypical ideas about people on the basis of their accents. Advertisers draw on these ideas in the UK, using country accents to indicate the wholesome nature of food products, or more prestigious accents such as **RP** (see Chapter 8) to promote financial services. Country accents can also used to denote lack of intelligence with the stereotypical image of the 'country bumpkin'. The connection between gender and lack of intelligence is signified not only by accent but also by patterns of stress and intonation, as can often be seen in film and television characterisations of silly women. Negative attitudes to female voices are so strong that the former British Prime Minister Margaret Thatcher took great pains to change her own voice:

> making it lower in pitch, less 'swoopy' in range and slower in rate. This collection of deliberate modifications can best be understood as a response to the perceived disadvantages suffered by the unreconstructed female speaker, who is stigmatised as 'shrill' (high pitch), 'emotional' (broad intonational range) and 'lacking in authority'.
>
> (Cameron 1995: 170)

In the United States, lack of intelligence is associated with women with southern accents who may be perceived as 'sweet, pretty and not very bright' (Lippi-Green 1997: 215). Lippi-Green also suggests that southern accents in general are associated with native wit rather than educated intelligence and with images of dim-wittedness or villainy. In Britain, however, villainy may be associated with a Birmingham[2] accent. The *Daily Mail* (1 October 1997) reports that 'crime suspects with a Birmingham accent are twice as likely to be considered guilty'. The fact that these two different and distant accents (southern-states American and Birmingham English) can both have over-tones of criminality suggests that this is an attribute which resides in the minds of those who judge, rather than being inherent in the accents or their speakers.

Urban accents in the UK tend to have low status in the eyes of British speakers, coming at the bottom of a hierarchical pecking order with speakers with urban accents judged low on intelligence and competence. As one elocution teacher put it: 'people still think that if you have a London accent then you're common' (quoted in *The Observer Review*, 24 March 1996). In Chapter 8 we saw that the New York accent, 'Noo Yawkese', is similarly stigmatised and its speakers regarded as less trustworthy than those using the more standard American accent of the mid-west.

Criticism of New York accents includes an objection to the loss of 'r' in words such as *sugar* (*shuguh*) or *never* (*nevuh*). This objection provides a contrast with British English accents, where 'r' has largely disappeared from the pronunciation of such words. Indeed, 'r' pronunciation tends to be stigmatised, which was not always the case. Lynda Mugglestone (1995) describes the loss of 'r' in England and attitudes towards its loss during the nineteenth century. Speakers without 'r' were variously described as 'vulgar', 'illiterate' and 'lower-class' whereas those with 'r' were 'elegant', 'polished' and 'educated'. The poet Keats was apparently criticised as illiterate and ignorant for creating rhymes such as *thorns* and *fawns*, or *thoughts* and *sorts* by those who refused to acknowledge that the sound pattern was changing. Now the change is virtually complete, at least for accents in England, with 'r' pronunciation seen as belonging to the stereotypical, rural 'country bumpkin' accent. Thus, one small unit of sound can provoke different responses according to time and place. Such questions of salience (what is regarded as important and whom it is import-ant to) are part of what we all learn when we learn our native language.

To find out what kind of attitudes to language and its speakers are gener-ally shared by members of a particular speech community, researchers have devised a method of testing called **matched guise**. Matched guise tests may follow different formats according to the subject of the experiment, but they aim to get people to make evaluations of different groups of speakers based on the different languages or language varieties they use. Researchers using matched guise techniques in experiments get their informants to judge speakers' characteristics based on what they hear. Measures are taken to control other factors that might influence the judgement, such as the age, gender, or voice quality of the speakers, so that the judges are reacting only to the language variety or varieties under consideration. They will then respond with the attrib-utes that are typically ascribed to the users of those varieties. Tests carried out in the UK reveal attitudes which consistently attribute speakers with RP accents with qualities such as intelligence and confidence, while speakers with regional accents are attributed with qualities such as sincerity or friendliness. The differ-ence in perception is one of status versus solidarity. Speakers who score high on the status scale tend to score low on the solidarity scale; that is, they are not seen as being particularly friendly or sincere. Speakers who score high on the solidarity scale tend to score low on the status scale; that is, they are not seen as being particularly intelligent or confident. Interestingly however, there are contexts in which high-status accents such as RP are not valued. The British *Evening Standard* (18 March 2002) reported on Dominic Scott-Barrett, an actor who, in an audition for a BBC drama, was rejected because his accent was a bit too 'posh'. He was told by the director that the BBC now needed 'accents the audience can understand and relate to'. Whereas the BBC may be endearing itself to a major sector of its audience with such a turnaround in attitude and policy, Dominic Scott-Barrett remains unimpressed, terming it an instance of 'political correctness gone mad'.

Attitudes which rate speakers on the status and solidarity scales also exist in the United States. Giles and Coupland (1991) report a 1990 study in Kentucky where Kentucky students were asked to evaluate standard American and Kentucky accented speakers. The Kentucky speakers scored high on soli-darity, low on status; standard American speakers scored low on solidarity, high on status.

It seems then that attitudes are consistently held and widely spread within various communities and that attitudes to languages or language forms are inextricably linked to attitudes to the speakers. The article in *The Times Weekend*, quoted above, which talks about English attitudes to the Welsh language also talks about the attitudes of the English to the Welsh people:

> English denigration of things Welsh is almost as old as history . . . Just the word 'Welsh' has all too often been a term of abuse, implying thievery, trickery, lasciviousness, mendacity and a tendency to run away from debts.

Attitudes to the Welsh language (the resentment and mistrust) are tied up with these attitudes to the people themselves, and we talk about the language as a cover for talking about the people. Lippi-Green explains this relationship with reference to stereotypes associated with southern accents in the US:

> we use accent to talk about bundles of properties which we would rather not mention directly. When a northerner appropriates a pan-southern accent to make a joke or a point, he or she is drawing on a strategy of condescension and trivialisation that cues into those stereotypes so carefully structured and nurtured: southerners who do not assimilate to northern norms are backward but friendly, racist but polite, obsessed with the past and unenamored of the finer points of higher education.[3]
>
> (Lippi-Green 1997: 215)

It's important to remember that people who are unfamiliar with the language variety in question may find it difficult, if not impossible, to make the kinds of evaluations which appear in the research and in popular opinion as expressed in the press. Aesthetic qualities such as 'elegance' or 'vulgarity' are not ones that necessarily travel beyond the confines of the speech community but they seem to reside within the socially conditioned ear of the hearer, not in the language form itself.

ACTIVITY 11.2

Broadcast media such as television, film and radio use different accents to portray different characteristics or personality traits. During your regular viewing or listening, note which accents are used in connection with which kind of character portrayal and check whether there are any regular patterns in such portrayals. You could also concentrate on commercials. Do you notice any patterns of accent variation connected to the type of product being advertised?

11.3 The effects

We have seen that attitudes to languages and language varieties can be related to social and cultural identity, to power and control, to notions of prestige and solidarity, and that our attitudes are often influenced by conventionally held stereotypes of language forms and their speakers. Our ability to respond to different types of language are not always negative. Giles and Coupland also talk about our perceptions being related to 'uncertainty reduction'. When you meet someone for the first time, you try to work out what the other person is like so that you know how to respond to them and how to behave appropriately. Listening to the way they talk is one of the factors you can use in forming an impression about them and the formality of the social situation, and you can adapt your behaviour, including your linguistic behaviour (your speech style) to match theirs. It's also useful to be able to manipulate your speech styles in other situations; for example you may want to give an impression of status by adopting a more prestigious style when you want to make a complaint about goods or services. Hopefully, the person you're making the complaint to will then attribute you with the qualities that are conventionally associated with prestige accents and see you as intelligent, capable, confident and so on. This in turn will influence their behaviour and bring about a speedy and satisfactory resolution to your problem. In this latter example, the impression of status will be based on the stereotypes that the hearer has learnt to associate with different forms of language as they relate to different groups of people. We need, then, to be aware of how our attitudes are linked to stereotypes, and what role they may play in our analysis and expectations of other people.

There may be occasions when our perceptions of a speaker's personal attributes are considered welcome. A survey quoted in the *Glasgow Herald* (28 October 1997) reports that, in Britain, speakers with Scottish accents are rated the highest on sex appeal. In other cases, an attributed character trait may look superficial. A report in *The Guardian* (26 October 1991) about a court case against a doctor states: 'in court she admitted her temper matched her red hair and Belfast/Glasgow accent'. This association between (uncontrolled) temper and accent seems fairly trivial until you remember that this is a court case for slander, where someone's ability to control their temper might be an important consideration. At perhaps a more serious level, we saw earlier how a Birmingham accent or a southern states accent is linked with criminality. In the United States, negative and criminal stereotypes are also associated with Spanish-accented speakers; the more negative the stereotype, the heavier the accent. This stereotype is reinforced in the media, where

Mexican-Americans are portrayed negatively: 'recent stereotypes in film and television ... have one thing in common: Mexican Americans are almost always portrayed as violent: they are drug-pushers, gang-members, pimps' (Lippi-Green 1997: 236). As with many stereotypes, such perceptions can have far-reaching effects. Lippi-Green records the evidence of a research student who was discussing language styles with a businessman whose job was to hire sales personnel. The businessman was positive that he wouldn't hire anyone with a Mexican accent. His reason for this was that he 'wouldn't buy anything from a guy with a Mexican accent' and therefore assumed that his customers wouldn't either. Job prospects can also be considered in relation to other speakers. Speakers with a southern accent with its connotations of dimwittedness have reported discrimination in employment contexts, and speakers of 'Noo Yawkese' find their accents a liability: in the words of the *Washington Post* (16 December 1997), 'natives of New York can get rich faster if they sound like they are from someplace else'. In Britain, reports in the press indicate that the way people speak also affects their job prospects. *The Daily Telegraph* (12 March 1994) covers the story of an employee of a Birmingham company who was fired for having a Birmingham accent, and a survey by the Institute of Personnel and Development confirms that 'employers tend to look down their noses at those who speak in the accents of Liverpool, Glasgow and Birmingham' (*The Guardian*, 3 January 1993). However, there are occasions when issues of solidarity are more important than issues of status, and less prestigious accents are sought. The same *Guardian* report suggests:

> in some other trades, standard English is a disadvantage. The disc jockey John Peel, a profile reveals, is the son of a middle class Cheshire cotton broker who sent him to public school. He upgraded to Scouse only later, when he got into turntables.[4]

British Telecom was also reported as locating new telephone sales jobs in the north of England because of a 'belief that regional accents exude honesty' (*The Guardian*, 8 April 1997). Politicians are not immune from prevailing attitudes to accents either. Those who traditionally appeal to lower-status groups may emphasise their non-prestige accents if they have them, or adopt features from them if they haven't, while politicians who traditionally appeal to high-status groups may adapt their language to prestige norms. People can, then, manipulate norms for their own ends. Those who are less fortunate, however, may find themselves in a double bind. Giles and Coupland record that research in Canada, the United States and Britain indicates that people with low-status accents are regarded negatively for employment in high-status jobs, but positively for employment in low-status jobs. They are therefore doubly likely to be kept at the bottom of the job market.

Another major area of social life where language attitudes can be important is that of education. Lippi-Green (1997), commenting on attitudes to Hawaiian **creole** English in the United States, illustrates how this variety has been described as a 'speech defect' or classed as a **pidgin**. Negative attitudes have resulted in calls for an educational ban, not only in the classroom but anywhere within the school environment, an attitude which stigmatises both the language and its speakers. And such effects can be far-reaching. Teachers' perceptions of pupils' language can influence their assessment of pupils' ability:

> Overall, research indicates that the perception of children's so-called 'poor' speech characteristic leads teachers to make negative inferences about their personalities, social background and academic abilities.
>
> (Giles and Coupland 1991: 45)

Negative inferences in turn may influence attainment. On the other side of the coin, attitudes can affect students' perceptions of teachers. Lippi-Green (1997) outlines a study in which undergraduate students were divided into two groups and asked to listen to a recording of introductory lectures. With the recording one group was shown a picture of an Asian woman lecturer and the other group was shown a picture of a Caucasian woman lecturer. Both pictures were evaluated equally in terms of physical attractiveness. The recordings were however the same, both made by a native American English speaker; only the pictures differed. In their evaluations of the lectures, the students rated the lecture with the picture of the Asian woman as being more foreign accented than that with the picture of the Caucasian woman. Not only that, the students also scored lower on a comprehension test where they believed the lecturer was Asian. Remember that the recordings were identical, so the students couldn't actually have heard any difference at all; they only thought they did. And their lower expectation of an Asian lecturer was enough to interfere with their comprehension and learning. So it seems that complaints about accent and pronunciation have more to do with the complainant's perception of the speaker than with the utterance itself.

ACTIVITY 11.3

Investigate for yourself the attitudes that people have to a variety of accents. Record four speakers with different accents reading the same passage. Make sure they are all approximately the same age and are either all men or all women (to control for the effects of age and gender). Play the tapes to ten people, making sure that they are all of the same approximate age and the same gender as the speakers. After each tape, have your informants fill in a questionnaire asking them to name the accent they have just heard and then to rate the speaker on: (1) how pleasant the accent was: very pleasant, pleasant, neutral, unpleasant, very unpleasant (2) how prestigious it was: very prestigious, prestigious, neutral, unprestigious, very unprestigious (3) how intelligent the speaker was: very intelligent, intelligent, neutral, unintelligent, very unintelligent. You could add some open-ended questions such as 'Describe the house this person might have' and 'What sort of job might this person have?' (adapted from Stockwell 2002).

11.4 Summary

In this chapter we have looked at the way our attitudes to language can be focused on any level of language use. As we said at the beginning of the chapter, our attitudes to language are far from trivial and we have seen how they may be influential in our assessments of the characteristics of individuals and social groups. These assessments can then be carried over into the decisions that are made in important areas of our lives such as law and order, employment, education and equality of opportunity. Awareness of how attitudes might be formed or manipulated may not make us immune to them, but it may help us to evaluate their influence on our own practices.

Notes

1   As, for example, in a discussion on English usage on BBC Radio 4's *Today*, 19 March 1997. Incidentally, *gotten* still exists in some traditional British English dialects, where it is also stigmatised.
2   Birmingham is a large industrial city in the British Midlands.
3   Lippi-Green points out that stereotypes of southern African-Americans are different from these.
4   Public schools in England are in effect private schools; they charge fees and have high status. 'Scouse' is the term for the Liverpool accent and dialect. It has low status in mainstream society but has, or had, high credibility in the popular music industry.

Suggestions for further reading

Cameron, Deborah (1995) *Verbal Hygiene*, London: Routledge. A thorough, interestingly presented and easy to read look at attitudes to language and those who seek to regulate it.

Lippi-Green, Rosina (1997) *English with an Accent: Language, Ideology and Discrimination in the United States*, London: Routledge. An absorbing coverage of the far-reaching effects of language attitudes and representation of language varieties in the United States.

Giles, Howard and Coupland, Nikolas (1991) *Language: Contexts and Consequences*, Milton Keynes: Open University Press. Chapter 2 covers a wide range of academic research on language attitudes around the world and the methodologies used to discover them.

Glossary

accent   features of speakers' pronunciation that can signal their regional or social background.

active and **passive**   are terms which refer to the voice of the verb. In the active voice the sentence has a structure where the 'doer' (agent) of the action is in the subject position and the 'done-to' (affected) is in the object position. This contrasts with the passive where the 'done-to' is in subject position and the agent becomes optional. *Active*: 'Tom hit Bob'; *Passive*: 'Bob was hit by Tom' or 'Bob was hit'.

address forms   expressions used to refer to a person when you are talking to them directly. Address forms can vary according to the context of use and the relationship between the speaker and hearer. Variation can involve the use of 'titles' such as *Ms, Dr* or *Reverend*; whether or not a person is called by their first name; and in some languages, the form of the second person pronoun as in the *tu/vous* distinction in French. (See also **honorific**.)

adjective   a class of words which is generally used to describe or modify a noun. The adjectives in the following examples are in small capitals: 'The LUCKY cat ran away'. 'The PERSIAN cat ate my trout.' 'That cat is BIG.'

agent   see **active**.

Amerindian   a general name for the languages spoken by the native peoples of North and South America.

arbitrariness of the sign   Saussure argued that there was no inherent connection between combinations of sounds or letters and the concepts which they refer to. The fact that different languages label concepts differently, for example French speakers using *arbre* for what the English speakers call *tree*, supports this.

asymmetry/asymmetrical   see **symmetry**.

audience design   the notion that speakers will take into account whom they are addressing and alter their speech style accordingly.

auxiliary verb   see **modal auxiliary verb**.

back channel support   the feedback that listeners give to speakers, by verbal expressions such as *mmm*, *uhuh*, *yeah*, and by nodding, frowning or other facial and body gestures.

BBC   The British Broadcasting Corporation (BBC) is the oldest and most prominent television and radio broadcasting company in the UK, with several national television and radio channels. Supported by public funds, it has a reputation for good quality programming which reflects established norms and values.

code   a term sometimes used instead of 'language' or 'dialect' to refer to a linguistic system of communication. There are also non-linguistic communication codes such as dress codes or gesture codes.

codification   a process where scholars analyse and record the vocabulary and grammatical patterns of a language. For English, much of this codification took place in the eighteenth century. The vocabulary and grammatical patterns that were written down in dictionaries and grammar books then became 'rules'.

collocation   refers to the co-occurrence of words. Some words are in frequent collocation such as *happy* and *event* as in 'happy event'. Collocation can also affect the meaning of a word in a particular context. For example *white* in collocation with *wine* denotes a different colour from *white* in collocation with *snow*.

compound   a term used to describe a noun created by combining two other nouns. The meaning of the compound derives only partly from the meaning of the words that make it up. For example, a *blackberry* is a dark purple rather than a black berry.

commonsense/common sense discourse   see **discourse**.

connotation   the personal associations conjured up by a word, although they are not strictly part of its definition. For example, a *spinster* is an adult female human who has never been married, but for many people this word also carries connotations of 'old', 'unattractive' and 'not sexually active'.

consonant   a speech sound made by partially or completely obstructing the airflow from the lungs. The italic letters in the following examples represent some of the consonant sounds in English: '*s*at', '*bel*ie*v*e', '*m*a*n*'.

convergence   a process in which speakers change their speech to make it more similar to that of their hearer, or to that of other people in their social group. When applied to the convergence of whole dialects or accents it is also termed **levelling**.

covert prestige   covert means 'hidden' or 'non-obvious'. Sometimes speakers use a seemingly less prestigious or non-standard language variety to identify with a group that uses that variety. Thus, the language variety of that group can have a covert prestige.

creole   see **pidgin**.

crossing   a process in which speakers of one group occasionally use the speech patterns of another group as a means of identifying with some aspect of that group (see also **covert prestige**).

dialect   a variety of a language that can signal the speaker's regional or social background. Unlike accents which differ only in pronunciation, dialects differ in their grammatical structure – *Do you have . . .?* (US) versus *Have you got . . .?* (UK) – and in their vocabulary: *sidewalk* (US) versus *pavement* (UK).

disambiguate   to indicate more exactly what a term refers to in a particular context (see also **topical ambiguity**).

discourse   used in linguistics with a range of meanings. It can refer to any piece of connected language which contains more than one sentence. It is also sometimes used to refer specifically to conversations. In sociology, it can be used to refer to the way belief systems and values are talked about, as in 'the discourse of capitalism'. The prevailing way that a culture talks about or **represents** something is called the **dominant discourse**, that is, the '**commonsense**' or 'normal' representation.

divergence   a process in which speakers choose to move away from the **linguistic norms** of their hearer or social group. This can involve using a style or **language variety** not normally used by the group or even speaking an entirely different language.

dominant discourse   see **discourse**.

epistemic modal forms   see **modal auxiliary verb**.

euphemism   the use of an inoffensive or more 'pleasant' term as a substitute for one which might be unpleasant or taboo. For example, *passed away* is a euphemism for *died*. Euphemism can also be used to promote a more positive image, for example, *air support* for *bombing* or *pre-owned* for *second-hand*.

field   see **register**.

first person pronoun   see **pronoun**.

generic   generally, an expression which is used to refer to a class of things. For example, a distinction is drawn between the generic use of *man* in

Man has walked the earth for millions of years where this term refers to humans in general and *I now pronounce you man and wife* where this term refers only to male humans.

genre   a 'kind' or 'type'. As used in discourse analysis it can refer, for example, to writing genres such as thrillers, scientific writing or recipes. It can also refer to other media genres such as talk show, documentary and soap opera.

glottal stop   a **consonan**t made by a tight closure of the vocal chords followed by an audible release of air. It can be heard in several British accents where this consonant replaces the /t/ in a word such as *butter* pronounced *buh-uh*. The phonetic symbol for a glottal stop is /ʔ/.

grammatical gender   Some languages attribute masculine, feminine (and sometimes neuter) genders to their nouns, as in French *la gare* (the station – feminine), and *le soleil* (the sun – masculine). This type of gendering is called grammatical for two reasons. Firstly, the gender differentiation often has no correlation with 'natural' gender (there is nothing inherently masculine of feminine about a railway station or the sun), and therefore exists only in the language's grammatical system. Secondly, in languages which made use of such gender differentiation, there is typically grammatical agreement between the noun and its modifiers. Thus, if a noun is masculine, any determiners or adjectives that modify it must also be masculine, as in *le train brun* (the brown train). The same applies to the noun when it is feminine (as in *la table brune* – the brown table) or neuter.

hedges   linguistic devices such as *sort of* and *I think* which 'dilute' an assertion. Compare *he's dishonest* and *he's sort of dishonest*; *she lost it* and *I think she lost it*.

homophone   see **lexical item**.

honorific   in general refers to the use of language to express respect or politeness. More specifically it can refer to certain **address forms** which express respect such as *Sir/Madam, Your Highness, Reverend* and the 'formal' version of *you* in languages which make that distinction.

ideology   a set or pattern of beliefs.

implicature   a meaning which can be extracted but is implicit rather than explicit. For example, *a dog is for life, not just for Christmas* implies that some people regard dogs as a short-term rather than a long-term responsibility.

informant   someone who acts as source of linguistic data or information.

ingroup   a social group to which the speaker belongs. The **outgroup** comprises people who do not belong to that group. For example, gang members may use certain expressions with each other that mark them as members of a particular gang or ingroup. At the same time, the use of these expressions can differentiate them from members of other gangs, the outgroups in that situation.

language norm   see **linguistic norm**.

language variation/variety   see **linguistic variation**.

language variety   see **linguistic variety**.

langue   Saussure's term for the perfect knowledge of a language that he believed we all have in our heads, in contrast to what he thought of as the corrupt versions of language we actually produce, which he called **parole**.

levelling   see **convergence**.

lexical item   term used by linguists for one of the senses of 'word'. This term is useful because while *loves* and *loved* are two different words in terms of their form, they still represent the same lexical item, the verb *to love*. Notice that we can also have two words with the same phonological form but which represent two different lexical items. An example is: *bark*$_1$ as in 'the bark of a dog' and *bark*$_2$ as in 'the bark of a tree'. Words like *bark*$_1$ and *bark*$_2$ are said to be **homophones**.

lexis   vocabulary.

linguistic norm   generally, a norm refers to 'standard practice'. **Speech communities** can differ with respect to the linguistic norms being followed. These norms can involve grammar (e.g. whether or not *I don't know nothing* is acceptable); pronunciation (e.g. whether or not *pie* is pronounced as 'pah'); vocabulary (e.g. whether the pedestrian walkway is called the *sidewalk* or the *pavement*); and the appropriate social use of language (e.g. whether or not you should address your parents as *Sir* and *Ma'am*).

linguistic variation   term referring to the many ways that language systems can change or vary with respect to their grammar, pronunciation and vocabulary. Language systems change over time. They also change or vary according to the geographical or social identity of their users and according to the situations in which they are used. See also **linguistic variety**.

linguistic variety   term with several meanings, but generally referring to an identifiable language system which is used in particular geographic or social situations and has its own linguistic norms. For example, the variety of English spoken in Birmingham, Alabama, will differ from that spoken in Birmingham, England. Within a geographic region there may also be varieties based on social class or occupation. Similarly, the variety of English used in casual conversations will differ from that used in academic writing.

marked   generally speaking, 'marked' means noticeably unusual. More specifically, marked terms refer to anything which deviates from the norm and this deviation is signalled by additional information. **Unmarked** linguistic forms are neutral in so far as they **represent** the 'norm', and carry no additional information. For example, the unmarked form *nurse* is often assumed to refer to a woman. To refer to a nurse who is a man, the additional term *male* is often added: *male nurse* (the marked form). The notion of markedness has also been applied to pairs of opposites such as *tall* and *short*, where *tall* is considered to be the unmarked term. We can see this in certain constructions where the use of the unmarked term seems more 'natural'. Compare: *How tall are you?* to *How short are you?* and *She's five feet tall* to *She's five feet short*.

matched guise experiment   method of investigating people's attitudes to different languages. It involves **informants** listening to several recordings of the same 'script' spoken by the same speaker (or by other speakers matched for voice quality) but using a different language for each recording. The informants are then asked to judge each speaker's personal characteristics based on what they hear. Matched guise experiments can also be adjusted to elicit people's attitudes to different voice qualities, **accents** or **dialects**.

metaphor/metaphorical   figurative expression where a word or phrase from one area of meaning (semantic field) is used to refer to something from a different semantic field. Metaphorical expressions transfer some features from the first semantic field to the second. For example, *Her uncle is a snake* transfers features associated with snakes such as stealth, danger, evil, to a person. Rather than asserting that her uncle actually is a snake, it implies that he is like a snake in some respects. This contrasts with **simile**, where the comparison is made explicit rather than implied: *Her uncle is* LIKE *a snake*.

modal auxiliary verb   the modal auxiliary verbs of English are *will*, *shall*, *would*, *should*, *can*, *could*, *must*, *may*, *might*. Modal auxiliaries have several meaning functions. One important meaning function is epistemic. That is, speakers use modals to express their attitude towards the 'certainty' of what they are saying. Note the meaning difference between *That is a bird* and *That could be a bird*.

mode   see **register**.

multiple negation   see **negation**.

negation   sentences can be negated in English by using *not*: *I knew* versus *I did not (didn't) know*. They can also be negated by the use of other negative words like *nothing*, *never*, *nowhere*: *I knew nothing*. The grammar of standard American and British English does not allow a sentence like *I didn't know nothing* because it contains *multiple negation*, the use of *not* plus the negative word *nothing*. However, the grammatical rules of other **dialects** of English, as well as other languages such as Italian and Spanish, require the use of multiple negation.

Newspeak   term coined by George Orwell in his novel *Nineteen Eighty-Four*, where it referred to a special vocabulary invented by a totalitarian regime to manipulate people's thinking. This term has now passed into common usage to mean, loosely, new words or uses of words, but more specifically new words or uses of words in political jargon or propaganda.

nominalisation   grammatical process of forming a **noun** from another word class: for example *organisation* is nominalisation of the **verb** *organise*, *happiness* is a nominalisation of the **adjective** *happy*.

norm   see **linguistic norm**.

noun   class of words which, generally speaking, name people or things, but more importantly share certain grammatical characteristics. For example, in English nouns (in small capitals) can be preceded by *the*: *the* MUSIC. They can be marked for plural: CAT/CATS. They can be modified by **adjectives**: *the big* BRIDGE.

noun phrase   a phrase with a **noun** or **pronoun** as its 'head'. A noun phrase can consist of a single noun or pronoun or a noun which has been pre-modified and/or post-modified by other words or phrases. The following are examples of noun phrases (the 'head' is in small capitals): FIDO, HE, *the* DOG, *my big* DOG, *that expensive* DOG *from the pet shop*.

number   a grammatical category marking contrasts between the number of entities being referred to. English makes a number distinction between **singular** (one) and **plural** (more than one) as in: singular *cat* and plural *cats*, singular *I* and plural *we*. Number can also be marked on **verbs** as in singular *I am* and plural *We are*.

orthography   the writing system of a language and how words are spelled. For example, in English orthography both *so* and *sew* have different spellings even though they sound the same when spoken.

outgroup   see **ingroup**.

parole   Saussure's term for the language we actually produce, which may not match the system of **langue** in our brains because, Saussure believed, of errors we make in the actual production of speech.

passive   see **active**.

phoneme   the smallest significant sound unit in a language. For example *bat*, *sat*, and *pat* are different words in English because they differ in their first sound unit. The sounds /b/, /s/ and /p/ are three of the phonemes of English. English has approximately forty-four phonemes, although this number varies slightly between accents.

phonetics/phonetic the study of speech sounds, especially how they are made by speakers and perceived by hearers. Analysing the phonetics and phonology of a language generally involves looking at speakers' pronunciations.

phonology/phonological the study of the sound systems of languages. It looks at what sounds are significant for a language (its **phonemes**) and the permissible ways that sounds can be combined in words. For example the phonology of English would permit a word such as *tump* but not *mptu*. Analysing the **phonetics** and phonology of a language generally involves looking at speakers' pronunciations.

pidgin simplified form of language (in terms of both vocabulary and grammar) which arises when speakers of different languages need a common means of communication, usually for trading purposes. Pidgins are not fully fledged languages and have no native speakers. A *creole*, while it may have developed from a pidgin, is a fully fledged language with native speakers. In its most 'standard' or **prestige variety**, a creole will closely resemble one of the original languages from which it came.

plural see **pronoun** and **number**.

possessive words or phrases indicating possession. In English this is indicated either by *'s* as in *Jane's book* or by possessive determiners such as *my/our/your/his/her/their book*.

post-vocalic 'r' post-vocalic means 'after a **vowel**'. A speaker whose accent does not have post-vocalic 'r' will pronounce the 'r' only when it occurs before a vowel, as in *arise*, *trap* or *rip*. However, speakers whose accents contain a post-vocalic 'r' will pronounce the 'r' also in words where it occurs after a vowel at the end of a word, as in *floor*, and in words where it occurs after a vowel and before another consonant, as in *smart*.

presupposition a background assumption embedded within a sentence or phrase. The assumption is taken for granted to be true regardless of whether the whole sentence is true. For example *We will introduce a fairer funding formula* presupposes that the current funding formula is not fair.

prestige variety when used with respect to language it refers to a variety which society associates with education and high social status.

pronoun a class of words which can replace a **noun** or **noun phrase** in a sentence. This is an example from the English pronoun system:

	Singular	*Plural*
first person	I/me	we/us
second person	you	you
third person	he/him, she/her, it	they/them

received pronunciation or **RP**   the **accent** which is generally used by news-readers on national television in the UK. Sometimes called a 'BBC accent' or an 'educated British accent'. An RP accent is not marked for a particular region of Britain, but is marked for relatively 'high' social class. It is thought that only about three per cent of the British population normally use RP.

register   the way that language can systematically vary according to the situation in which it is used. Different registers can be characterised by their sentence structure, pronunciation and vocabulary. Three factors that determine variation in register have been proposed: *field*, which refers to the subject matter of the discourse; *tenor*, which refers to the role being played by the speaker and the resulting level of formality in the situation; and *mode*, which usually refers to the medium of communication, e.g. speech or writing.

represent/representation   as used in discourse analysis, it is basically how the speaker chooses to refer to something or someone. For example the same act could be represented as *terminating a pregnancy* or *killing an unborn baby* depending on the worldview of the speaker. Similarly, the same person could be represented as either a *terrorist* or a *freedom fighter*. See also **euphemism**.

rhetoric/rhetorical   the use of language to persuade or convince the hearer.

RP   see **Received Pronunciation**.

second person pronoun   see **pronoun**.

semantic derogation   a process in which a word can take on a second meaning and/or **connotations** which are negative or demeaning. Examples in English are the words *mistress*, *madam* and *spinster*. Compare these to their masculine counterparts *master*, *sir*, *bachelor*.

sign   the **arbitrary** combination of concept and label which exists in the minds of members of a **speech community**. Saussure called the 'concept' half of the sign the **signified**, while he referred to the 'label' half as the **signifier**.

signified   see **sign**.

signifier   see **sign**.

simile   expression in which something is figuratively compared to something else. Unlike a metaphor, where the comparison is implied, the comparison in a simile is made explicit by the use of expressions such as *as, as if, like*. For example: *You're as red as a beet. He's working as if there's no tomorrow. She's like a tiger defending her young.*

singular   see **pronoun** and **number**.

speech community   a human group, defined either geographically or socially, whose members share a common **language variety** and set of **linguistic norms**.

speech event   a specific unit or exchange of speech which has a well-defined structure, for example a greeting or a sermon.

stratified/stratification   division into layers, where a layer can be 'above' or 'below' another layer. In terms of social stratification, people in any one layer share certain social characteristics and are 'equals' but differ from and are not 'equal' to people in other layers. One example of social stratification by class is: upper, middle and lower or 'working' class.

style-shifting   people do not always talk in the same way. They can shift their speech styles and this can involve using different words, pronunciations or even grammatical forms. Notice the style differences between: *singin'* and *singing*; *verdant* and *green*; *So I says . . .* and *So I said . . .* See also **audience design** and **register**.

symmetry   as used in linguistics, an equal balance between expressions; *asymmetry* is an imbalance between expressions. For example, standard English shows symmetry between the **first person** singular and plural **pronouns** *I*/*me* versus we/us (two forms for each). However, it shows asymmetry between the first and **second person** pronouns. There are four forms for the first person pronouns: *I*/*me* and *we*/*us* but only one form for the second person pronouns: *you*. Asymmetry can be seen also in some **address forms**: only *Mr* for men but *Mrs*, *Miss* and *Ms* for women. Symmetry and asymmetry can also refer to the distribution of speakers' rights to talk in given situations. In a trial, speakers' rights are asymmetrical. Lawyers have more rights to ask questions than the witnesses.

syntactic/syntax   grammatical rules which determine how words can be combined into phrases and sentences. For example, the syntactic rules of English permit the phrase *the nice book* but not **book the nice* and the sentences *Jane is happy* and *Is Jane happy?* but not **Is happy Jane?*

tenor   see **register**.

tense   way that grammatical information about time can be marked on verbs. In English there are two tenses, present: *I leave* and past: *I left*. Future time is not expressed by tense marking but by other constructions such as *I will leave* or *I am going to leave*.

thesaurus   a book of words arranged by meaning categories.

third person pronoun   see **pronoun**.

topical ambiguity   situation where the hearer needs to know the topic of the discussion in order to interpret a word correctly. For example, *a hit* means one thing in the context of talking about pop songs, another when talking about baseball, and yet another when talking about the internet.

transitive/intransitive   kind of verb used in a clause. A transitive verb requires a direct object in order to make sense, whereas an intransitive verb does not. For example, in *Lucy loves Fred*, 'Fred' is the direct object of the verb 'love'. 'Love' is a transitive verb and would be incomplete without its direct object, as you can see from *Lucy loves* . . . On the other hand, in *Fred snores*, 'snores' is an intransitive verb; there is no direct object and the verb is complete on its own.

transitivity (model) model, used in the analysis of utterances, to show how the speaker's experience is encoded. In the model, utterances potentially comprise three components. (1) *Process*, which is typically expressed by a verb. (2) *Participants* in the process. The participant who is the 'doer' of the process represented by the verb is known as the *actor*. The *goal* is the entity or person affected by the process. (3) *Circumstances* associated with the process. In utterances such as *she cried <u>loudly</u>* or *he jumped <u>from the cliff</u>*, the underlined components provide extra information about the process, and can be omitted.

unmarked see **marked**.

variation see **linguistic variation**.

variety see **linguistic variety**.

verb grammatical class of words, which commonly refer to 'acting' or 'doing', although many verbs such as *to seem* or *to know* do not quite fit into this meaning category. More importantly, verbs take characteristic forms or endings such as those marking tense and voice, and they perform a specific function in a sentence. The verbs in the following sentences are in small capitals: *She was elected president. I am walking quickly. He laughed a lot. They might want some. I have seen her. Bob seems nice. sit there.* See also **modal auxiliary verb**.

vernacular this word comes from the Latin meaning 'of the home'. It refers to the indigenous language or dialect of a speech community, for example, the 'vernacular of Liverpool' (UK), or 'Black English vernacular' (US). It is often used in contrast to the standard or prestige variety of a language.

voice see **active**.

voiced/voiceless distinction used to classify **consonants**. Voiced consonants are produced with vocal cords vibrating as in the first consonants of *bat, din, zap*. Voiceless consonants are produced without vocal cord vibration as in the first consonants of *pat, tin, sat*.

vowel speech sound made with no obstruction to the air flow from the lungs. The bold letters in the following examples represent some of the vowel sounds in English s**a**t, t**o**p, h**ea**lth, s**i**lly.

References

Alladina, Safder and Edwards, Viv (1991) *Multilingualism in the British Isles*, London: Longman.

Allport, G. (1990) 'The Language of Prejudice', in P. Escholz, A. Rosa and V. Clark (eds) *Language Awareness*, New York: St Martins Press.

Andersen, Roger (1988) *The Power and the Word*, London: Paladin.

Andersson, Lars-Gunnar and Trudgill, Peter (1992) *Bad Language*, Harmondsworth: Penguin.

Applebaum, A. (2000) 'Paddy melt', *Slate*, 30 May. http://slate.msn.com/id/83330/. Accessed March 2003.

Atkinson, K. and Coupland, N. (1988) 'Accommodation as ideology', *Language and Communication*, 8.

Australian Broadcasting Company (1999) Transcript: *Lingua Franca*, broadcast 29 May 1999. http://www.abc.net.au/rn/arts/ling/stories/s28631.htm. Accessed March 2003.

Baron, Dennis (1990) *The English-only Question*, New Haven, CT: Yale University Press.

BBC (2003) Transcript: *Newsnight*, broadcast 6 February, 22:09 GMT. http://news.bbc.co.uk/1/hi/programmes/newsnight/2732979.stm. Accessed March 2003.

Becker, J. (1988) 'The success of parents' indirect techniques for teaching their preschoolers pragmatic skills', *First Language*, 8: 173–82.

Bell, Allan (1984) 'Language style as audience design', *Language in Society*, 13: 145–204.

Bolinger, Dwight (1980) *Language – The Loaded Weapon*, London: Longman.

Breines, W. (1997) 'Combatting middle-ageism', *Radcliffe Quarterly*, 83 (2).

British National Party website: http://www.bnp.org.uk/.

Bryson, Bill (1994) *Made in America*, London: Secker & Warburg.

Bucholtz, M. (1999) 'Why be normal?: Language and identity practices in a community of nerd girls', *Language in Society*, 28 (2).

Burchfield, R.W. (1996) *The New Fowler's Modern English Usage*, 3rd edn, Oxford: Clarendon Press.

Butler, R. N. (1969). 'Age-ism: another form of bigotry', *The Gerontologist*, 9: 243–6.

Cameron, Deborah (1992) *Feminism and Linguistic Theory*, 2nd edn, London: Macmillan.

Cameron, Deborah (1994) '"Words, words, words": the power of language', in Sarah Dunant (ed.) *The War of the Words*, London: Virago.

Cameron, Deborah (1995) *Verbal Hygiene*, London: Routledge.

Cameron, Deborah (1998) *The Feminist Critique of Language*, 2nd edn, London: Routledge.

Carroll, J. B. (ed.) (1956) *Language, Thought and Reality*, Cambridge, MA: MIT Press.

Casagrande, J. (1948) 'Comanche baby language', reprinted in D. Hymes (ed.) (1964) *Language in Culture and Society*, New York: Harper & Row.

Chambers, J. and Trudgill, P. (1980) *Modern Dialectology*, Cambridge: Cambridge University Press.

Cheshire, Jenny (1982) *Variation in an English Dialect*, Cambridge: Cambridge University Press.

Cheshire, Jenny, Edwards, Viv and Whittle, Pamela (1993) 'Non-standard English and dialect levelling', in James Milroy and Lesley Milroy (eds) *Real English: The Grammar of English Dialects in the British Isles*, London: Longman.

Cheshire, Jenny and Milroy, James (1993) 'Syntactic variation in non-standard dialects: background issues', in James Milroy and Lesley Milroy (eds) *Real English: The Grammar of English Dialects in the British Isles*, London: Longman.

Coates, Jennifer (1989) 'Gossip revisited: language in all-female groups', in Jennifer Coates and Deborah Cameron (eds) *Women in their Speech Communities*, London: Longman.

Coates, Jennifer (1993) *Women, Men and Language*, 2nd edn, London: Longman.

Coates, Jennifer (1996) *Women Talk*, Oxford: Blackwell.

Cockcroft, Robert and Cockcroft, Susan M. (1992) *Persuading People: An Introduction to Rhetoric*, London: Macmillan.

Cohn, Carol (1987) 'Slick 'ems, glick 'ems, Christmas trees and cookie cutters: nuclear language and how we learned to pat the bomb', *Bulletin of Atomic Scientists*, 43 (June): 17–24. On-line version at http://www.geocities.com/: 1–11. Accessed 4 November 2002.

Coupland, N., Coupland, J. and Giles, H. (eds) (1991) *Language, Society, and the Elderly: Discourse, Identity, and Ageing*, Oxford: Blackwell.

Coupland, N. and Nussbaum, J. (1993) *Discourse and Lifespan Identity*, London: Sage.

Coupland, J., Nussbaum, J. and Coupland, N. (1991) 'The reproduction of aging and agism in intergenerational talk', in N. Coupland, H. Giles and J. Wiemann (eds) *Miscommunication and Problematic Talk*, London: Sage.

Cox Report: see DES (1989).

Cromer, R. (1991) *Language and Thought in Normal and Handicapped Children*, Oxford: Blackwell.

Crowley, Tony (1989) *The Politics of Discourse: The Standard Language Question in British Cultural Debates*, London: Macmillan.

Crystal, David (1987) *The Cambridge Encyclopedia of Language*, Cambridge: Cambridge University Press.

Crystal, David (2001) *Language and the Internet*, Cambridge: Cambridge University Press.

DeFrancisco, Victoria (1991) 'The sounds of silence: how men silence women in marital relations', *Discourse and Society*, 2 (4): 413–24.

DES (1989) *English for ages 5–16* [*Cox Report*], London: DES.

Deuel, Nancy (1996) 'Our passionate response to virtual reality', S. Herring (ed.) *Computer Mediated Communication: Linguistic, Social and Cross-cultural Perspectives.* Amsterdam and Philadelphia: John Benjamins: 129–46.

Dunant, Sarah (ed.) (1994) *The War of the Words*, London: Virago.

Eckert, P. (1988) 'Adolescent social structure and the spread of linguistic change', *Language in Society* 17: 183–207.

Eckert, Penelope (1997) 'Gender and sociolinguistic variation', in Jennifer Coates (ed.) *Language and Gender: A Reader*, Oxford: Blackwell.

Edwards, Viv (1986) *Language in a Black Community*, Clevedon: Multilingual Matters.

Edwards, Viv (1997) 'Patois and the politics of protest: Black English in British classrooms', in Nikolas Coupland and Adam Jaworski (eds) *Sociolinguistics: A Reader and Coursebook*, London: Macmillan.

Ervin-Tripp, Susan (1979) 'Children's verbal turntaking', in E. Ochs and B. Schieffelin (eds) *Developmental Pragmatics*, New York: Academic Press.

Ervin-Tripp, Susan (1980) 'Sociolinguistic rules of address', in John Pride and Janet Holmes (eds) *Sociolinguistics*, Harmondsworth: Penguin.

Fairclough, Norman (1989) *Language and Power*, London: Longman.

Fairclough, Norman (1995) *Media Discourse*, London: Edward Arnold.

Fasold, Ralph (1984) *The Sociolinguistics of Society*, Oxford: Blackwell.

Fishman, Pamela (1980) 'Conversational insecurity', in Howard Giles, Peter W. Robinson, and Philip M. Smith (eds), *Language: Social Psychological Perspectives*, Oxford: Pergamon Press.

Fishman, Pamela (1983) 'Interaction: the work women do', in Barrie Thorne, Cheris Kramerae and Nancy Henley (eds) *Language and Sex: Difference and Dominance*, Rowley, MA: Newbury House.

Fletcher, P. (1988) *A Child's Learning of English*, Oxford: Blackwell.

Franklin, B. (ed.) (1995) *The Handbook of Children's Rights*, London: Routledge.

Gal, Susan (1998) 'Cultural bases of language-use among German-speakers in Hungary', in Peter Trudgill and Jenny Cheshire (eds) *The Sociolinguistics Reader*, vol. 1, London: Arnold.

Giles, Howard and Coupland, Nikolas (1991) *Language: Contexts and Consequences*, Milton Keynes: Open University Press.

Giles, Howard and Powesland, Peter (1975) *Speech Style and Social Evaluation*, London: Academic Press.

Giles, Howard and Sinclair, Robert (1979) *Language and Social Psychology*, Oxford: Blackwell.

Gleason, J. (ed.) (1997) *The Development of Language*, 4th edn, Boston, MA: Allyn & Bacon.

Graddol, David and Boyd-Barrett, Oliver (eds) (1994) *Media Texts: Authors and Readers*, Clevedon: Multilingual Matters.

Gullette, Margaret (1997) *Declining to Decline: Cultural Combat and the Politics of Midlife*, Charlottesville: University Press of Virginia.

Gumperz, John (1982a) *Discourse Strategies*, Cambridge: Cambridge University Press.

Gumperz, John (ed.) (1982b) *Language and Social Identity*, Cambridge: Cambridge University Press.

Gumperz, John J. and Levinson, Stephen C. (1996) *Rethinking Linguistic Relativity*, Cambridge: Cambridge University Press.

Gurak, Laura (1996) 'The rhetorical dynamics of a community protest in cyberspace: what happened with Lotus Marketplace', in S. Herring (ed.) *Computer Mediated Communication: Linguistic, Social and Cross-cultural Perspectives*. Amsterdam and Philadelphia: John Benjamins: 265–78.

Halliday, M. A. K. (1972) *Language as a Social Semiotic*, London: Edward Arnold.

Hansard (2002) http://www.publications.parliament.uk/pa/cm200102/cmhansrd/cm020703/debtext/20703–03.htm#20703–03_dpthd0. Accessed March 2003.

Harris, M. and Coltheart, M. (1986) *Language Processing in Children and Adults*, London: Routledge.

Harris, R. (2003) *Writing with Clarity and Style: A Guide to Rhetorical Devices for Contemporary Writers*, Los Angeles: Pyrczak Publishing.

Harris, Roy (1988) *Language, Saussure and Wittgenstein*, London: Routledge.

Heller, Monica (1982) 'Negotiations of language choice in Montreal', in John J. Gumperz (ed.) *Language and Social Identity*, Cambridge: Cambridge University Press.

Hewitt, Roger (1986) *White Talk, Black Talk*, Cambridge: Cambridge University Press.

Høeg, Peter (1996) *Miss Smilla's Feeling for Snow*, London: The Harvill Press.

Holtgraves, Thomas and Dulin, Jeffrey (1994) 'The Muhammad Ali effect: differences between African Americans and European Americans in their perceptions of a truthful bragger', *Language and Communication*, 14 (3): 275–85.

Honey, John (1997) *Language is Power: The Story of Standard English and its Enemies*, London: Faber & Faber.

Hooten, Jon (2002) 'Fighting words: the war over language', in *PopPolitics*: 1–7. http://www/poppolitics.com/articles/2002–09–10-warlanguage.shtml. Accessed 16 January 2003.

Hudson, R. (1980) *Sociolinguistics*, Cambridge: Cambridge University Press.

Hutchby, Ian (1996) 'Power in discourse: the case of arguments on a British talk radio show', *Discourse and Society*, 7 (4): 481–97.

James, Deborah and Clarke, Sandra (1993) 'Women, men, and interruptions: a critical review', in Deborah Tannen (ed.) *Gender and Conversational Interaction*, Oxford: Oxford University Press.

James, N. (ed.) (1998) 'The mouth and the method', *Sight and Sound*, 8 (3).

Jasper, Lee 'Open letter to David Blunkett', *Blink*. http://www.blink.org.uk/pdescription.asp?key=140&grp=21. Accessed 16 January 2003.

Jenkins, Nancy and Cheshire, Jenny (1990) 'Gender issues in the GCSE oral English examination: part 1', *Language and Education* 4: 261–92.

Kleyman, P. (2001) 'Media ageism: the link between newsrooms and advertising suites', *Aging Today*, March–April.

Kollock, Peter and Smith, Marc (1996) 'Managing the virtual commons: cooperation and conflict in computer communities', in S. Herring (ed.) *Computer Mediated Communication: Linguistic, Social and Cross-cultural Perspectives*. Amsterdam and Philadelphia: John Benjamins: 109–28.

Labov, William (1966) *The Social Stratification of English in New York City*, Washington, DC: Centre for Applied Linguistics.

Labov, William (1972a) *Sociolinguistic Patterns*, Philadelphia: University of Pennsylvania Press.

Labov, William (1972b) 'The social stratification of (r) in New York City department stores', in *Sociolinguistic Patterns*, Philadelphia: University of Pennsylvania Press.

Labov, William (1972c) 'The linguistic consequences of being a lame', in *Language in the Inner City*, Pennsylvania: University of Pennsylvania Press.

Labov, William (1972d) 'The social motivation of a sound change', in *Sociolinguistic Patterns*, Oxford: Blackwell.

Labov, William (1994) *Principles of Linguistic Change*, Oxford: Blackwell.

Lakoff, G. and Johnson, M. (1980) *The Metaphors We Live By*, Chicago: University of Chicago Press

Lakoff, Robin (1975) *Language and Woman's Place*, New York: Harper & Row.

Lakoff, R. (2000) *The Language War*, Berkeley: University of California Press

Lawrence, D. H. ([1928] 1961) *Lady Chatterley's Lover*, Harmondsworth: Penguin.

Lee, David (1992) *Competing Discourses: Perspective and Ideology in Language*, London: Longman.

Leith, Dick (1992) *A Social History of English*, 2nd edn, London: Routledge.

Lippi-Green, Rosina (1997) *English with an Accent: Language, Ideology and Discrimination in the United States*, London: Routledge.

Littlebear, Richard (1999) 'Keeping indigenous languages alive', in Reyhner, Jon, Gina Cantoni, Robert N. St Clair and Evangeline Parsons Yazzie (eds), *Revitalizing Indigenous Languages*, Flagstaff: Northern Arizona University: 1–5. http://jan. ucc.nau.edu/~jar/RIL_1.html. Accessed 31 January 2003.

Livingstone, Peter and Lunt, Sonia (1994) *Talk on Television: Audience Participation and Public Debate*, London: Routledge.

Lucy, J. A. (1992) *Language Diversity and Thought: A Reformulation of the Linguistic Relativity Hypothesis*, Cambridge: Cambridge University Press.

Mackinnon, Donald (1996) 'Good and bad English', in David Graddol, Dick Leith and Joan Swann (eds) *English: History Diversity and Change*, London: Routledge.

McMahon, A. (1994) *Understanding Language Change*, Cambridge: Cambridge University Press.

Maxim, J. and Bryan, K. (1994) *Language of the Elderly*, London: Whurr.

Mertz, Elizabeth (1982) 'Language and mind: a Whorfian folk theory in United States language law', *Sociolinguistics Working Paper* no. 93, Duke University, July: 1–10.

Mills, Sara (1995) *Feminist Stylistics*, London: Routledge.

Milroy, James and Milroy, Lesley (1985) *Authority in Language: Investigating Language Prescription and Standardisation*, London: Routledge & Kegan Paul.

Milroy, James and Milroy, Lesley (eds) (1993) *Real English: The Grammar of English Dialects in the British Isles*, London: Longman.

Milroy, James and Milroy, Lesley (1998) 'Mechanisms of change in urban dialects: the role of class, social network and gender', in Peter Trudgill and Jenny Cheshire (eds) *The Sociolinguistics Reader*, vol. 1, London: Arnold.

Milroy, Lesley (1987) *Language and Social Networks*, 2nd edn, Oxford: Blackwell.

Minkel, J. R. 'A way with words: do languages help mould the way we think?', *Scientific American* 25 March 2002: 1–3. http://www.sciam.com/print-version. cfm?articleID=00009A6B-B402-1CDA-B4A88. Accessed 4 November 2002.

Montgomery, Martin (1996) *An Introduction to Language and Society*, 2nd edn, London: Routledge.

Moore, Stephen and Hendry, Barry (1982) *Sociology*, Sevenoaks: Hodder & Stoughton.

Moores, Shaun (1993) *Interpreting Audiences: The Ethnography of Media Consumption*, London: Sage.

Morley, David (1980) *The 'Nationwide' Audience*, London: British Film Institute.

Morley, David (1992) *Television, Audiences and Cultural Studies*, London: Routledge.

Mugglestone, Lynda (1995) *Talking Proper: The Rise of Accent as Social Symbol*, Oxford: Clarendon Press.

Mühlhäusler, Peter and Harré, Rom (1990) *Pronouns and People: The Linguistic Construction of Social and Personal Identity*, Oxford: Blackwell.

Naipaul, S. (1976) *The Adventures of Gurdeva and Other Stories*, London: André Deutsch.

'New improved Nukespeak' (1990) *Bulletin of Atomic Scientists* 46 (3): 4–5. http:// www.thebulletin.org/issues/1990/jf90/jf90bulletins.html. Accessed 16 January 2003.

Nkweto Simmonds, Felly (1998) 'Naming and identity', in Deborah Cameron (ed.) *The Feminist Critique of Language*, 2nd edn, London: Routledge.

Ochs, E. (1991) 'Misunderstanding children', in N. Coupland, H. Giles and J. Wiemann (eds) *Miscommunication and Problematic Talk*, London: Sage.

Ochs, Elinor (1993) 'Constructing social identity: a language socialisation perspective', *Research on Language and Social Interaction*, 26 (3): 287–306.

Orwell, George ([1946] 1962) 'Politics and the English language', in *Inside the Whale and Other Essays*, Harmondsworth: Penguin.

Orwell, George ([1949] 1984) *Nineteen Eighty-Four*, London: Secker & Warburg.

Parmar, Pratiba (1982) 'Gender, race and class: Asian women in resistance', in Centre for Contemporary Cultural Studies, *The Empire Strikes Back*, London: Hutchinson.

Quirk, Randolph and Stein, Gabriel (1990) *Language in Use*, London: Longman.

Rampton, Ben (1995) *Crossing: Language and Ethnicity among Adolescents*, Harlow: Longman.

Richardson, Kay and Corner, John (1986) 'Reading reception: mediation and transparency in viewers' accounts of a TV programme', *Media, Culture and Society*, 8: 485–508.

Rosewarne, D. (1984) 'Estuary English'. *Times Educational Supplement*, 19 October.

Rowling, J. K. (1997) *Harry Potter and the Philosopher's Stone*, London: Bloomsbury.

Sacks, Harvey (1995) *Lectures on Conversation*, Oxford: Blackwell.

Scannell, Paddy (1988) 'The communicative ethos of broadcasting'. Paper presented to the International Television Studies Conference, July 1988.

Schiffman, Harold F. (1996) *Linguistic Culture and Language Policy*, London and New York: Routledge.

Shuy, Roger, Wolfram, Walt and Riley, William (1968) *Field Techniques in an Urban Language Study*, Washington, DC: Centre for Applied Linguistics.

Simpson, Paul (1993) *Language, Ideology and Point of View*, London and New York: Routledge.

Skotko, Brian (1997) 'Something to talk about: the relationship between language and thought from a cross-cultural perspective', in *Exploring the Mind*, Duke University: 1–13. http://www.duke.edu/~pk10/language/ca.htm. Accessed 4 November 2002.

Spender, Dale (1980) 'Talking in class', in Dale Spender and Elizabeth Sarah (eds) *Learning to Lose*, London: Women's Press.

Spender, Dale ([1980] 1990) *Man Made Language*, London: Pandora.

State of the World (2000) http://www.simulconference.com/clients/sowf/dispatches/dispatch2.html. Accesses 20 March 2003.

Stockwell, P. (2002) *Sociolinguistics: A Resource Book for Students*, London: Routledge.

Stubbe, Maria and Holmes, Janet (1995) 'You know, eh and other "exasperating expressions": an analysis of social and stylistic variation in the use of pragmatic devices in a sample of New Zealand English', *Language and Communication*, 15 (1): 63–88.

Stubbs, Michael (ed.) (1985) *The Other Languages of England*, London: Linguistic Minorities Project.

Suzuki, Y. (2002) *Nihongo no deki nai Nihonjin (Japanese who can't use Japanese correctly)*, Tokyo: Chuokoron-Shinsha.

Swann, Joan (1989) 'Talk control: an illustration from the classroom of problems in analysing male dominance in education', in Jennifer Coates and Deborah Cameron (eds) *Women in their Speech Communities*, Longman: London.

Swift, J. ([1726] 1994) *Gulliver's Travels*, Harmondsworth: Penguin.

Tannen, Deborah (1990) 'Gender differences in topical coherence: creating involvement in best friends' talk', in Bruce Dorval (ed.) *Conversational Organisation and its Development*, Norwood, NJ: Ablex.

Tannen, Deborah (1991) *You Just Don't Understand: Women and Men in Conversation*, Virago: London.

Thatcher, M. (1983) Speech to Confederation of British Industry Annual Dinner, 19 April. Margaret Thatcher Foundation. http://www.margaretthatcher.org/Speeches/displaydocument.asp?docid=105295. Accessed March 2003.

Thomas, Beth (1988) 'Differences of sex and sects: linguistic variation and social networks in a Welsh mining village', in Jennifer Coates and Deborah Cameron (eds) *Women in their Speech Communities*, London: Longman.

Thomas, Linda (1996) 'Variation in English grammar', in David Graddol, Dick Leith and Joan Swann (eds) *English: History, Diversity and Change*, London: Routledge.

Thornborrow, Joanna (1997) 'Having their say: the function of stories in talk show discourse', *TEXT*, 17(2): 241–62.

Thornborrow, Joanna and Wareing, Shân (1998) *Patterns in Language: An Introduction to Language and Literary Style*, London: Routledge.

Thorsheim, H. and Roberts, B. (1990) 'Empowerment through story-sharing: communication and reciprocal social support among older persons', in H. Giles, N. Coupland and J. Wieman (eds) *Communication, Health and the Elderly*, Manchester: Manchester University Press.

The Times (1992) *The Times English Style and Usage Guide*, London: Times Newspapers.

Tout, K. (ed.) (1993) *Elderly Care: A World Perspective*, London: Chapman & Hall.

Trudgill, Peter (1972) 'Sex, covert prestige and linguistic change in the urban British English of Norwich', *Language in Society*, 1: 179–95.

Trudgill, Peter (1974) *The Social Differentiation of English in Norwich*, Cambridge: Cambridge University Press.

Trudgill, Peter (1983a) *Sociolinguistics: An Introduction to Language and Society*, Harmondsworth: Penguin.

Trudgill, Peter (1983b) 'Acts of conflicting identity: the sociolinguistics of British pop-song pronunciation', in *On Dialect: Social and Geographical Perspectives*, Oxford: Blackwell.

Trudgill, Peter (1990) *The Dialects of England*, Oxford: Blackwell.

Trudgill, Peter and Chambers, J. K. (eds) (1991) *Dialects of English: Studies in Grammatical Variation*, London: Longman.

Trudgill, Peter and Hannah, Jean (1994) *International English: A Guide to the Varieties of Standard English*, 3rd edn, London: Edward Arnold.

Turner, G. (1973) *Stylistics*, Harmondsworth: Penguin.

United Nations (2001) The International Criminal Tribunal for the former Yugoslavia, Indictment Case No. IT-01–51-I, The Hague, Netherlands. http://www.un.org/icty/indictment/english/mil-ii011122e.htm. Accessed March 2003.

US English (2002) http://www.us-english.org/foundation. Accessed July 2002.

Van Dijk, Teun A. (1987) *Communicating Racism: Ethnic Prejudice in Talk and Thought*, London: Sage.

Van Dijk, Teun A. (1991) *Racism and the Press*, London: Routledge.

Van Dijk, Teun A. (1993) *Elite Discourse and Racism*, London: Sage.

Wardhaugh, Ronald (1992) *An Introduction to Sociolinguistics*, 2nd edn, Oxford: Blackwell.

Watts, D. (1987) *The West Indies: Patterns of Development, Culture and Environmental Change since 1492*, Cambridge: Cambridge University Press.

Watts, R. (2002) 'From polite language to educated language: the re-emergence of an ideology', in R. Watts and P. Trudgill (eds) *Alternative Histories of English*, London: Routledge: pp. 155–72.

Whorf, B. L. (1939) 'The relation of habitual thought and behaviour to language', in J. B. Carroll (ed.) (1956) *Language Thought and Reality*, Cambridge, MA: MIT Press.

Williams, A. and Kerswill, P. (1999) 'Dialect levelling: change and continuity in Milton Keynes, Reading and Hull', in P. Foulkes and G. Docherty (eds), *Urban Voices*, London: Arnold.

Winokur, J. (2001) 'Aging in America' MSNBC.com http://www.aging.msnbc.com. Accessed March 2003.

Wolfram, Walt and Schilling-Estes, Natalie (1998) *American English*, Oxford: Blackwell.

Wooden, R. (2000) *Recasting Retirement: New Perspectives on Aging and Civic Engagement*, San Francisco: Civic Ventures.

Zimmerman, Dan and West, Candace (1975) 'Sex roles, interruptions and silences in conversation', in Barrie Thorne, Cheris Kramerae and Nancy Henley (eds) *Language and Sex: Difference and Dominance*, Rowley, MA: Newbury House.

Index